The Memoir of General Toussaint Louverture

The Memoir of General Toussaint Louverture

Translated and edited by
Philippe R. Girard

OXFORD
UNIVERSITY PRESS

Oxford University Press is a department of the University of
Oxford. It furthers the University's objective of excellence in research,
scholarship, and education by publishing worldwide.

Oxford   New York
Auckland   Cape Town   Dar es Salaam   Hong Kong   Karachi
Kuala Lumpur   Madrid   Melbourne   Mexico City   Nairobi
New Delhi   Shanghai   Taipei   Toronto

With offices in
Argentina   Austria   Brazil   Chile   Czech Republic   France   Greece
Guatemala   Hungary   Italy   Japan   Poland   Portugal   Singapore
South Korea   Switzerland   Thailand   Turkey   Ukraine   Vietnam

Oxford is a registered trademark of Oxford University Press
in the UK and certain other countries.

Published in the United States of America by
Oxford University Press
198 Madison Avenue, New York, NY 10016

© Oxford University Press 2014

First issued as an Oxford University Press paperback, 2017

All rights reserved. No part of this publication may be reproduced, stored in
a retrieval system, or transmitted, in any form or by any means, without the prior
permission in writing of Oxford University Press, or as expressly permitted by law,
by license, or under terms agreed with the appropriate reproduction rights organization.
Inquiries concerning reproduction outside the scope of the above should be sent to the
Rights Department, Oxford University Press, at the address above.

You must not circulate this work in any other form
and you must impose this same condition on any acquirer.

Library of Congress Cataloging-in-Publication Data
Toussaint Louverture, 1743–1803.
The memoir of general Toussaint Louverture / translated and edited by Philippe Girard.
pages cm
Includes index.
English and French parallel text.
ISBN 978-0-19-993722-6 (hardcover : alk. paper); 978-0-19-063635-7 (paperback : alk. paper)
1. Toussaint Louverture, 1743–1803.   2. Generals—Haiti—Biography.   3. Revolutionaries—
Haiti—Biography.   4. Haiti—History—Revolution, 1791–1804.   I. Girard, Philippe R.,
editor, translator.   II. Toussaint Louverture, 1743–1803. Memoires du general Toussaint
Louverture.   III. Toussaint Louverture, 1743–1803. Memoires du general Toussaint Louverture.
English. IV. Title.
F1923.T69A313 2014
972.94'03092—dc23
[B]
2013027028

Frontispiece: British officer Marcus Rainsford, who personally met Toussaint Louverture, drew this portrait. It dates from the last years of the British occupation of Saint-Domingue (probably 1798). Inigo Barlow then engraved the portrait, and it was published as part of an English-language history of the Haitian Revolution in 1805. Louverture's British-inspired uniform is fanciful, as if Rainsford was trying to appropriate Louverture and his revolution for England.
Marcus Rainsford, *An Historical Account of the Black Empire of Hayti* (London: Albion Press, 1805), 241.

CONTENTS

Acknowledgments vii

Introduction 1

Preface to the Transcript and English Translation 45

Map of Place Names Mentioned in the Memoir 48–49

Original Transcript and English Translation 50–51

Memoire du General Toussaint Louverture:
   Transcript 52

Memoir of General Toussaint Louverture:
   English Translation 53

Index 171

ACKNOWLEDGMENTS

I would like to thank David Geggus for providing his expert opinion on the manuscript and for supporting me in my (failed) attempt to obtain NEH funding for this project and my (successful) quest for a publisher. Isabelle and Gildvin Hiélard provided lodging while I was doing research in Paris in 2009. The history department at McNeese State University financed my research at the University of Puerto Rico's Nemours collection in 2011. A Shearman endowed professorship financed part of my research at the Archives Nationales d'Outremer in 2012.

The Memoir of General Toussaint Louverture

Introduction

On 24 August 1802, the Haitian revolutionary general Toussaint Louverture entered the Fort de Joux, a foreboding medieval castle located in the Jura Mountains near the French-Swiss border. Born a slave in the French colony of Saint-Domingue (Haiti), Louverture had played a leading role in the Haitian Revolution and become governor general for life of the colony by 1801. But his meteoric career had come to an abrupt end when he was deported to France in June 1802 because the first consul of France, Napoléon Bonaparte, suspected him of marching for independence.

The Fort de Joux. The fort was renovated extensively in the late 19th century, but Toussaint Louverture's cell can still be visited.
Photograph by Christophe Finot, from commons.wikimedia.org/wiki/File:Fort_de_ Joux_-_05

One after the other, Louverture crossed five successive layers of fortifications. Each gate closed behind him with the sharp snap of a coffin slamming shut until he found himself in his cell, a dank and dark room tucked behind the keep. A small window that gave onto a courtyard where other prisoners took their daily walks was his only link to the outside world. To prevent an escape, it was obstructed with two sets of iron bars, bricks, wire netting, and storm shutters.[1] He felt, he later wrote, as if he had been buried alive. He was right: Aside from visits to the neighboring cell for his daily shave, Louverture never again crossed these doors alive.

Despite his difficult material circumstances, Louverture was initially hopeful that he could obtain a court-martial and secure his release. To do so, he employed a potent tool that this previously illiterate man had learned to master: the written word. As August turned into September, he wrote a lengthy text addressed to his captor Bonaparte that is his main political and literary legacy. This is the memoir that is analyzed, reproduced, and translated in this book.

Louverture's memoir is an important primary source for historians who generally struggle to retrace the history of the Haitian Revolution and other slave revolts because the vast majority of documents were authored by the dominant classes. The memoir gives a voice to the people victimized by slavery and racism, starting with Louverture, arguably the most relevant historical figure of African descent in world history, but also a complex man whose past and personality remain largely a matter of debate and speculation.

Though the memoir was written by a man who could not be fully frank because he was in captivity, it contains important information about Louverture's career and political agenda. Scholars have long debated whether Louverture, who grew up at the intersection of African, American, and European influences, should be seen as a black nationalist, a Creole, or a son of the French Revolution; the memoir helps us better understand how he juggled these multiple identities. Because Louverture was a former slave and a planter who both combated and enabled forced labor, scholars have also debated whether he should be seen as a herald of emancipation or a reactionary figure: He defended his labor policies in his memoir. Finally, because Louverture claimed much political autonomy as governor yet never declared independence, historians disagree on whether his long-term goal was the creation of Haiti: Louverture addressed that question directly in his memoir.

The memoir is also a layered literary work that Louverture painstakingly crafted, revised, and copied during his captivity. It is a rare example of a French-language slave narrative, a genre that is more common in the English language. But this is a slave narrative with a twist because it incorporates few of the typical ingredients found in slave narratives like the one by Frederick Douglass.[2] Louverture did not describe his upbringing, the moment when he became aware of being a slave, or the circumstances of his manumission. He chose to focus on his actions as the leader of a post-emancipationist world rather than commiserate on the abuse he had suffered as a slave. And yet, the memoir is also a very personal work enlivened by genuine and forceful *cris du cœur*.

Last but not least, the memoir is a linguistic artifact from an era in which French and African languages combined to form Kreyòl, the vernacular of Haiti and many former French colonies today. Because few written samples of early Kreyòl have survived—especially substantial texts written in their own hand by native Kreyòl speakers—the memoir is a veritable Rosetta stone that allows us to plunge into the prehistory of Haitian Kreyòl.

THE RISE AND FALL OF TOUSSAINT LOUVERTURE

"I was a Slave, I dare to declare it." Such is the only mention of Toussaint Louverture's origins in his memoir. The statement, with its capitalized "Slave" and its forceful "dare," was a defiant reminder of Louverture's humble past, but it stood surprisingly isolated in the text, as if Louverture chose not to let his past enslavement define his life. Other sources indicate that he was born on the Bréda sugar plantation near Cap-Français (Cap-Haïtien) around 1743, the son of two slaves imported from the kingdom of Allada (present-day Benin) as part of the Atlantic slave trade.[3]

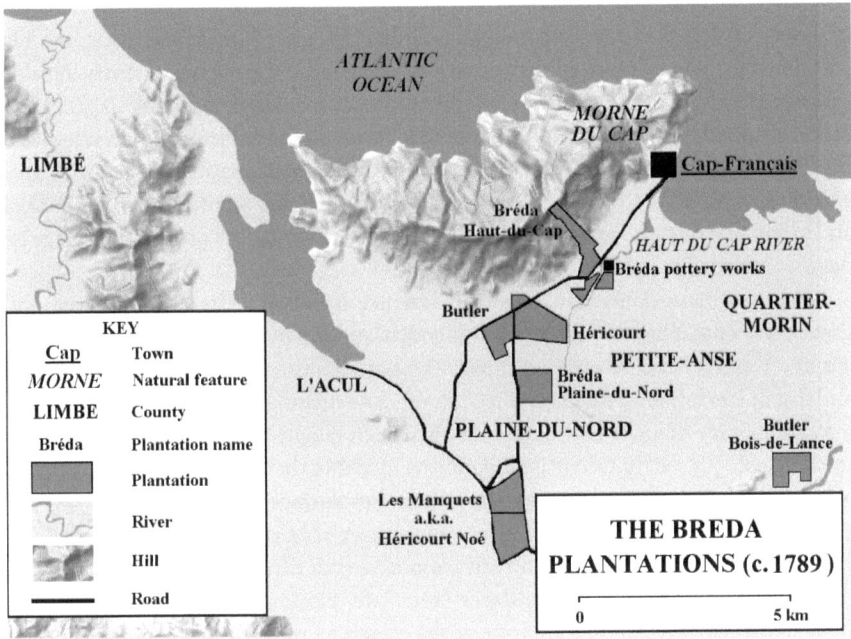

The Bréda plantations (c. 1789). Toussaint Louverture was born on the Bréda plantation in Haut-du-Cap (immediately southwest of Cap-Français) and lived there until the outbreak of the Haitian Revolution.
Map by Philippe Girard and Jean-Louis Donnadieu

During his years as a slave, Louverture coped by creating an extended kinship network that he later tapped during the Haitian Revolution. Several of his relatives are mentioned in the memoir, starting with "a respectable father aged one hundred and five." This passage may seem perplexing since archival documents indicate that both of Louverture's parents actually died in 1774. But Louverture was instead referring to his godfather Pierre Baptiste, who played a central role in his life and whom he regarded as a surrogate father.[4] Other relatives mentioned in the memoir include his wife and children, his brother Paul, his nephews Charles Belair and Bernard Chancy, and his niece's husband André Vernet, all of whom became officers in his army during the Haitian Revolution.

Sometime before 1776, Louverture was manumitted in circumstances that have yet to be elucidated. He then acquired at least one slave and leased a dozen others from his son-in-law, including possibly Jean-Jacques Dessalines, who later became his most prominent general and the first leader of independent Haiti.[5] He mentioned none of this in the memoir and his other writings, possibly because he wished to remain a convincing champion of abolitionism in the eyes of the general public. Similarly, the narrative of the British abolitionist Olaudah Equiano may have falsely included a Middle Passage scene to hide the fact that Equiano was born in the New World, not Africa, and that he had owned slaves.[6] Memoirs are as much the creation of a convenient identity as a faithful retelling of the past.

Though a freedman, Louverture remained on the plantation where most of his relatives continued to live in bondage, including his sons Placide and Isaac and his wife Suzanne, whom he often mentioned in his memoir. During his captivity, he also explained to an envoy of Bonaparte that "he had lost 11 children, including six girls" and that he had only five children left, two of them born out of wedlock. He did not reveal the identity of these two illegitimate children in his memoir, possibly for fear that they would be arrested by the French, but one suspects that they were his children Gabriel and Marie-Marthe, who were actually the legitimate offspring of a previous marriage he never mentioned in public.[7]

Some historians claim that Louverture learned to read while he was still a slave and that he was taught by his master or by his godfather, who himself had been educated by Jesuits. There are indeed striking similarities between the handwriting of Louverture and that of Pierre Baptiste and his wife Suzanne, a relative of his godfather. Alternatively, a contemporary thought that Louverture had been taught by a French soldier visiting the Breda plantation. But there is no definitive evidence that Louverture could read and write, or even sign his name, before the Haitian Revolution.[8]

According to his son Isaac, it was only after this revolution began in 1791 that Louverture learned how to read from a French officer; indeed, the first signature that is undoubtedly his dates from late 1791, when he was almost 50.[9] Louverture's belated education (one of the memoir's most important sub-themes) was clearly on his mind when in 1797 he questioned the black race's alleged mental shortcomings. "Blacks surely are ignorant and crude, since the lack of education can only produce ignorance and crudeness," he replied to a racist planter. "But should we hold the blacks responsible for their lack of education, or should we blame those who prevented them from acquiring it with threats and terrible punishments?"[10]

In his memoir, Louverture claimed that he was worth "about six hundred and forty-eight thousand francs" by the time the Haitian Revolution broke out. Such a sum seems enormous for a man generally assumed to have been a freedman of modest means in the 1780s. One possible explanation for the discrepancy is that, when mentioning the beginning of the "Revolution," Louverture was not referring to the August 1791 slave revolt that is now viewed as the beginning of the Haitian Revolution, but to the August 1792 storming of the Tuileries palace in France, by which point he had indeed begun the political and financial ascent that would make him a wealthy man in subsequent years.[11] For Louverture to cite Louis XVI's overthrow rather than the slaves' rebellion as the true beginning of the Haitian Revolution is revealing of his monarchist leanings, which were evident in his early career.[12] Some Freudian slips in the memoir also underline how much Louverture was shaped by the pre-revolutionary world of the Ancien Régime. He occasionally wrote of "Port-au-Prince" even though the city's name was republicanized to "Port-Républicain" in the 1790s. More surprisingly, he used the qualifiers "le nommé" and "sieur," which had been used before the Revolution to underline a person's racial background, even though such pejorative terms were no longer supposed to be used in the more egalitarian era of the Revolution.

Louverture's role in the major slave revolt that broke out in Saint-Domingue in August 1791 remains mysterious. Contemporaries variously alleged that he waited to see how events would unfold before committing to the cause of abolition, or that he was part of a royalist conspiracy. Louverture later claimed that he had actually been a partisan of emancipation from the outset, but he did not belabor that point in his memoir, probably because he did not want to come across to Napoléon Bonaparte as a radical firebrand.[13]

In 1793–94, two years into the Haitian Revolution, Louverture joined the Spanish army operating out of nearby Santo Domingo (today's Dominican Republic) when a war broke out between revolutionary France and monarchist Spain. For obvious reasons, he did not remind his French captors in the memoir that he had once served in a foreign army. He instead chose to emphasize his 1794 switch to the French army (around the time France abolished slavery) and the ensuing years he spent battling a joint Spanish and British invasion of Saint-Domingue, which bolstered his case as a loyal servant of the French Republic. This also allowed Louverture to spend much time retracing his various *faits d'armes*, which he did with the evident relish of an elderly general.

The 1790s saw Louverture's wealth increase, his military exploits multiply, and his political clout grow. The decade was also the time when he affirmed himself as an author. Hundreds of letters and proclamations from this period bear his name. But virtually all of these documents were drafted by secretaries and merely signed by Louverture, who had only recently learned how to read, and we know of only eight documents that he personally wrote in Saint-Domingue. In practice, Louverture wrote in his own hand only for practical reasons (he had no secretary with him), for minor issues (such as grocery lists), for personal issues (one letter was apparently intended for his mistress), and when the subject was too sensitive to involve a third party (two of the letters deal with a plot to expel a French agent in October 1798).[14]

Some illiterate officers like Louverture's nephew Moïse could be deceived by secretaries who misrepresented their ideas, but Louverture was educated enough to retain control of his prose even when he did not personally pen a letter. A French visitor who met him in Cap-Français was impressed by his "literary intelligence. I saw him orally explain in a few words the summary of his letters, refashion poorly drafted sentences, and face several secretaries who would alternatively present their drafts to him." "He would never have signed a letter without first understanding or weighing each word," noted another witness.[15] Louverture did not employ secretaries because he could not write, but because he could not write *well*: He wanted his letters to Parisian officials to be couched in formal French, a language he never fully mastered in writing. So self-conscious was Louverture about his lack of formal schooling that he mentioned it three times in the memoir.

It was to ensure that the next generation of Louvertures would be fully fluent in French that in 1796 Toussaint Louverture sent his sons Placide and Isaac to a government-financed school in France. "I am most grateful for the instruction that [the minister of the navy and the colonies] also chose to give my children," he wrote in 1797, "because if I cannot leave them a fortune, they will have, thanks to the government, a fine education that is worth more than the most brilliant fortune. If I had not myself received a Christian education...I would be lost among the crowd." "You negroes, try to learn the manners" of white colonists, he proudly told his black officers. "This is what you get from being educated in France; my children will be like that."[16]

By the time the British evacuated their last troops from Saint-Domingue in 1798, Louverture had become the leading political and military figure in the colony, where this former slave eventually claimed the title of governor. Over the following three years, he attempted to revive the plantation economy of Saint-Domingue, once the most prosperous in the New World, but severely affected by revolutionary violence and the abolition of slavery. The stern manner with which he treated former slaves made him unpopular with plantation field hands, but he emphasized the success of his labor policies in the opening lines of his memoir. "Agriculture and commerce were flourishing, the island had attained a degree of splendor that no one had ever seen previously, and all of this I dare to say was the result of my labors." His economic accomplishments reflected well on his record as governor, but the state of the colonial economy was also a litmus test for the merits of emancipation. Reactionaries were adamant that no sugar could be produced without slaves, so by insisting that plantations were doing well (better, even) since the official abolition of slavery in 1794, Louverture was trying to prove the economic viability of free labor. Though his claims of unprecedented prosperity were somewhat exaggerated (the plantation economy had only begun to recover), they clearly struck a chord: Looking back years later on his decision to remove Louverture from office, Bonaparte acknowledged that he should probably have left this efficient administrator in place.[17]

Other steps taken by Louverture to secure his power were more controversial. From 1798 to 1801, he conducted a secret diplomacy with Great Britain and the United States that could easily have been construed as treason (both countries were at war with France) and thus went unmentioned in the memoir.[18] He also exiled several French envoys that were his direct superiors, invaded the neighboring Spanish colony of Santo Domingo against the wishes of Bonaparte, and drafted a daring constitution that made him governor general for life, without seeking France's prior approval. In his memoir, Louverture could not omit such events, of which Bonaparte was well aware, but he tried to justify his decisions as the well-intended policies of a French public servant who had to make decisions without daily guidance from the distant metropolis because the ongoing state of war in Europe had interrupted normal communications by sea. He cleverly explained, for example, that it had become necessary to issue a constitution because Bonaparte had left the colony in a state of

An allegorical rendering of the presentation of the 1801 constitution. Toussaint Louverture stands at the center.
Library of Congress LC-USZ62-7861

legislative abandon. "Yes, it is true, I made a mistake," he confessed during his captivity. "But my intentions were pure."[19]

Late in 1801, concerned that Louverture was rapidly positioning himself for independence, Bonaparte sent a massive expedition to unseat his wayward governor and perhaps restore slavery.[20] Led by Bonaparte's brother-in-law Victoire Emmanuel

Leclerc, the expedition landed near Cap-Français in February 1802. Fighting soon erupted between Leclerc, who was itching for a fight that would bring him riches and glory, and Louverture, who refused to yield his post and suspected that Bonaparte's ultimate goal was the restoration of slavery. The city of Cap-Français, once known as the "Paris of the Antilles," was burned to the ground when Leclerc tried to land his troops. To justify why he had fought a French army led by Bonaparte's own brother-in-law, Louverture's memoir described in considerable detail the circumstances that surrounded the arrival of the Leclerc expedition. Leclerc, he explained, had caused the outbreak of fighting by violating proper procedure and landing unannounced.

Louverture went on to give a first-person account of the ensuing campaign between his and Leclerc's armies in the spring of 1802, including the battles of Ravine-à-Couleuvre (figure 4) and Crête-à-Pierrot, which have remained the high-water mark of Haiti's military history. Louverture took this opportunity to

The battle of Ravine-à-Couleuvre (1802). During this battle, Louverture's forces ambushed a French column led by General Donatien de Rochambeau.
Library of Congress LC-USZ62-17250

accuse French troops of summarily executing some rebel prisoners, as indeed happened. Less truthfully, he declined all responsibility for the massacres of white civilians that plagued the campaign, even though he had actually ordered his subordinates to kill white planters.[21]

The spring campaign ended in a draw in May 1802 when Louverture and Leclerc, their armies exhausted by three months of brutal combat, met in Cap-Français and signed a truce. In keeping with the general arc of his argument, Louverture implied in his memoir that he could easily have kept on fighting but had agreed to a ceasefire to avoid further bloodshed and save the colony. In reality, he had been abandoned by most of his subordinates and had no hope of a quick victory.[22]

The ceasefire granted immunity to Louverture, who retired to his plantations near Ennery in western Saint-Domingue. A month later, however, Leclerc had him arrested and deported to France. Louverture dedicated many pages of his memoir to his arrest, an event that was still fresh and painful in his mind. He emphasized the pillages that preceded and followed his capture and the treachery of the French officers who arrested him after giving him their word of honor that he would be safe, accusations that are consistent with the historical record (Louverture, on the other hand, seems to have been unaware that his subordinate Dessalines had denounced him to Leclerc, because he described him in very positive terms throughout the memoir).[23] Louverture also denounced as a fake a letter seized by Leclerc in which Louverture allegedly expressed his intention to resume his revolt at a later date.

Louverture hoped that the pillages, Leclerc's promise, and the lack of evidence would prove that his imprisonment was illegitimate and thus secure his release. More personally, the memoir was also an opportunity for Louverture to comprehend how he could have fallen for Leclerc's simple trap, a surprising lack of foresight that has puzzled historians ever since. "It was to deceive me, then," he mused aloud. "And if [Leclerc] wanted to deceive me why did he not use ruses and finesse only, and not his word and the protection of the French government?" What Louverture did not know was that the deportations were actually part of a larger plan by Bonaparte to deport all leading officers of color from the French Caribbean and that the first consul fully agreed with Louverture's summary arrest. Among the many victims of the racist turn in Bonaparte's colonial policies, one may cite Thomas-Alexandre Dumas, a mixed-race Dominguan general and father of the novelist who, after a stay in prison, was taken off active duty despite his written pleas to Bonaparte.[24]

Louverture and his family reached the military port of Brest in western France in July 1802. He immediately dictated letters to complain about his arrest and to beg French authorities to take good care of his relatives. "If my wife [Suzanne] had not been forced to follow her spouse" in exile, he wrote Leclerc, "she could have helped the large family we have in Saint-Domingue, most of whom are girls. Left on their own, without guides, what will become of these unfortunate persons?" "A fifty-three year old housewife deserves the indulgence and goodwill of a liberal and generous nation," he wrote Bonaparte. "I alone must be responsible for my conduct."[25] Taking full responsibility for his actions in the hope of shielding his loved ones from the French government's reprisals remained one of Louverture's main goals when drafting his memoir.

Louverture's pleas fell on deaf ears. After a month's delay, his son Placide, who had fought by his side during the spring 1802 campaign, was sent to a prison in nearby Belle Ile. There, he shared a cell with Jean-Baptiste Belley, who in less prejudiced times had been the first black deputy to the French National Assembly. Louverture's other relatives were sent to Bayonne and ultimately Agen in southwestern France. Though they were treated humanely, they were subjected to a lifelong exile; only his niece ever returned to Haiti. Louverture was not informed of his relatives' whereabouts, nor they of his, which caused understandable anguish.[26]

For fear that a formal court-martial would create political unrest in Saint-Domingue, Bonaparte decided that Louverture would be held without trial in the Fort de Joux, where he would be unlikely to find means of escape since this prison was located far from France's Atlantic ports. The procedure was far from unusual: Under Bonaparte, both metropolitan France and the colonies saw the multiplication of measures aimed at placing criminal and political prisoners beyond the reach of normal laws in a kind of 19th-century Guantánamo.[27]

At dawn on 13 August 1802, Louverture was discreetly transferred ashore in Landerneau, northeast of Brest. Worried that sympathizers might help him abscond on the way to Joux, French authorities whisked him away at full speed through provincial roads in an enclosed carriage. Several authors mention that Louverture spent a night at the Temple prison in Paris, not far from where Bonaparte worked, but he actually passed far to the south of the capital.[28] The historic meeting between the first consul and the man often described as the "black Napoléon" never took place.

As Louverture traveled all the way to Joux on the opposite side of France, each local military commander was tasked with providing a large escort while the convoy crossed his district. In the Loire region, General Paul Thiébault was so eager "to see this man who was extraordinary in his way" that he woke up at 2:00 A.M. when Louverture's carriage stopped in Tours to change horses. Believing that his destination was Paris, Louverture explained to Thiébault in his "negro talk" that he was eager to meet the first consul. Noting that he wore three jackets despite the stifling heat inside the carriage, the general thought to himself, "poor devil.... I will let someone else reveal to you your destiny. Thankfully, you won't suffer long, because the first cold wind that blows through the battlements of the Fort de Joux will be for you the kiss of death."[29]

In comparison with the first half-century of Louverture's life, about which very little is known, his captivity in Joux is particularly well documented. In addition to the memoir and his other writings, one can rely on a steady stream of instructions and reports by the directors of the prison, Bonaparte's envoys, local civilian and military officials, and the French government that deal with the most minute aspects of Louverture's daily routine. Personal recollections by witnesses who met the famous prisoner are also available.[30]

Security in Joux was tight. Louverture, by far the most prominent of the prisoners held in the prison, was kept in his own cell and isolated from other inmates. He was guarded by a squad of 19 riflemen and officers who had standing orders to shoot unannounced visitors on sight. Even these security measures were not deemed enough by the French government in Paris, which closely supervised the actions of local authorities. After hearing that two prisoners had recently managed to escape, the minister of war demanded that surveillance measures be doubled, and Louverture's knife and razor were taken away.[31]

Louverture and his servant Mars Plaisir, the only member of his entourage who had accompanied him to Joux, relied on each other for moral support. "We feared that we would soon be dead," Plaisir later recounted. He would do his best to lift his master's spirits, who reciprocated when Plaisir's own morale sank. "Seeing the grandeur of his soul, I would jump and embrace him.... And throughout our captivity we never ceased to talk about all of you [Louverture's family] and cry that we could not see you." But Plaisir was sent away just weeks after his arrival in Joux, and Louverture had to face the rest of his captivity without a familiar face.[32]

Despite the precariousness of his situation, Louverture remained resilient at first because he still hoped to obtain his release. As soon as he arrived in Joux, he asked for writing materials so that he could defend himself. Despite Bonaparte's express orders, Louverture obtained paper and ink, and over the following weeks he wrote several versions of his memoir along with nine letters, with only partial assistance from a secretary. Since documents written in his own hand are exceedingly rare, the fall of 1802 was by far the single most intensive period of writing in his life.[33]

Thankfully for Louverture, the director of the prison, Baille, was a dutiful but humane gaoler. He fed Louverture better than other captives, gave him a daily allowance of two bottles of wine, and used his own money to buy sugar (Louverture had a sweet tooth). He also regularly brought in doctors from Pontarlier. Louverture, who was not allowed to speak to his guards or other prisoners, must have looked forward to Baille's daily visits, when the two men spent hours discussing Caribbean politics.[34]

It was during one of these encounters that, late in August, Louverture announced that he had "important things" to say to the French government. Louverture meant that he wished to defend his record in person, but a jubilant Bonaparte, who had heard tales that Louverture was fabulously rich, immediately sent his aide-de-camp Marie-François Auguste de Caffarelli du Falga to Joux to enquire about the location of his secret "treasures." Two days later, Caffarelli was in Louverture's cell. "He is a 5'1" negro, slender," he reported, "very black... with very prominent cheekbones, a flat nose, but quite long.... He seems calm, tranquil and resigned in his prison; he suffers a lot from the cold. When I introduced myself to him, he saluted me very politely, and then invited me to sit down."[35]

Caffarelli expected Louverture to humbly seek the forgiveness of his French masters. He found instead a combative man who managed to portray his controversial record as governor of Saint-Domingue in a positive light. He adamantly denied having ever betrayed France. Questioned about his financial assets, he insisted that "I had a lot of animals, I own a lot of land, but I never had much cash." "This man is very sure of himself, and he repeats exactly the same thing one or two days apart," marveled Caffarelli. "Either he tells the truth, or he is a very deep liar who has thought about his argument for a long time."[36]

Only one painful incident seemed to faze Louverture. To punish and humiliate him, the minister of war had decreed that Louverture should no longer be allowed to wear his French general's uniform. "While he was talking, the commander of the fort [Baille] brought in the clothes that had been made for him," reported Caffarelli. "He was surprised when he realized that it was not a uniform, and stayed for a moment without talking, then took them, put them on his bed, and resumed the conversation. But he was so preoccupied with this matter that I could not take his mind off it." Another account is more direct. He "refused at first and insulted the officer," remembered a guard. "Then all of a sudden he took off his jacket and threw it to the envoy,

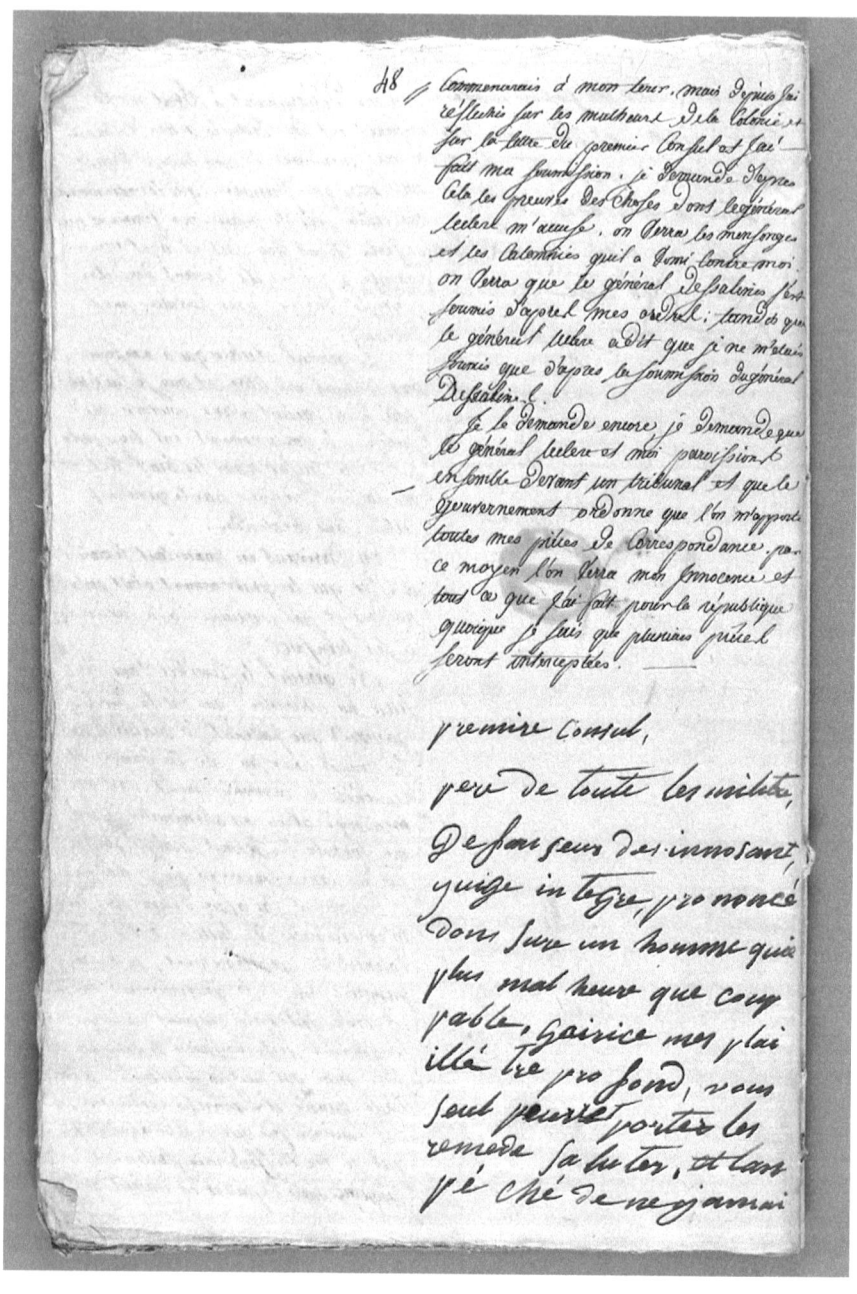

The next-to-last page of the D manuscript illustrates the difference between the handwriting of Jeannin (top of the page) and Louverture (bottom of the page).
Courtesy of the Archives Nationales d'Outremer, Dossier 1, EE1734, ANOM

saying, 'here, take this to your master.'"[37] As a self-made man, Louverture was very sensitive to any social or racial slight, so this insult must have deeply hurt his pride.

After six days of lengthy discussions with the prisoner, Caffarelli returned to Paris empty-handed. He had not managed to convince Louverture to confess his sins and reveal the location of his treasure. All he had to show for his efforts was a document in which Louverture had placed all his hopes: his memoir.

LOUVERTURE'S MEMOIR: LITERARY ANALYSIS

The memoir written during Louverture's captivity is a 21-page, 16,000-word document. According to Daniel Desormeaux, who oversaw a French edition of the memoir in 2011, Louverture "drafted in one setting, without any corrections, Memoirs in which he emphasized, with the self-assurance typical of memorialists, his central role." The writing process was actually far more convoluted. Four contemporary versions exist, labeled here A, B, C, and D. Manuscripts A, B, and C are in a folder at the Archives Nationales in Paris, which also contains three preparatory documents in Louverture's hand, as well as most of the letters he wrote in captivity; manuscript D is at the Archives Nationales d'Outremer in Aix-en-Provence.[38]

Manuscript A was penned by a secretary. It bears many corrections and marginal notations in the secretary's hand, particularly in its opening and closing segments, as if it had been dictated, then proofread and edited on Louverture's orders; it is also incomplete as it does not include a final section found in other versions. It was most likely a first draft. Manuscript B, written by the same secretary, is a second version that bears a few additional marginal notations, some in Louverture's own hand, as well as an "addendum to this memoir" that extends the main narrative by a few pages, and then a final paragraph in Louverture's hand that was initialed by him. Manuscript D is identical to manuscript B aside from minor textual variations, a single marginal notation in Louverture's hand, and a slightly revised closing paragraph. It was apparently the official copy sent to Bonaparte, because the secretary employed a more elegant handwriting, Louverture signed the document with his full signature, and the D manuscript is kept in the same folder as a letter in which Caffarelli mentions delivering the "enclosed" memoir to French authorities in Paris.[39]

Manuscript C is the only version entirely in Louverture's hand. Its content resembles that of manuscripts B and D, but with a few notable exceptions. Louverture corrected his secretary's factual mistakes (which largely pertain to his lack of knowledge of Dominguan politics and place names), refined a few sentences, and employed a syntax and spelling that differed markedly from his secretary's and standard French. He deleted two passages, the first of which digressed from the account of his arrest and the second of which was an oblique criticism of the French government that he may have found too daring on second thought. He also significantly expanded the closing pages of his memoir to include anecdotes that bolstered his case. The C manuscript bears no marginal notations by third parties and is presumably the last, most authentic version, which Louverture kept for his own records (it is not signed). This is the version reproduced in this book.

Louverture wrote the bulk of his memoir between 24 August 1802, when he reached Joux, and 11 September 1802, when Caffarelli arrived from Paris to interrogate him (he may have thought of its contents during the two months he had spent at sea or in Brest, but there is no documentary evidence of this). He revised the memoir after meeting with Caffarelli, which probably explains the disorganized structure of the closing pages. The memoir was finished by the 16th of September, when he entrusted the D manuscript to Caffarelli before he left for Paris.[40] Even manuscript C, the copy made by Louverture for his own records, must have been drafted before or during Caffarelli's stay, because several segments match the D manuscript word for word.

According to a 19th-century mixed-race Haitian historian who was eager to emphasize the historical importance of his kin, it was the mixed-race general Martial Besse who helped Louverture draft his memoir, a claim often recycled since then; but Besse did not reach the Fort de Joux until after Louverture's death.[41] In his report, Caffarelli actually indicated that Louverture "dictated the memoir before I arrived in Joux to a secretary from the sub-prefecture [of Pontarlier]."[42] His name was Jeannin. "I wrote memoirs dictated by [Louverture] during his captivity," Jeannin later explained. The two men apparently developed a close relationship. "Several times I went to Pontarlier to get a doctor for him, and I arranged for him to have a bathtub to use, because no one but me and the commander of the prison could talk to him." Jeannin's signature, like Louverture's, bore two lines and three dots (a symbol usually associated with freemasonry), which may explain their bond.[43]

Since the memoir was written with the help of a secretary, it is important to determine whether the resulting work is truly Louverture's or whether it was largely mediated. Potential interference is a constant problem in slave narratives, a genre to which Louverture's memoir is related: Consciously or not, white narrators can reframe issues and rub out uncomfortable truths. Such does not seem to have been the case here. Louverture's memoir was not the testimony of an illiterate slave interviewed by an author who was his social superior, but a report that was "dictated" (per Caffarelli and Jeannin's accounts) by a general to a secretary who played the role of a scribe, much in the same way that Bonaparte dictated his memoirs during his own captivity in Saint Helena or Christopher Columbus defended his governorship before King Ferdinand when he was jailed after his third voyage. The many marginal notations and corrections, some of them in Louverture's own hand, indicate that he carefully proofread Jeannin's drafts to correct occasional mistakes and ensure that the finished product matched what he had in mind word for word and even letter for letter. While dictating his memoir, Louverture had mentioned staying at a "hatte" (a cattle ranch), a Caribbean term that Jeannin had incorrectly rendered as "hutte" (a hut) in manuscript D; Louverture corrected the errant vowel in manuscript C. The arguments that Louverture used in his memoir and during his conversations with Baille and Caffarelli are also remarkably similar.[44]

Self-censorship is a more likely problem. Louverture, like most politicians, knew how to portray the truth in a manner compatible with his political goals. The precarious environment in which he found himself in August and September 1802 called for particular caution, since he was a prisoner who could legitimately fear being executed as a traitor if he revealed anything that was compromising; his relatives' fate was also on his mind. This drastically limited his ability to speak his mind in a document addressed to the powerful first consul of France, who held his life in his hands. For example, he omitted in manuscript C a paragraph that criticized officials in Brest for issuing him "old, half-rotten soldier rags"; after Caffarelli's visit and the confiscation of his uniform, he must have understood that this humiliation had been ordered by Paris itself and that it was best not to complain about the matter. Louverture also frequently used the passive voice and the indeterminate "they" (French: "on") to avoid accusing anyone in particular, leaving General Leclerc as the only identifiable villain in the memoir, even though, as Louverture knew, he was largely the executioner of Bonaparte's policies.

Ascertaining the authenticity of the memoir's style (as opposed to its content's) is also important because the memoir is the only lengthy piece of writing in Louverture's hand and the only way to reproduce his manner of speaking. As governor, Louverture had made extensive use of secretaries, but according to a contemporary, he "dictated separately to his secretaries, in Kreyòl, what they would write in French," so the formal French employed in his official correspondence was most likely not his.[45] Similarly, transcripts made in the 1790s of his conversations with French agents were airbrushed to make him speak in formal French. "Toussaint speaks only Kreyòl and barely understands French, he is perfectly incapable of employing the language that is ascribed to him," protested a French agent after reading the transcript.[46]

The style of manuscript C indeed varies noticeably as the text progresses. The opening pages are written in formal, grammatically accurate French, however badly misspelled, and are reminiscent of the official letters drafted by Louverture and his secretaries during his governorship. These pages were revised extensively by Jeannin, starting with manuscript A, which explains the polished style. But some later passages differ markedly from standard French. They happen to be more fiery, as if Louverture, caught up in his narrative, forgot that he was addressing a head of state and pushed aside the sentences suggested by his secretary to employ a language that was more personal (a Frenchman who met him in Saint-Domingue noted that he would occasionally switch from French to Kreyòl when he struggled to express his thoughts).[47] This is particularly true of two extended segments that Louverture wrote with little or no input from Jeannin. The first only surfaced in manuscript D, the third version of the memoir, too late to be polished by Jeannin. The second segment is unique to manuscript C and was written by Louverture entirely on his own.

Two excerpts demonstrate this stylistic shift (spelling has been corrected in the translation). The first, which appears at the beginning of the memoir, was written in formal French and is stylistically identical to Louverture's official writings. The second, taken from the segment that first appeared in manuscript D, incorporated Kreyòl variations, such as the use of the infinitive form of verbs, and was presumably more representative of Louverture's personal style.

> It is my duty to give to the French government an exact account of my conduct. I will recount the facts with all the naiveté and the frankness of a former military man,

while adding the thoughts that will arise naturally, in a word I will tell the truth even if it were against my interests. . . .

Arrested arbitrarily without hearing me or telling me why; took all my assets; plundered all my family in general; seized my papers and kept them; embarked me naked as worm; spread the worst calumnies on my account. Based on this I am thrown at the bottom of a cell.

According to his contemporaries, Louverture loved to employ metaphors, so the rich imagery that surfaces in the more authentic passages of the memoir must have been representative of his style. After complaining of being "naked as worm" in the passage above, Louverture went on to compare his captivity to dismemberment.[48] "Isn't it like cutting the leg of someone and telling him: 'walk'?" he complained. "Isn't it like cutting his tongue and telling him: 'talk'?" The various anecdotes he inserted at the end of manuscript C to illustrate the concepts of preparedness and forgiveness, in the manner of a Christian parable, were a rhetorical device he often employed when speaking to plantation workers.

What happened to the various versions of the memoir after they were finished remains unclear. Louverture presumably handed over the neatly written, signed D manuscript to Caffarelli so that he could hand-deliver it to Bonaparte. He probably kept with him the earlier drafts (manuscripts A and B), his personal copy

First page of the C manuscript. This 21-page manuscript was written entirely in Louverture's hand.
Courtesy of the Archives Nationales, Paris, folder 1, AF/IV/1213, AN

(manuscript C), and personal copies of letters he had written to Bonaparte, some of which were later seized during searches of his cell. The prison commander who visited Louverture's cell after his death, Amiot, also mentioned finding a memoir "secretly hidden under a hat on Toussaint's head, sewn into a piece of cloth," which was in very poor condition. Amiot made a copy for himself and sent the original to the minister of war, who passed on to Bonaparte the "papers that were found on Louverture after his death in the folds of a handkerchief that covered his head."[49] It is possible that Amiot was referring to the C manuscript, which is in the worst shape of the four surviving versions, though it does not appear to have been folded. Alternatively, the memoir found on Louverture's body was a fifth version that was thrown away because of its poor condition. In the 1850s, an author mentioned that the French general Etienne Desfourneaux also owned a copy, which might be some unknown sixth version or possibly the copy made by Amiot for his own records.[50]

Mentioned by the French abolitionist Henri Grégoire as early as 1818, then published in fragments in 1845, Louverture's memoir was first published in its entirety by the Haitian historian Joseph Saint-Rémy in Paris in 1853 under the title *Mémoires du Général Toussaint l'Ouverture écrits par lui-même*. Born in the French colony of Guadeloupe, Saint-Rémy was a naturalized Haitian citizen and a self-described black nationalist who wished to demonstrate Louverture's greatness; a secondary goal was to discredit the French emperor Napoléon III by emphasizing that his uncle Napoléon I had treated Louverture dishonorably. Saint-Rémy's edition, complete with extensive footnotes, has remained the main reference for generations of historians and casual readers ever since. It was reprinted several times in Haiti and in France; an English translation was also published in 1863 and then reprinted many times.[51]

However frequently used, the Saint-Rémy edition suffers from a major flaw: Though entitled *Memoirs of General Toussaint l'Ouverture written by himself*, it was based on the D manuscript redacted with the help of the secretary Jeannin, rather than the C manuscript in Louverture's hand. One may suspect that Saint-Rémy, who lived in an era of rampant racism, hesitated to reproduce a version whose spelling and grammar did not conform to proper usage (to satisfy his "patriotic pride," he even thought of rewriting the memoir entirely to better match the literary canons of his time).[52] Two recent French editions include the C manuscript, but one, following Saint-Rémy's lead, willfully modernized its spelling and content, while the other was marred by several transcription errors.[53]

Stylistically, the memoir falls halfway between oral and written literature, as if Louverture's secretary had been feverishly jotting down notes while Louverture was reminiscing aloud about the Leclerc expedition. "The troops who surrendered to General Leclerc, had they received their orders from me? Had they consulted me?" he asked. "No. Well, those who did bad things had not consulted me either." This is particularly true of the C manuscript, which, unlike Jeannin's copies, has almost no punctuation and is not divided into paragraphs, giving a breathless feel to the text. Some sentences are long, even by French standards, in part because Louverture cited letters and related conversations in the third person while interjecting personal comments. A passage regarding Louverture's enemy Lubin Golart contains no fewer than four distinct layers in the manner of a matryoshka doll: The account of the Leclerc expedition is interrupted by a flashback explaining that Golart had been hiding, which is interrupted by a recapitulation of Golart's career, which is interrupted by an anecdote about an assassination attempt.

[1] If General Leclerc had had good intentions, would he have welcomed in his army the person named Golart (...)
[2] this dangerous rebel,
[3] who would arrange for owners to be assassinated on their plantations; who invaded the town of Môle Saint-Nicolas; who shot on General Clervaux who commanded the town, on General Maurepas and his brigadier chief; who waged war in this region; who incited the cultivators of Jean-Rabel, Moustique, and the heights of Port-de-Paix to rebel; who even had the audacity to shoot at me a bullet that cut off the feather in my cap
[4] (mister Bondère, a doctor who was accompanying me, was killed by my side, my aides-de-camp had to dismount)
[3] as I was marching against him to get him to submit to his chief and to retake the territory and the town that he had invaded; this brigand, at last, after sullying himself with all sorts of crimes,
[2] had hidden in a forest until the arrival of the French squadron.

The result is a discursive narrative that brings to mind modern stream-of-consciousness novels. Though it is better organized, the early part of the memoir, which recounts the arrival of the Leclerc expedition from Louverture's perspective, remains intensely personal and clouded by the fog of war as Louverture explained how he attempted to react to unexpected events day by day. The segment added at the end in manuscript C, though ostensibly addressed to Bonaparte, could almost be described as the personal ruminations of a man who again and again mulled over the fact that he had been outmaneuvered by Leclerc and mistreated by the French government—daydreaming or even therapy more than official report.

LOUVERTURE'S MEMOIR: HISTORICAL ANALYSIS

The manuscript written by Louverture during his captivity in Joux is generally described as his "memoirs" after the title of the Saint-Rémy edition. The use of the plural form gives the text an autobiographical character. For Daniel Desormeaux, Louverture was a memorialist in the French literary tradition who wanted to retrace his life one last time before his death in order to leave behind a "political testament." Deborah Jenson also used the plural "memoirs" in her book on the writings of Haitian revolutionary leaders, though her characterization of the memoir as a political tract designed to influence French policy is far more convincing. In a 2009 edition, Jacques de Cauna noted that the term "mémoires" was inaccurate, but he employed it nonetheless.[54]

Manuscript C actually bears the title "mémoire" in the singular form, meaning "petition" or "report" rather than "autobiography." This was no misspelling: Jeannin also used the singular in the other three versions, and Louverture described the document as "my report" when sending it to Bonaparte.[55] The title is quite apt for a text that says remarkably little about Louverture's early life and seeks primarily to retrace his recent career in order to obtain his release. "It is my duty to give to the French government an exact account of my conduct," he made clear from the opening line, before using the term "account" another 13 times in the memoir. Louverture did not yet know in August 1802 that he would never leave Joux alive. His primary goal was not to retrace his life for future generations but to prove to the French government that he was in the right, as he had done on previous occasions in the 1790s when he had sent lengthy printed reports to the French government to salvage his career.[56]

Though the memoir is at times disorganized, no doubt because it was written and revised in a few weeks, one can nevertheless identify four sections organized in the manner of a legal brief because Louverture's stated goal was "to be brought before a tribunal or court martial, where General Leclerc will also be made to appear, and that we be judged after both being heard."

The first and longest section is a chronological account of the period from the landing of the Leclerc expedition in February 1802 to Louverture's arrival in Brest five months later. Its main purpose is to denounce his arrest as unjustified and irregular. Its tone is argumentative and unapologetic. Throughout, Louverture blamed Leclerc's highhandedness for backing him into a corner but was careful to flatter Bonaparte (one suspects that Louverture's opinion of the first consul was less complimentary, but he knew better than to insult his captor and arbiter). Aside from a few logical inconsistencies, individual points are cogent and convincing; Louverture would have made a great lawyer. "He does not answer directly the questions asked of him," complained Caffarelli during his interrogation. "He ignores them or goes off-topic."[57]

Louverture was also a skilled politician who must have understood that he was not in prison solely because he had violated the clauses of his ceasefire with Leclerc: Bonaparte had sent a large army to remove him from office and evidently objected to his policies as governor. In the second part of his memoir, which was greatly expanded in the D version (possibly after Caffarelli's pointed criticisms during his visit to Joux gave Louverture a deeper understanding of the reasons for Bonaparte's anger), he thus spent much time justifying the decisions that had provoked the wrath of Bonaparte, as if the memoir was one-half of a long-distance dialogue with the first consul. This section is quite chaotic as it again retraces the arrival of the Leclerc expedition, mentions his record prior to that date, and defends his 1801 constitution, only to return once again to the French landing, but its purpose is clear: to present his policies as governor as exemplary of his innate loyalty. The section fulfilled the purpose normally served by character witnesses in a trial (Louverture even listed people, like General Etienne Laveaux, who could "vouch for me").

The third section expressly focuses on Louverture's record prior to 1802, and particularly his military exploits against the British, so as to claim some extenuating circumstances. In the manner of a lawyer's closing argument, the last section, entitled "addendum to this memoir," re-emphasizes his main points and underlines the value of forgiveness before ending with a plaintive plea for the first consul's mercy that he wrote in his own hand in manuscripts B, C, and D. It is possibly the memoir's most moving passage. Unfortunately, Louverture's legal efforts were doomed from the outset since Bonaparte had already decided not to hold a trial.[58]

Louverture, who was accused of being a traitor to France, repeatedly insisted on his loyalty in the memoir. Prudently omitting his role in the 1791 slave uprising, his service in the army of Bourbon Spain in 1793–94, and his secret diplomacy with Great Britain and the United States from 1798 to 1801, he instead reminded Bonaparte that he had helped France repulse a British invasion of Saint-Domingue in 1794–98. He also did his best to justify his controversial 1801 constitution, which turned Saint-Domingue into a quasi-sovereign dominion. Today, Louverture is widely seen as a precursor to Haiti's independence, but his memoir is replete with references to "the colony," "the fatherland," and "French" colonial troops. To him, the spring 1802 campaign was not a war of self-determination but a civil war in which Leclerc had forced "Frenchmen to fight Frenchmen." Whether he was sincere in his embrace of colonialism or hid his true intentions will forever remain a matter of debate, but it is worth noting that, judging by the linguistic and religious references in the memoir, Louverture was thoroughly assimilated into French culture.[59]

The memoir was not solely a defense of Louverture's record. He occasionally went on the offensive to remind the first consul that he was being ungrateful toward a public servant who had done great things for France at a time when the colony was virtually abandoned to its own devices. His service against the British from 1794 to 1798 clearly helped him in his regard. So did his labor record.

Present-day readers might expect the last major manuscript of the leading figure of the Haitian Revolution to be an impassioned defense of universal emancipation, which France had officially abolished in a 1794 law, but "slavery" (mentioned only twice), "liberty" (mentioned only twice in this meaning), and "abolition" (never mentioned) are largely absent from the text. Louverture was of course too astute to broach this topic at a time when Bonaparte was restoring slavery in parts of the French colonial empire, but the memoir also reminds us of the more conservative aspects of Louverture's labor record, which are often overlooked today. When he had tried to restart the plantation sector after achieving full control of the colony in 1800–01, Louverture had faced much opposition on the part of former slaves. In response, he had forced field hands to remain on the same plantation for life, much like medieval serfs.[60] This was a major step back from his revolutionary ideals, which he described with astonishing frankness in a passage of his memoir that is the best and most concise summary of his social views:

> If I made my people work, it was to make them appreciate the price of liberty without license, it was to prevent the corruption of morals; it was for the general happiness of the island, and in the interest of the republic, and I indeed succeeded because you could not see in the entire colony a single idle man and the number of beggars had diminished.

Louverture's desire to restart the plantation economy—for the greater good of a colony dependent on exports of tropical crops but also to serve his personal interests as a landowning planter—explains his hostility toward the rebels who threatened the stability of the plantation sector. The memoir nominally cites Lubin Golart, "who would arrange for plantation owners to be killed on their estate" and Lamour Derance, "who incited the cultivators to rise up." The memoir is the perfect illustration of the central divide in early Haitian society, which Michel Rolph-Trouillot has described as "the war within the war," between an elite attached to the economic superstructures inherited from the colonial era and popular classes eager to break up the plantation system and turn to subsistence agriculture.[61]

Politically, Louverture's preference was for an enlightened dictatorship run, to paraphrase Plato, by a philosopher-king. Even in this age of revolutions, many statesmen thought that the common people were too uneducated and shortsighted to know what was good for them and that, in Simón Bolívar's terms, a "terrible power" (a strong centralized government) was needed to avoid the perils of factionalism and mob rule.[62] This was the essence of the argument made by U.S. Federalists like Alexander Hamilton; Bonaparte, who had seized power to restore order after the excesses of the French Revolution, was not far behind.

Louverture was often accused in his time of being a devious leader, and indeed his correspondence is a study in multiple identities. His willingness to constantly adapt his public persona to survive in the Darwinian environment of the Haitian Revolution puts into question whether the principles articulated in the memoir ever reflected Louverture's real views. His love for Bonaparte, however strongly expressed, was likely counterfeit; his opposition to independence remains a matter of debate; but his stated desire to force former slaves to continue working on plantations was probably genuine since it was consistent with the stern policies he had embraced as governor.[63]

Historians must check the accuracy of each of Louverture's claims but also ask themselves *why* he was lying, because his misrepresentations and omissions help us divine what he was hoping to demonstrate, as if there was a shadow memoir hidden underneath the lines in the manner of a medieval palimpsest. Louverture covered topics that he knew would please Bonaparte (such as his labor policies) and issues that had so angered Bonaparte that he could not eschew them (his 1801 constitution). But he left out others for reasons we can only guess. He did not mention his African ancestry—possibly because he was ashamed of it. He did not mention his first family—possibly so that they would not be arrested.

The themes that were probably most representative of Louverture's worldview were those he brought up repeatedly in his memoir even though they brought him no immediate benefit: honor, race, family, nostalgia, and God. Words such as "rank," "duty," "frank," and especially "honor" feature prominently in the memoir, mentioned four, eight, ten, and twenty times, respectively. Louverture saw himself not as a former slave, but as a French officer abiding by a specific code of conduct, which explains the anger with which he recounted the humiliating experience of being dragged away like a captive after his arrest. "To reward me for all these services they arrest me arbitrarily in Saint-Domingue like a criminal, they tie me up and bring me on board without any regards for my rank," he complained. This was probably Louverture's most potent argument in the memoir, since it reminded Bonaparte that he was not treating his captive in a manner behooving an honorable officer. In a racial context in which individuals of African descent were often assimilated with barbarism, Louverture was keen to point out that he was the civilized one.

Louverture was a man who longed for "respect," a word he used eight times in the memoir and that was part of the send-off that ended his letters ("honneur/respect" is also a traditional Haitian greeting). In this context, the confiscation of his uniform during his captivity and orders that he no longer be addressed as "general" must have hurt him considerably.[64] In a subtle jibe at his captors, Louverture always referred to individuals by their proper title in the memoir; he also made a distinction between people who addressed him as "Toussaint Louverture" and those who called him "Toussaint" as if he were still a slave with no last name of his own.

Louverture was convinced that he knew the underlying reason for his dishonorable arrest and disrespectful treatment: As a black officer, he had not been judged worthy of the privileges normally awarded to a man of his rank. Four direct accusations of racism appear in the memoir. "Surely I owe this misunderstanding to my color," he asserted, adding later that "because I am black and ignorant, I must not count as one of the soldiers of the Republic.... If I were a white man, after serving like I served, all these misfortunes would not have happened to me." Louverture rarely accused his white interlocutors of racism in his official correspondence.[65] Such a salvo was thus highly unusual, especially considering that Louverture was in a delicate situation and needed to assuage the first consul rather than hurl accusations, however accurate (Bonaparte was indeed in the process of reestablishing racial inequality in French colonies). This was evidently an issue that was so foremost in his mind that he could not hold back.

Aside from these bursts of anger, the memoir is tinged with sadness. References to his family abound, not surprisingly since Louverture was a doting husband and father who had high hopes for his progeny. "They make me the unhappiest man in the world by denying me my liberty and by separating me from what is dearest to me in the world," he lamented, "from a cherished family that made my life happy." One immediately thinks of William Wordsworth's description of Louverture as "Toussaint, the most unhappy man of men!" in a sonnet written in August 1802, just as Louverture was laboring on his own memoir.[66]

Deep in his heart, a person as politically astute as Louverture must have sensed that his petition had no chance of succeeding: Bonaparte, who had sent two-thirds of the French navy to recall Louverture because of fundamental policy differences, was unlikely to be swayed by a memoir whose centerpiece was a vocal denunciation of his brother-in-law. One wonders if for Louverture the writing process was, at least subconsciously, a grieving mechanism. "By dictating this memoir," wrote Jacques de Cauna, "the prisoner breaks out of his cell and returns to his country."[67] His memoir was filled with dispatches, decision points, and "orders," a term that appeared 94 times, as if Louverture replaced himself in the thick of the action in order to relive his glory days vicariously. His accounts of the battles he fought against the French army of Leclerc were surprisingly numerous and precise; in some instances, vanity even led him to exaggerate his role in rebel victories such as Crête-à-Pierrot (in which

Louverture played a secondary role), even though reminding Bonaparte of his armed resistance clearly undermined his case.

Louverture's biographers have long disagreed on whether his ostentatious Catholic piety was genuine or whether he was a false Christian and a closet practitioner of Vodou. A 1785 slave register (the only known document to describe him as a slave) actually mentioned that he was very devout and "eager to proselytize," while the memoir clearly placed him within the Euro-Christian cultural framework typical of the black elite of Saint-Domingue.[68] There are two specific references to "God" in the memoir and 10 to "le mal" (which can be translated as "evil"), as well as one passage paraphrasing the Bible (Isaiah 5:20). "Africa" is never mentioned; a reference to the Carthaginian general Hannibal could be over-interpreted as an indictment of European imperialism in Africa, but it seems more representative of 18th-century European officers' penchant for quoting Greek and Roman classics (Louverture was particularly fond of Spartacus). Louverture, to the end, portrayed himself as a member of the French cultural and political elite. His linguistic choices in the memoir confirm this.

LOUVERTURE'S MEMOIR: LINGUISTIC ANALYSIS

Over the past three decades, our knowledge of the Haitian Revolution has progressed considerably, but one major problem remains: the unequal distribution of sources. White planters, bureaucrats, and generals have left behind a large archival treasure trove, but the black population of Haiti is comparatively absent from the record, except in the official correspondence of the leading black and mixed-race revolutionaries, which is usually mediated by white secretaries. Lower-class revolutionaries are mute; their leaders speak through interpreters. This archival blank spot is problematic for the linguists attempting to retrace the origins of Haiti's main language, Kreyòl, since virtually all colonial-era documents were written in French. For lack of sources, some linguists have tried to reconstruct colonial-era Kreyòl by comparing present-day Kreyòl with European and African languages, but this roundabout method makes it impossible to determine conclusively which of several competing theories on the origins of Haitian Kreyòl is correct—specifically, whether Kreyòl descends primarily from French or from African languages.[69] Only archival documents can settle the matter, which is another reason why Louverture's memoir is so valuable: It allows us for the first time to recreate the way a Haitian revolutionary spoke.

During the colonial era, three types of languages were commonly spoken in Saint-Domingue: the West and Central African languages of the *bossales* (slaves born in Africa), metropolitan French (including regional variations), and Haitian Kreyòl, which belonged to a family of Afro-French languages common to all French colonies from Louisiana to Réunion Island in the Indian Ocean.

African languages should normally have predominated since *bossales* represented a majority of the slave population in pre-revolutionary Saint-Domingue, but this was far from the case. The diversity of African languages limited their appeal as a communication tool. Newly arrived slaves were so uprooted that they failed to preserve or impose their native tongues. Social prejudices against the *bossales*, who occupied the lowest rank of the colonial hierarchy, also explain the rapid demise of African languages. In practice, African languages were mostly used in mountain communities of plantation runaways (to this day, practitioners of the Afro-Caribbean religion of Vodou still employ tidbits of African languages when they are possessed by spirits).[70]

Educated elites in Saint-Domingue, whether white or colored, spoke standard metropolitan French, along with a few Caribbean terms that described their unique environment (such as the word "hatte" for "ranch" that so puzzled Jeannin). In many ways, standard French was even more widely used in the colonies than in France itself, where regional dialects still predominated in the provinces, because immigrants to the colony had to adopt a common tongue to understand one another.[71]

Kreyòl was used primarily by Caribbean-born people of color and veteran white colonists. Contrary to chroniclers visiting from Europe, who often dismissed Kreyòl as mere "jargon" and "negro talk," Caribbean-born whites, who had grown up speaking Kreyòl with their enslaved nannies, liked to emphasize the "finesse" and the "grace" of this expressive language. Unfortunately, because Kreyòl was an oral language, early written examples are very rare and not always authentic: The most frequently cited pre-revolutionary example of Haitian Kreyòl is a song written by a French colonist according to the norms of French poetry.[72]

The revolutionary period is richer, but many of the Kreyòl-language documents that have survived were drafted by white authors. These include translations of proclamations by various French officials (including Bonaparte) and a guidebook for would-be colonists. Far more interesting are petitions by field laborers and transcripts of Kreyòl speeches made by Louverture and other rebel leaders, but they are short and few.[73] It was only after independence that some Kreyòl-language texts written by Haitians appeared in print. Even then, the vast majority of Haitian literature

One of the better-known portraits of Toussaint Louverture, which features his prominent lower jaw. Often derided as a racial caricature, this portrait is actually similar to a contemporary portrait now held by the New-York Historical Society. See Paul Youngquist and Grégory Pierrot, eds., *Marcus Rainsford: An Historical Account of the Black Empire of Hayti* (1805; reprint, Durham, NC: Duke University Press, 2013), xlvii.
Library of Congress LC-USZ62-7862

was written in French well into the 20th century, when a long-delayed nationalist renaissance finally brought about the development of a written Kreyòl literature.[74]

Which of these languages did Louverture speak? According to Isaac Louverture, his father had learned the language of his Allada ancestors as a child, but Isaac's claims that Louverture proudly spoke Ewe-Fon as an adult are not credible given his general hostility toward African mores and the absence of corroborating sources. Louverture did not speak English (contrary to his Anglophone colleague Henry Christophe, who later became king of Haiti) and does not seem to have learned Spanish (even though he served in the Spanish army for a year). He occasionally used gibberish Latin to impress his subordinates, but his knowledge of this language was minimal.[75]

Louverture spoke Kreyòl better than any other language, but he relegated it to the oral sphere, using it specifically to deliver speeches to the black rank and file. When addressing whites, he spoke exclusively French, a language he associated with France, formal settings, the written realm, and authority. "I was very poorly received one day when I tried to speak to him in the local patois [Kreyòl]," noted a French visitor, "because he only used it to harangue the cultivators or his soldiers." Contemporaries were unfortunately vague when describing his French; Bonaparte's envoy Caffarelli, who spent hours interrogating Louverture in Joux, simply explained that "his way of narrating is hard to follow because he has a hard time expressing himself."[76]

However tragic on a personal level, Louverture's exile was a linguist's dream because his captivity and limited access to a secretary forced him to personally pen multiple letters, drafts, and particularly the lengthy C manuscript. The most obvious characteristic of the memoir to a present-day French reader is that Louverture misspelled virtually every word of it. Some of these mistakes were simply typos ("gouvernememet" for "gouvernement") or reflected his lack of formal schooling when encountering difficult words ("piétater" for "pied-à-terre"), but a careful analysis of the text shows that there is more to Louverture's idiosyncratic spelling than partial literacy. Many apparent mistakes were in fact phonetic approximations that allow us to recreate, two centuries after the fact, Louverture's accent and manner of speaking, as if someone had tape-recorded his conversations with Jeannin. Such is the key to deciphering Louverture's memoir.[77]

Some of Louverture's non-standard pronunciations possibly had a physical cause since he suffered from prognathism (a prominent lower jaw) and had lost many teeth in a battle. But they also reflected old French norms, as indicated by the archaic spellings that he still employed even though they had fallen out of favor in metropolitan France (such as "isle" for "île" and "ii" for "y"). Louverture spoke in an old-fashioned way, either because he was elderly, or because he wanted to imitate the accent of the aristocrats (who occasionally refused to adopt new pronunciations), or, more likely, because old pronunciations had survived in the colonies long after they had become outmoded in metropolitan France. These remnants of 17th- and 18th-century French fashioned Haitian Kreyòl, as well as the French spoken in other colonies such as Louisiana Cajun and Québécois French.[78] For example:

- Louverture often wrote "respecte" instead of "respect," which indicates that he pronounced the final /kt/, as was common in the 18th century, instead of /ɛ/, as is the norm in modern French.

- Louverture elided many /ʀ/ ("conte" for "contre"). Such was often the case in everyday 18th-century French ("mécredi" for "mercredi") and in present-day Kreyòl, where /ʀ/ is either eliminated ("bonjou" for "bonjour") or becomes /w/ ("gwo" for "gros").
- Louverture simplified some groups of consonants that he found hard to pronounce, transforming /ks/ into /s/ for example ("sanctions" for "sanctions") or eliminating /s/ altogether ("résitance" for "résistance"). Such simplifications were common in 18th-century French and still are in present-day Kreyòl ("dezas" for "désastre").
- Like Jeannin, Louverture systematically indicated the imperfect tense with "oi" instead of "ai" ("je marchois" instead of "je marchais") and presumably pronounced this final syllable as /we/ instead of /e/, even though this pronunciation had fallen out of favor in metropolitan France during the Revolution. Similarly, in colonial-era Kreyòl, as well as in present-day Kreyòl and Québecois, the word "moi" is not pronounced /mwa/ but /mwe/ or /mwɛ̃/.
- Louverture added /u/ sounds or replaced /o/ with /u/ ("au goumente" for "augmenter"). This must have been a colonial remnant of an archaic French pronunciation because the sound /u/ had often been used in lieu of /o/, /y/, and /œ/ in pre-revolutionary France, a practice that is still evident in present-day Kreyòl ("nouaj" for "nuage").
- Louverture often pronounced /œ/ as /e/ in his memoir ("jai cé" for "je sais"), which is also true of his letters ("couragé" for "courageux") and his wife's ("vous mé démandé" for "vous me demandez").[79] This shift, common in present-day Kreyòl, likely reflects the fact that distinctions between the sounds /œ/, /e/, and /ɛ/ had only recently emerged in metropolitan French.
- Other vowels and semi-vowels used in the memoir are also typical of present-day Kreyòl. Louverture replaced /u/, /œ/, and /yi/ with /i/ ("tiys jour" for "toujours," "regitter" for "rejeter," "li" for "lui"), which is still the case in present-day Kreyòl ("piti" for "petit"), especially in the countryside.

Louverture's manner of speaking thus seems to have been inspired by antiquated French more than Ewe-Fon. The memoir also supports the theory that connects Kreyòl to regional variations of French, particularly the accents and dialects of western regions such as Normandy and Aquitaine that played a leading role in the settlement of the colony. Louverture seemed particularly influenced by the accent of the Aquitaine region, which provided 40 percent of Saint-Domingue's white colonists, including his wife's former master, the Comte de Noé, and his plantation overseer, François Bayon de Libertat.[80] Norman variations are also noticeable, possibly due to the fact that some members of Louverture's entourage, such as his ambassador Joseph Bunel de Blancamp, were from Normandy. For example:

- Louverture pronounced the final letters "t," "s," and "r," which are normally silent in Parisian French but are often pronounced in southwestern France ("Brunette" for "Brunet," "honnet gence" for "honnêtes gens," "premiere consul" for "premier consul"). To this day, in Kreyòl, the final /s/ in "mwens" is pronounced (from the French "moins"), as is the final /t/ in "abit" (from the French "habit").
- In southwestern France, the letter "o" is often pronounced as an open /ɔ/ rather than a closed /o/. This is reflected in present-day Kreyòl ("wòz" for "rose"). Louverture probably spoke this way, but this pronunciation is hard to detect in the memoir since French spelling does not distinguish between /o/ and /ɔ/.
- Louverture almost always wrote "geurre" instead of "guerre," which suggests that he pronounced the letter "g" as /ʒ/ or /dʒ/ rather than a hard /g/, which would correspond to modern-day Kreyòl ("ladjè" or "lagè" for "la guerre"). Kreyòl also occasionally

- pronounces /k/ and /s/ as /ʃ/ or /tʃ/ ("tchè" or "kè" for "coeur," "chonjé" or "sonjé" for "songer"), which is specific to the accent of the Auvergne region in France, but such a shift is not detectable in the memoir, possibly because Louverture, who had lost many teeth, struggled to form sounds in the upper-front part of his mouth.
- Louverture often elided certain vowels, particularly "i" ("pusque" for "puisque") and "e" ("soulevment" for "soulèvement"), which is commonly done in Norman and popular French and is also typical of Kreyòl ("tèlman" for "tellement").
- Louverture consistently added nasal sounds like /ɔ̃/, /ɑ̃/, /ɛ̃/, and /jɛ̃/ ("ingnoré" for "ignorer"). Nasalizing words was characteristic of 18th-century Norman speakers and remains common in present-day Kreyòl, particularly in its rural variety ("agronnom" for "agronome"). Even then, Louverture must have used more nasal sounds than was customary because he felt the need to explain that "he spoke through his nose because of a Vodou curse."[81]

Present-day Kreyòl vocabulary incorporates some Spanish and English loan words, which is not surprising given the proximity of Jamaica, the Dominican Republic, Cuba, and the United States. Louverture, who was closely involved with these countries during his lifetime, was also sometimes, though infrequently, influenced by Spanish and English pronunciation and vocabulary. For example:

- Louverture consistently misspelled the name of his Grenada-born subordinate Henry Christophe ("Christopher," "Christophete"), most likely because he tried to pronounce it with an English accent.
- Louverture employed the French word "principe," which normally means "principle" in French, to mean "beginning," possibly because he was influenced by the meaning of "principio" in Spanish.
- As noted above, he used /u/ instead of /y/ and /e/ instead of /œ/, which would be characteristic of a Spanish speaker.

African influences, which some scholars see as central to the formation of Kreyòl, seem absent from the memoir. Louverture employed a vocabulary that was essentially French with a few foreign loan words (such as "hatte," derived from the Spanish "hato," or "herd"). He did simplify French grammar and conjugation, but it is not clear whether he was consciously replicating Ewe-Fon grammatical forms, he was simply baffled by the complex rules of French grammar, or, more convincingly, he was using the speech patterns of the colonial population's lower classes. Some white masters willfully talked down to slaves in simplified French (the way one would address a child); grammatical simplifications were also common in the popular French spoken by lower-class whites. "It is the former variety of French [plebeian speech] rather than the latter [elite French] that formed the speech input the slaves transformed into Creole," notes Albert Valdman.[82] Examples of this process abound in the memoir:

- Louverture frequently split words ("en voier" for "envoyer"). This suggests that he treated the first syllable as a distinct word that could be elided altogether, as is the norm in Kreyòl ("voye" for "envoyer"). Inversely, he treated as one word many article-noun combinations ("dumal" for "du mal") and liaison-word combinations ("les zotre"). Both processes are understandable mistakes for a person transcribing oral French phonetically and are very common in present-day Kreyòl ("legliz" for "l'église," "zwazo" for "oiseaux").

- Louverture often confused the masculine and feminine forms of words ("un nasamblé" for "une assemblée"). Similarly, present-day Kreyòl has largely abandoned the distinction between masculine and feminine.
- In the passages of his memoir that deviate the most from standard French, Louverture simplified the negative form ("il m'auroit pas traité" for "il ne m'aurait pas traité"), dropped articles ("balle a raflé" for "la balle a raflé"), dropped pronouns ("nai pas resu" for "je n'ai pas reçu"), and dropped prepositions ("si grand nombre" for "en si grand nombre"), all of which are characteristic of present-day Kreyòl, as well as popular French.
- In Kreyòl-influenced passages, Louverture also stopped conjugating verbs and used the infinitive form instead ("mes plai et tre profond" for "mes plaies sont très profondes"). The use of the infinitive in Kreyòl was already well established in the colonial era and has remained the norm in present-day Kreyòl.

The language employed by Louverture in some passages of his memoir, though displaying many characteristics of Kreyòl, is not Kreyòl. It should more properly be described as "creolized French," that is, the language of a person trying to speak French but influenced by his native Kreyòl (Jenson uses the expression "maroon French," Desormeaux "mixed-race language," and Saint-Rémy "negro talk").[83] It is quite different from a speech that Louverture delivered to a black audience in southern Saint-Domingue and for which he employed standard Kreyòl to establish his working-class bona fides.[84]

Toussaint and Suzanne Louverture reuniting with their sons Placide and Isaac in February 1802. At left is their French teacher, Jean-Baptiste Coisnon.
Library of Congress LC-USZ62-7859

Z'autres pas té connois mai ben, parceque moi te au Cap. N'a pas Nègres au Cap qui batt premier pour libre.... C'est Rigaud io, c'est Milatre pîtôt qui vlé faire z'autres tourner esclaves. C'est cila-io qui té gagné esclaves qui faché voir io libres. N'a pas moi qui té esclave moi-même, tout comme z'autres.

(You don't know me because I was in Cap-Français. There is no black man in Cap who fought earlier than me for liberty.... Rigaud and the Mulattoes are the ones who want to make slaves of you. It is those who had slaves who are unhappy to see you free, not me, who was a slave just like you.)

That Louverture tried his best to employ standard French when writing a petition to the first consul of France is understandable (linguists describe this habit of shifting from a language to another based on the subject matter and the addressee as "code-switching"). But creolized French was his default written language even when the recipient was not French and the subject matter was not official: He employed it in a letter to his subordinate Jean-Jacques Dessalines, who spoke little French, and in a private letter to his wife Suzanne, who also wrote to her husband in creolized French rather than Kreyòl. Louverture also wrote to his children in French (through a secretary), and they replied in standard French, which they spoke and wrote fluently after studying for years in Paris.[85] It is even possible, though not certain, that Louverture also spoke French to his family members, at least when others were present, because the French teacher who witnessed the moment when Louverture reunited with his children in February 1802 was able to understand their conversation (in present-day Haiti, Kreyòl is normally preferred within the informal environment of a family gathering).[86]

Louverture's language of choice was thus not the Ewe-Fon of his ancestors (which he had learned as a child but did not practice because African languages were associated with the despised African-born *bossales*), nor Kreyòl (which he spoke fluently but used mainly when addressing lower-class laborers), nor elite metropolitan French (which he understood but could not exactly replicate), but the laborious, creolized French of an up-and-coming former slave trying to hide his humble roots. The memoir thus reveals the existence of an intermediate language between French and Kreyòl, a kind of "aspiring French" that was used by lower-class whites and upwardly mobile blacks.

Louverture's preference for French may come as a surprise since embracing Kreyòl is a central part of Haitian nationalism these days, but it is consistent with Louverture's social background and aspirations. Until recently, elite Haitians often favored French because they associated it with intellectual and economic superiority, and ambitious *nouveaux riches* who lacked education tried to hide their shortcomings in French by "hyper-correcting" (adding sounds or suffixes that they mistakenly viewed as characteristic of French).[87] Similarly, Louverture added extraneous /ʁ/ sounds ("jambre" for "jambe") and needlessly complicated groups of consonants ("sageste" for "sagesse") and vowels ("ésiuié" for "essuyé") to artificially "Frenchify" his memoir.

Louverture's linguistic choices speak to the tortured relationship that he and other black revolutionaries had with the French métropole. Though it is the only truly Haitian language, Kreyòl was long denigrated as the sub-French of the slaves, and official documents like Haiti's declaration of independence were written in formal French even though (or because?) it could not be understood by the lower classes. Similarly, urban Kreyòl, though less authentic because it is heavily influenced by French, is often seen as more elegant, or "silky" ("kreyòl swa"), while its rural counterpart, however true to Haiti's roots, is also dubbed "rèk" and "su" (rough, acidic) because it is associated with the lower classes.[88] These contradictions, at the heart of the Haitian soul, are evident in Louverture's memoir, in which he defiantly trumpeted his antiracist message while apologizing for his lack of education in the language of his masters.

LOUVERTURE'S PASSING

Louverture hoped that his memoir would convince Bonaparte to free him. He was sadly misguided. Bonaparte had personally instructed Leclerc to deport all leading black officers and was in no way displeased by Louverture's exile; he had even specified that Louverture should be shot if caught with arms in hand.[89] The geopolitical context did not help Louverture, since the summer of 1802 was marked in Saint-Domingue by a major labor uprising and a yellow fever epidemic that ravaged the ranks of the French expeditionary army. Deluged with dispiriting accounts of the human and financial cost of subduing the revolt started by Louverture, French officials viewed him as a criminal who should consider himself lucky to even be alive. "Make him understand the enormity of his crime," Bonaparte had instructed his envoy Caffarelli.[90]

The memoir had consequently little impact in Paris. The minister of the navy concluded that "no important confession results from this report [by Caffarelli] and the memoir made by Toussaint to justify himself."[91] French officials underlined only the passages relating to Louverture's alleged treasure and dedicated much energy pursuing leads on its possible location. When the search for the treasure reached a dead end, Bonaparte lost interest and stopped mentioning his fallen rival in his correspondence. For all intents and purposes, Louverture had now ceased to exist in his eyes.

After vainly waiting three weeks for a response, Louverture wrote again to Bonaparte on 9 October 1802 to beg for clemency in terms that recycled several themes of the memoir. "I am not educated, I am ignorant, but my father [godfather] who is presently blind has shown me the path of virtue. I beg you in the name of God and humanity to look positively upon my petition because I have been punished with a crown of thorns and the most marked ingratitude." "Please refresh the first consul's memory," he also added for Caffarelli's benefit. No reply came. During his years as governor, Louverture had often complained that Bonaparte refused to write to him directly; Bonaparte's silence in the fall of 1802 must have been a painful reminder of past snubs. (Unbeknownst to Louverture, his godfather was drowned in Saint-Domingue around the same time).[92]

In the absence of a response from the first consul, Louverture continued the lonely and monotonous life of a state prisoner. He may have planned to write another memoir because he asked for one of his sons to be sent to him, "either to serve as a secretary, or to serve him and console him," but his request was denied.[93] Aside from the prison director Baille and the secretary Jeannin, his only visitors were a doctor and a surgeon from Pontarlier who regularly made the trip to Joux to pull out some of his remaining teeth. But in October, a mysterious priest managed to sneak into his cell by passing as a doctor, and Louverture lost his visitation privileges. So concerned were local authorities about a possible escape that they kept a vagabond in jail for four months simply because they found his presence in the region suspicious.[94]

"My friends, a man must never forget the humiliations he has suffered," Louverture had once told his officers.[95] In this context, the multiple indignities he suffered during his captivity must have left him boiling with anger. To lessen the risk of bribery and escape, Paris demanded that Louverture's valuables be confiscated. He had to give away all the cash he had on him or undergo a body search. On orders from the minister of the navy, his watch was confiscated and replaced by "one of these cheap wooden clocks, of the cheapest kind, which are enough to indicate the passage of time."[96] Louverture, who had longed all his life to be treated with respect by his white contemporaries, described the episode as the worst "humiliation" of his life. He initially asked Baille for a receipt so that he could get back his belongings "when he would get out of jail." Then, after thinking the matter over, he realized that this day would never come. "The day I am executed, send all my belongings to my wife and children," he wrote sullenly.[97]

In a last-ditch attempt, Louverture sent yet another letter to Bonaparte on 26 October 1802 to promise that the "supreme being" (a euphemism for "God" employed by deists during the French Revolution) would reward him if he showed forgiveness.[98] The first consul's response was uncompromising: He asked that Louverture's writing materials be taken away at once. Again threatened with a body search, Louverture had to give away nine notebooks, along with three letters he had hidden in his pants (Louverture possibly managed to hide the C manuscript under the handkerchief wrapped around his head). "He seemed very bothered by the confiscation of his papers," noted Baille.[99] Louverture had been effectively silenced. The 26 October letter is the last document he ever wrote.

For two weeks after his cell was searched, Louverture was very agitated and angry. He would bang his feet on the ground and, Baille reported, say "the most indecent things" about his foe, General Leclerc (who, he would have been happy to learn, was actually dying of yellow fever in Cap-Français at that very moment).[100] Then, losing the last remnants of his combativeness, he began to complain of unceasing fevers and pains and announced that he no longer wished to get out of bed because it was too cold.[101] The life of an impotent captive must have felt worse than death itself for a man who had once been absolute master of Saint-Domingue. Commanding was for him "an ecstasy, a need," his secretary had once noted. "For such a man, death must seem preferable to becoming a nobody."[102] Death was indeed the only thing to which he could now look forward.

Loneliness and melancholy overwhelmed the homesick prisoner. Louverture "was sad and somber, he spent most of his days looking through the small window, his head resting on his hand, leaning against the iron of the grate, plunged in a dark melancholy," a guard remembered. "The poor man thought of his country, his children! He was so desolate."[103] Some books claim that Louverture was jailed next to his fellow Dominguans André Rigaud and Martial Besse, but they only reached the prison of Joux after his death. Two other Caribbean exiles, Jean and Zamor Kina, did arrive in January 1803, but they never had a chance to meet Louverture, who did not even know that they were jailed one floor above him.[104] He was truly alone.

Nivôse, pluviôse, ventôse, the months of snow, rain, and wind in the French revolutionary calendar, came and went. For Louverture, accustomed to the endless summers of the tropics, the terrible winter of the Jura Mountains, the coldest region in France, was a frozen hell. He spent his days in front of a roaring fire in a vain attempt to warm up his dying body, but the light cotton clothes he had been issued to replace his uniform were not enough to protect him from the bite of the icy air. The stinginess of French officials did not help: His wood allowance was cut down in the midst of January to save a few francs.[105]

To make matters worse, the prison director Baille, whose personal kindness had somewhat mitigated the stern and petty measures inflicted by Paris, left his position on 1 December 1802. According to his temporary replacement, Jean Gazagnaire, "Toussaint sometimes ventures questions about his future destiny. I only gave negative answers." Gazagnaire was replaced in January 1803 by a young and aggressive officer named Amiot. The latter routinely ordered surprise searches of Louverture's cell in the middle of the night while the mortified captive stood by in frigid silence next to his torn-up bed.[106]

Amiot need not have worried about a possible escape. Louverture was an elderly and sickly man whose indomitable will had finally been broken by the vexatious measures of his captors. Time after time, he complained of fevers, headaches, stomachaches, and a dry cough that would not go away, but he no longer asked for doctors.[107] He might have derived some comfort from the knowledge that the rebels of Saint-Domingue were organizing and uniting their army. England had just begun a new war with France, and in November 1803, after a last climactic battle fought outside Cap-Français, at the doorstep of the plantation on which Louverture was born, a rebel army led by his former second Jean-Jacques Dessalines would defeat the remnants of the Leclerc expedition and declare Haiti's independence.

But Louverture never lived to see his native island gain its full sovereignty. On 7 April 1803, as prison director Amiot entered Louverture's cell to deliver his daily food allowance, he found him sitting by the remnants of a dead fire, his head leaning against the mantle. Doctors from Pontarlier pronounced Louverture dead later that day. The autopsy attributed his death to pneumonia and apoplexy (stroke). Some rumors allege that he had been poisoned on Bonaparte's orders or that Amiot had deliberately left him without food for four days, but there is no evidence to back such conspiracy theories. Put simply, Louverture died because his body was old and cold. He also died because his heart was broken.[108]

Auguste Nemours, a Haitian historian who wrote the most detailed account of Louverture's final months, described his end in Christian terms, overtly comparing his humiliation and agony to the Stations of the Cross.[109] The picture that emerges from the archives is more prosaic. The French Pontius Pilates were primarily concerned with security. Miserliness was also routine as authorities spent an inordinate amount of time calculating the expense of housing Louverture and other prisoners to the last franc and trying to locate Louverture's alleged treasure. There was no attempt

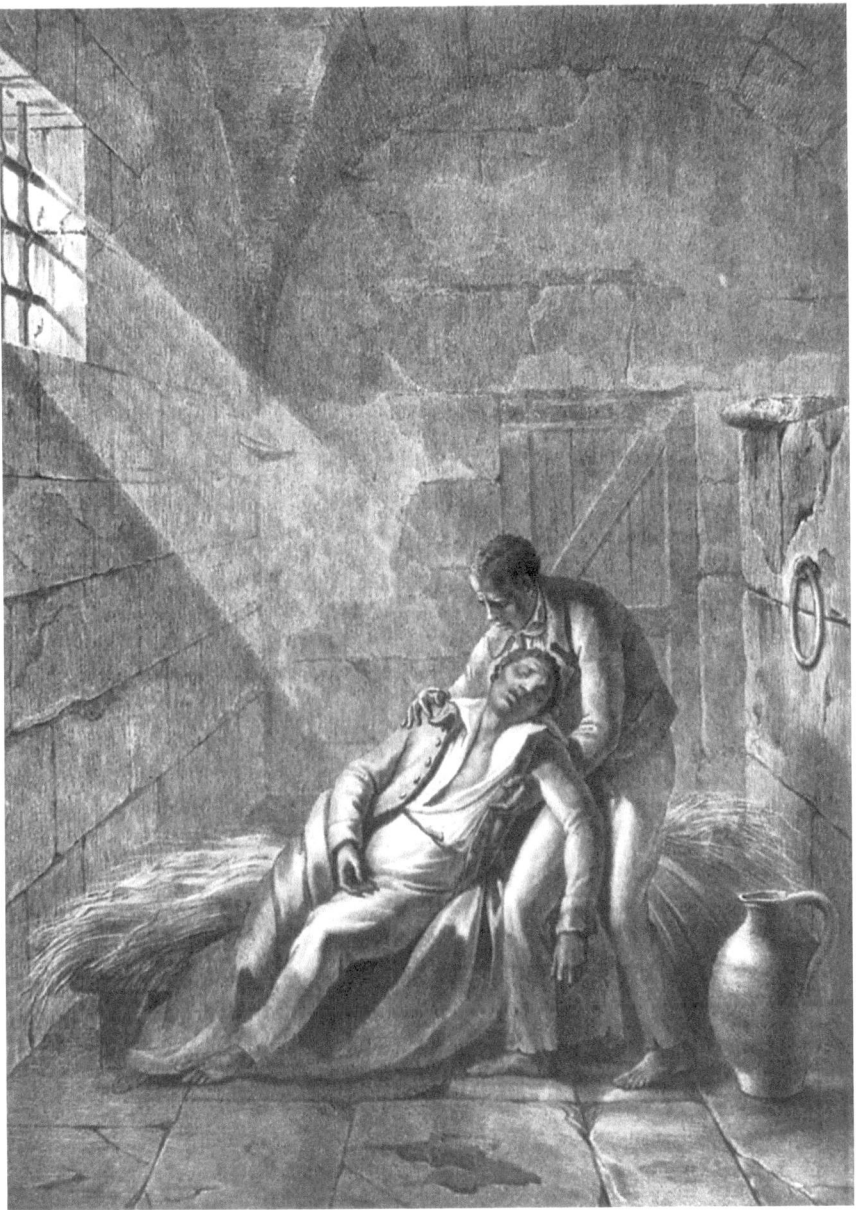

A posthumous rendering of Louverture's final hours. Louverture actually died alone because his servant Mars Plaisir had left the Fort de Joux in September 1802.
Library of Congress LC-USZ62-7863

to engage Louverture in a great ideological debate on the merits of emancipation and colonization, merely some accountants' squabbles over centimes and receipts. Humiliation was another theme, especially on the part of the minister of the navy, an insignificant and racist bureaucrat who scolded the director of the prison, Baille, for allowing Louverture to defend his record. "He only deserves the most profound scorn for his ridiculous pride."[110]

Silencing, indifference, and neglect marked the last months of Louverture's captivity. By denying him access to interlocutors, ignoring his letters and memoirs, and refusing to let him write, French authorities hoped to prevent him from expressing himself. This makes Louverture's memoir all the more important since it was his final attempt to tell his story.

LEGACY

Louverture's memoir is invaluable because it is a rare example of a former slave—arguably the most historically relevant former slave in world history—speaking out in his own voice. This text, first published 160 years ago, is widely known but poorly understood, particularly since few French speakers have read the more authentic C version, and English speakers only have access to an 1863 translation that is grossly inadequate. It is often portrayed as an autobiography when it was in fact a petition addressed to Bonaparte. It is a historical account, but one that must be approached with caution because of Louverture's desire to defend his record in a difficult personal context. It is a political tract with a surprising message: To the end, Louverture presented himself as a loyal servant of the French republic, a planter, and a military man abiding by the officers' code of honor, not as a slave rebel. He did bring race into the equation, but only to complain that racial discrimination had prevented him from being fully accepted into the French ruling sphere, not to outline a program of racial pride.

A literary critic's work consists in digging through various layers just as a geologist uncovers ancient strata of rocks. The memoir is particularly challenging in that regard because of its composite nature. On the surface, it is an administrative report filed with a superior. It is also, one layer below, a thinly veiled manifesto against the colonial policies of Bonaparte (though it is aimed at his brother-in-law to avoid offending the first consul) and an impassioned defense of Louverture's policies as governor. A third layer is composed of the narrative's gaps: the many elements in Louverture's life that he purposely omitted, which can be psychologically analyzed to try to deduce Louverture's innermost fears and hopes.

Another conclusion to be drawn from the memoir is linguistic. By establishing a "missing link" between present-day Kreyòl and 17th- and 18th-century regional and popular French, the memoir tends to undermine linguistic theories describing Kreyòl as a descendant of African languages. The memoir also points to the existence of a creolized French spoken by aspiring black elites during the late colonial era and confirms Albert Valdman's hypothesis that there was a "continuum ranging from that [Kreyòl] most distant from French... to that which shares many features with it."[111]

Haitian elites are often described as diglossic rather than simply bilingual because they employ French for prestige roles (such as education, literature, and politics) while relegating Kreyòl to informal speech.[112] By emphasizing that Louverture favored French in official settings while using Kreyòl to speak to social inferiors, the memoir allows us to trace back the origins of this diglossia to the revolutionary era. Louverture's preference for French will no doubt enrich the ongoing debates between those who view him as a black revolutionary fighting French imperialism and those who think, as his linguistic profile suggests, that he modeled his behavior on the planters and officers of the Ancien Régime and the French Revolution.

One of the most important developments in recent historiography has been the rise of Atlantic history: the study of the manifold interactions between Europe, Africa, and the Americas around 1500–1800. By bringing together national histories that were often analyzed in seclusion, Atlantic history has allowed us to underline the links between events such as the American, French, and Haitian revolutions. However, because Atlantic history was constructed by historians, cross-disciplinary (as opposed to transnational) studies have been the exception. Louverture's memoir forces historians to broaden their horizons and incorporate linguistics and literary criticism. Other approaches are possible; a political scientist, for example, might try to connect Louverture's views on government, race, and colonialism to Enlightenment ideals or African concepts of kinship and kingship.

The memoir is important for one final, more personal reason: It humanizes Louverture. Like many public figures, he maintained a public façade that was at once stern, austere, and inscrutable. He used the formal "vous" when writing to some family members, and his closest associates confessed to being unable to know his innermost thoughts. He remains, to a large extent, a cipher, a larger-than-life historical figure who can be hard to understand and even harder to love. Even making a physical connection is difficult. Many portraits of him exist, but his appearance varies dramatically from one portrait to the other because most were made by artists who had never met him. His body has proved to be equally elusive: It was buried in Joux after his death, but subsequent renovations of the fort destroyed his tomb, and the body subsequently vanished (a half skull of dubious origin was on display in his cell in the 1850s for the benefit of tourists). The plantation where he was born, now absorbed by the suburbs of Cap-Haïtien (formerly Cap-Français), has also vanished.[113]

Manuscript C is the only tangible way to make a connection with Louverture. Its tone is far more personal than his official correspondence, and it brings to the fore themes, like his anger at racial discrimination and his love for his family, that he rarely evoked in public. When holding the old, stained sheets of manuscript C, which he apparently hid on his body during searches of his cell, one can truly establish a rapport with the heartbroken leader languishing in Joux.

There is only one document comparable to Louverture's memoir in its tone, appearance, and emotional hold. It consists of a few sentences jotted down by Napoléon Bonaparte in his spidery handwriting while he too endured the agony of exile and imprisonment on the damp island of Saint Helena. Like Louverture, Bonaparte wrote these lines in the language of his victorious foe because he was trying to learn English in his waning years (Bonaparte had grown up speaking Corsican, but he normally expressed himself in standard French, which, like Louverture, he spoke with an accent). These last sentences, written in hesitant and grammatically incorrect English, are those of a lonely husband and father longing for his wife and son:[114]

> Lorsque je débarquerai en France je serai très content—When j shall land in France j shall be very content... my wife shall come near to me, my son shall be great and strong if he will be able to trink a bottle of wine at dinner j shall [toast] with him.... When you shall come, you shall see that j have ever loved you.

Bonaparte's body, now interred in a grandiose tomb at the Invalides chapel in Paris, has not vanished like Louverture's (his childhood home in Ajaccio, Corsica, also survived). But Louverture would surely have felt vindicated to learn that his captor, after being separated from his wife and offspring, experienced as much personal turmoil as Louverture did in his dying months.

NOTES

1. On the cell, see Baille to Denis Decrès (28 Sept. 1802), CC9B/18, Archives Nationales d'Outremer, Aix-en-Provence (ANOM); J. F. Dubois to Henri Grégoire (25 May 1823), NAF 6864, Bibliothèque Nationale, Paris (BNF).
2. Frederick Douglass, *Narrative of the Life of Frederick Douglass, An American Slave, Written by Himself* (Boston: Anti-Slavery Office, 1845).
3. On Louverture's early life, see Jean-Louis Donnadieu and Philippe Girard, "Toussaint Before Louverture: New Archival Findings on the Early Life of Toussaint Louverture," *William and Mary Quarterly* 70:1 (Jan. 2013), 41–78.
4. On the death of Louverture's parents, see François Bayon de Libertat to Pantaléon II de Breda (30 Apr. 1774), Dossier 12, 18AP/3, Archives Nationales, Paris (AN). On the godfather, see Isaac Louverture to M. de Saint-Anthoine (8 March 1842), NAF 6864, BNF; Thomas-Prosper Gragnon-Lacoste, *Toussaint Louverture* (Paris: Durand, 1877), 11, 15, 298.
5. On Dessalines, see Philippe Girard, "Jean-Jacques Dessalines and the Atlantic System: A Reappraisal," *William and Mary Quarterly* 69:3 (July 2012), 555.
6. Vincent Caretta, *Equiano the African: Biography of a Self-Made Man* (Athens: University of Georgia Press, 2005).
7. "Il a perdu onze enfants" from "Toussaint Louverture au Fort de Joux" (c. 17 Sept. 1802), *Nouvelle Revue Rétrospective* no. 94 (10 Apr. 1902), 13. On Louverture's first family, see Jean-Louis Donnadieu, "La famille 'oubliée' de Toussaint Louverture," *Bulletin de la Société Archéologique du Gers* 401 (Fall 2011), 357–365.
8. On learning how to read as a slave, see Thomas Madiou, *Histoire d'Haïti*, vol. 2 (Port-au-Prince: Courtois, 1847), 125; Gragnon-Lacoste, *Toussaint Louverture*, 10. For writing samples by relatives, see Jean-Baptiste to Moïse (10 Aug. 1800), Box 6:11, Borie Family Papers, (Phi)1602, Historical Society of Pennsylvania (HSP); Suzanne Louverture to Louverture (13 July 1794), 61J18, Archives Départementales de la Gironde, Bordeaux (ADGir). On a soldier as teacher, see Charles Malenfant, "Opinion sur les colonies" (c. 1801), Box 2/103, Rochambeau Papers, University of Florida, Gainesville.
9. On a French officer as the teacher, see Isaac Louverture, "Notes historiques sur Toussaint Louverture, manuscrit d'Isaac Louverture, notes intéressantes sur Banica etc." (c. 1819), p. 55, NAF 12409, BNF. For the first signature, see Jean-François

Papillon, Georges Biassou et al. to [French commissioners] (12 Dec. 1791), *D/ XXV/1, AN.
10. Toussaint Louverture, *Réfutation de quelques assertions d'un discours prononcé au corps législatif le 10 prairial, an cinq, par Viénot Vaublanc* (Cap-Français, c. 1797).
11. See "deu puis la revolution 10 aout 90[92?] je sui de même concecutivement au service de ma patris," in Louverture to Napoléon Bonaparte (9 Oct. 1802), Dossier 1, AF/IV/1213, AN.
12. On Louverture's royalist leanings, see Louverture, "Reponse Sentimentale pour Servir au Sujet de la Lettre sur la revolution de St. Domingue jeudy 8 aoust 1793" (27 Aug. 1793), Dossier 1511, aa55/a, AN.
13. On Louverture's whereabouts in 1791, see David Geggus, "Toussaint Louverture avant et après l'insurrection de 1791," in Franklin Midy, ed., *Mémoire de révolution d'esclaves à Saint-Domingue* (Montréal: CIDIHCA, 2006), 113–129. For Louverture's claim that he began the slave revolt, see Louverture, "Proclamation" (25 Apr. 1796), fr. 12104, BNF.
14. For a tentative list of documents signed by Louverture, see Joseph A. Boromé, "Toussaint Louverture: A Finding List of his Letters and Documents in Archives and Collections," Box 1, Joseph Borome papers, Sc MG 714, Schomburg Center, New York Public Library (SC-NYPL). For pre-1802 documents in Louverture's handwriting, see Louverture to Gabriel d'Hédouville (c. 1798), AF/III, 210, AN; Louverture to Jean-Jacques Dessalines (Oct. 1798), Autograph File T., Houghton Library, Harvard University (HL-HU); Louverture to Renne de Saba (17 Apr. 1799), Papers of Toussaint Louverture, Manuscript Department, Library of Congress, Washington, DC; Louverture to Etienne Dupuche (10 May 1800 and 24 Sept. 1801), Folder 6, Box 6, Borie Family Papers, (Phi)1602, HSP; Louverture to Augustin d'Hébécourt (6 March 1801), Ms. f Hait.69–29, Boston Public Library (BPL); Louverture to Henry Christophe (28 Apr. 1802) 61J18, ADGir. The British archives also have a transcript of a lost handwritten letter in "Council minutes" (22 Nov. 1799), CO 137/107, British National Archives, Kew (BNA).
15. On Moïse, see Philippe Roume to Louverture (21 Oct. 1799), CC/9A/26, ANOM. "Sa pénétration littéraire" from Michel-Etienne Descourtilz, *Voyage d'un naturaliste et ses observations*, vol. 3 (Paris: Dufart, 1809), 245. "Pour rien au monde il n'eût signé la lettre" from Pamphile de Lacroix, *Mémoires pour servir à l'histoire de la révolution de Saint-Domingue*, vol. 2 (Paris: Pillet, 1819), 206.
16. "L'instruction qu'il lui a plu également" from Louverture to Laurent Truguet (1 Feb. 1797), Dossier 1, EE1734, ANOM. "Vous autres nègres" from Lacroix, *Mémoires*, vol. 1, 400.
17. On the partial economic recovery, see Pierre Pluchon, *Toussaint Louverture* (Paris: Fayard, 1989), 400–422. For Bonaparte's regrets, see Barry O'Meara, *Napoléon en exil: relation contenant les opinions et les réflexions de Napoléon sur les événements les plus importants de sa vie* (Paris: Garnier, 1897), 276; Emmanuel de las Cases, *Le Mémorial de Sainte-Hélène*, vol. 1 (Paris: Gallimard, 1956), 769.
18. On Louverture's diplomacy, see Philippe Girard, "Black Talleyrand: Toussaint Louverture's Secret Diplomacy with England and the United States," *William and Mary Quarterly* 66:1 (Jan. 2009), 87–124.
19. "Oui, c'est vrai, j'ai fait une faute" from "Toussaint Louverture au Fort de Joux," 10.
20. On Bonaparte's intentions, see Philippe Girard, "Napoléon Bonaparte and the Emancipation Issue in Saint-Domingue, 1799–1803," *French Historical Studies* 32:4 (Fall 2009), 587–618.
21. On French atrocities, see R. Mends to John Duckworth (1 Apr. 1802), ADM 1/252, BNA; Lacroix, *Mémoires*, vol. 2, 150. For Louverture's orders to kill white civilians, see Louverture to Augustin Clerveaux (c. 30 Jan. 1802), in Guillaume Mauviel, "Mémoire

sur Saint-Domingue" (26 June 1805), p. 40, pièce 101, AF/IV/1212, AN; Louverture to Jean-Baptiste Domage (9 Feb. 1802), CC9B/19, ANOM.

22. On Louverture's military problems, see Philippe Girard, *The Slaves Who Defeated Napoléon: Toussaint Louverture and the Haitian War of Independence* (Tuscaloosa: University of Alabama Press, 2011), 134.

23. On money seized from the Louvertures, see Jean-Baptiste Brunet to Donatien de Rochambeau (15 June 1802), lot 224, Vente Rochambeau, Philippe Rouillac auction house (VR-PR). On Dessalines and the arrest, see Philippe Girard, "Jean-Jacques Dessalines et l'arrestation de Toussaint Louverture," *Journal of Haitian Studies* 17:1 (Spring 2011), 123–138.

24. On deportations, see Claude Bonaparte Auguste and Marcel Bonaparte Auguste, *Les déportés de Saint-Domingue: Contribution à l'histoire de l'expédition française de Saint-Domingue, 1802–1803* (Sherbrooke, Québec: Naaman, 1979). On Dumas, see Alexandre Dumas, *Mes mémoires*, vol. 1 (Paris: Michel Lévy, 1865), 193–196, 230–234.

25. "Si mon épouse n'avait pas été contrainte" from Louverture to Victoire Leclerc (18 July 1802), Folder 3C, Kurt Fisher Collection, Howard University. "Une mère de famille, à 53 ans," from Louverture to Bonaparte (20 July 1802), Dossier 1, AF/IV/1213, AN.

26. On the fate of Louverture's relatives, see Alexandre Berthier to Decrès (26 July 1802), Dossier 1, EE1734, ANOM; Auguste Nemours, *Histoire de la famille et de la descendance de Toussaint Louverture* (Port-au-Prince, HT: Imprimerie de l'Etat, 1941). Louverture's niece Louise Chancy made a visit to Haiti in 1821–25. For a letter enquiring about Louverture's whereabouts, see Isaac Louverture to Decrès (9 June 1803), CC9B/18, ANOM.

27. On convict law under Bonaparte, see Miranda Frances Spieler, *Empire and Underworld: Captivity in French Guyana* (Cambridge, MA: Harvard University Press, 2012), 82–84.

28. On Landerneau, see Joseph Caffarelli to Decrès (13 Aug. 1802), Dossier 1, EE1734, ANOM. For mistaken claims that Louverture spent a night at the Temple prison in Paris on 17 August, see Joseph Saint-Rémy, *Vie de Toussaint Louverture* (Paris: Moquet, 1850), 391; Victor Schoelcher, *Vie de Toussaint Louverture* (Paris: Ollendorf, 1889), 351; Pluchon, *Toussaint Louverture*, 522. On the actual route, see "Route proposée" (c. 1 Aug. 1802), Dossier 5410, F/7/6266, AN; Mars Plaisir to Isaac Louverture (3 Oct. 1815), NAF 6864, BNF.

29. "Son parler nègre" from Fernand Clamettes, ed., *Mémoires du général Baron Thiébault*, vol. 3 (Paris: Plon, 1893–1895), 302.

30. For official sources on Louverture's captivity, see AF/IV/1213 and 135AP/6, AN; CC9B/18, ANOM; Sc Micro R1527, SC-NYPL; 7Yd284 and B7/6 to B7/9, Service Historique de la Défense/Département de l'Armée de Terre, Vincennes (SHD-DAT); M696, Archives Départementales du Doubs, Besançon; Nemours Collection, University of Puerto Rico (NC-UPR). For personal accounts collected by Louverture's son Isaac, see NAF 6864 and NAF 12409, BNF; 6APC/1, ANOM. Many documents were printed in M. Morpeau, *Documents inédits pour l'histoire: Correspondance concernant l'emprisonnement et la mort de Toussaint Louverture* (Port-au-Prince: Sacré Coeur, 1920).

31. On security measures, see Baille, "Copie de la consigne du poste du donjon du château de Joux" (24 Aug. 1802), B7/6, SHD-DAT; Auguste Nemours, *Histoire de la captivité et de la mort de Toussaint-Louverture* (Paris: Berger-Levrault, 1929), 26.

32. "Cet aspect nous faisait présager une mort prochaine," from Mars Plaisir to Isaac Louverture (3 Oct. 1815), NAF 6864, BNF. For orders to send Plaisir away, see Berthier to Philippe-Romain Menard (31 Aug. 1802) B7/6, SHD-DAT. On his departure, see

Menard to Berthier (13 Sept. 1802), B7/8, SHD-DAT. On his later life, see Plaisir to Suzanne Louverture (18 Sept. 1815), TLF-2A1, NC-UPR.
33. On the request for writing material, see Baille to Menard (27 Aug. 1802), B7/6, SHD-DAT; J. de Bry to Jean-Antoine Chaptal (15 Sept. 1802), TL-2B1l, NC-UPR. For the ban on writing, see "Extrait des registres des délibérations des consuls de la République" (23 July 1802), 7Yd284, SHD-DAT. For Louverture's writings in Joux, see Louverture to Bonaparte (16 Sept. 1802), Dossier 1, EE1734, ANOM; Louverture to Suzanne Louverture (17 Sept. 1802), ibid.; Louverture to Marie-François Caffarelli (c. 17 Sept. 1802), *Nouvelle Revue Rétrospective*, no. 94 (10 Apr. 1902), 17; Louverture to Bonaparte (17 Sept. 1802), Dossier 1, AF/IV/1213, AN; Louverture to Berthier (17 Sept. 1802), ibid.; Louverture to Bonaparte (9 Oct. 1802), ibid. (two copies); Louverture to Caffarelli (9 Oct. 1802), ibid.; Louverture to Bonaparte (26 Oct. 1802), ibid.
34. On Baille's good treatment, see Baille to Menard (27 Aug. 1802), B7/6, SHD-DAT. On Louverture's isolation, see Micaut to de Bry (10 Jan. 1803), TL-2C2b, NC-UPR.
35. "Des choses importantes" from Baille to Menard (27 Aug. 1802), B7/6, SHD-DAT. "L'existence de ses trésors" from Bonaparte to Caffarelli (9 Sept. 1802), in Jean-Baptiste Vaillant, ed., *Correspondance de Napoléon Ier, publiée par ordre de l'empereur Napoléon III*, vol. 8 (Paris: Plon, 1858), 39. "Un nègre de la taille de cinq pieds un pouce" from "Toussaint Louverture au Fort de Joux," 1.
36. "Je n'ai jamais été riche en argent" from "Toussaint Louverture au Fort de Joux," 12. "Cet homme est maître de lui" from Caffarelli to [Bonaparte] (16 Sept. 1802), Dossier 1, AF/IV/1213, AN.
37. For orders on the uniform, see Berthier to Menard (31 Aug. 1802) B7/6, SHD-DAT. "Le commandant du fort lui apporta les habits" from "Toussaint Louverture au Fort de Joux," 15. "Toussaint refusa d'abord" from J. F. Dubois to Henri Grégoire (25 May 1823), NAF 6864, BNF.
38. "Il avait d'un seul trait" from Daniel Desormeaux, ed., *Mémoires du général Toussaint Louverture* (Paris: Classiques Garnier, 2011), 10. For manuscripts A, B, and C and various drafts, see Dossier 1, AF/IV/1213, AN. For manuscript D, see Dossier 2, EE 1734, ANOM. For a fifth version that is most likely posthumous, see "Mémoire du général Toussaint Louverture," West Mss. 6, Northwestern University Library.
39. "Ci-joint" from Caffarelli to [Berthier?] (24 Sept. 1802), Dossier 1, EE 1734, ANOM.
40. On adding to the manuscript, see "Toussaint Louverture au Fort de Joux," 4. On entrusting the manuscript to Caffarelli, see Louverture to Bonaparte (16 Sept. 1802), Dossier 1, EE1734, ANOM.
41. On Martial Besse as the author, see Joseph Saint-Rémy, *Mémoires du général Toussaint-L'Ouverture écrits par lui-même* (Paris: Pagnerre, 1853), 19. On Besse's arrival in Joux, see Jean-Antoine Chaptal to Decrès (14 May 1803), 8Yd638, SHD-DAT.
42. "Ecrit sous sa dictée" from Nemours, *Histoire de la captivité*, 249.
43. "J'ai également écrit sous sa dictée" from Jeannin to Isaac Louverture (24 Nov. 1810), NAF 6864, BNF. Whether Louverture was a freemason remains a matter of debate among historians.
44. On the conversations, see Baille to Decrès (28 Sept. 1802), CC9B/18, ANOM; Nemours, *Histoire de la Captivité*, 242, 249.
45. "Toussaint dictait séparément" from Schoelcher, *Vie de Toussaint Louverture*, 394.
46. "Toussaint ne parle que le créole" from Léger-Félicité Sonthonax to Directoire Exécutif (30 Jan. 1798), AF/III, 210, AN. For transcripts of conversations, see Louverture, "Rapport au directoire exécutif" (4 Sept. 1797), Pièce 12, Dossier 961, AF/III, 210,

AN; Jacques de Norvins, *Souvenirs d'un historien de Napoléon: mémorial de J. de Norvins* vol. 2 (Paris: Plon, 1896), 395.
47. On switching languages, see Lacroix, *Mémoires*, vol. 2, 206.
48. On Louverture's use of metaphors, see Lacroix, *Mémoires*, vol. 1, 410; Pluchon, *Toussaint Louverture*, 431; Jacques de Cauna, ed., *Toussaint Louverture et l'indépendance d'Haïti* (Paris: Karthala, 2004), 102. According to Desormeaux, *Mémoires*, 142, Louverture was inspired by the fact that Caffarelli had lost a hand and a leg in battle, but it was actually Caffarelli's brother Louis Marie Maximilien who suffered these wounds.
49. "Placée secrètement" from Amiot to Comte du Poul (24 Aug. 1814), 7Yd284, SHD-DAT. "Dans les plis d'un mouchoir" from Berthier to Bonaparte (2 June 1803), Dossier 1, AF/IV/1213, AN. No memoir is mentioned in the lists of Louverture's belongings in TL-3A2 and TL-2B6q, NC-UPR, possibly because it had no monetary value.
50. On Desfourneaux's copy, see Saint-Rémy, *Mémoires*, 18.
51. On Saint-Rémy, see Jacques de Cauna, ed., *Mémoires du Général Toussaint-Louverture commentés par Saint-Rémy* (Guitalens-L'Albarède: La Girandole, 2009), 11–15, 25; Desormeaux, *Mémoires*, 15–21, 51–61. For the edition and translation, see Joseph Saint-Rémy, *Mémoires du général Toussaint-L'Ouverture écrits par lui-même* (Paris: Pagnerre, 1853); John R. Beard and James Redpath, eds., *Toussaint Louverture: A Biography and Auto-Biography* (Boston: James Redpath).
52. "Amour-propre patriotique" from Saint-Rémy, *Mémoires*, 20.
53. For example, see p. 19, line 9 of the C manuscript: "aDi dition au presante memoire; sis le gouvernemenet a voit en voié un." Desormeaux, *Mémoires*, 196 (some words unwittingly corrected): "addition au presant memoire; si le gouvernement avoit envoié un." Cauna, *Mémoires*, 260 (willfully modernized): "Addition au présent mémoire / Si le gouvernement avait envoyé un."
54. "Testament politique" from Desormeaux, *Mémoires*, 83. On the memoir as memoirs, see also Daniel Desormeaux, "The First of the (Black) Memorialists: Toussaint Louverture," *Yale French Studies* 107 (2005), 131–145; Cauna, *Mémoires*, 17; Deborah Jenson, *Beyond the Slave Narrative: Politics, Sex, and Manuscripts in the Haitian Revolution* (Liverpool, UK: Liverpool University Press, 2011), 18.
55. Louverture to Bonaparte (17 Sept. 1802), Dossier 1, AF/IV/1213, AN.
56. For Louverture's petitions, see Louverture, "Rapport au Directoire Exécutif" (4 Sept. 1797), Pièce 12, Dossier 961, AF/III, 210, AN; Louverture to Directoire Exécutif (12 Nov. 1798), AF/III, 210, AN.
57. "Il ne répond pas directement" from "Toussaint Louverture au Fort de Joux," 4.
58. For the decision not to hold a trial, see "Rapport aux consuls concernant Toussaint Louverture" (23 July 1802), CC9/B23, ANOM; Leclerc to Decrès (26 Sept. 1802), B7/26, SHD-DAT.
59. On Louverture's views on independence, see Girard, "Black Talleyrand," 116.
60. On Louverture's labor record, see Louverture, [Règlement des cultures] (12 Oct. 1800), in Beaubrun Ardouin, *Etudes sur l'histoire d'Haïti*, vol. 4 (Paris: Dezobry and Magdeleine, 1854), 247–255.
61. "War within the war" from Michel Rolph-Trouillot, *Silencing the Past: Power and the Production of History* (Boston: Beacon Press, 1995), 40.
62. "Terrible power" from John Lynch, *Simón Bolívar: A Life* (New Haven, CT: Yale University Press, 2007), 67.
63. On Louverture urging cultivators to work, see the proclamations dated 18 May 1798, 5 Oct. 1798, 15 Nov. 1798, and 4 Jan. 1800 in CC9/A/19 and CC9/B/9, ANOM.
64. "Général" from [Decrès?] to Baille (27 Oct. 1802), CC9B/18, ANOM.

65. For previous accusations of racism, see Louverture, *Réfutation de quelques assertions d'un discours prononcé au corps législatif le 10 prairial, an cinq, par Viénot Vaublanc* (Cap-Français, c. 1797); Tobias Lear to James Madison (17 July 1801), 208 MI/2, AN; Pluchon, *Toussaint Louverture*, 549.
66. William J. Rolfe, ed., *Select Poems of William Wordsworth* (New York: Harper and Brothers, 1889), 89.
67. "Le prisonnier s'évade" from Cauna, *Mémoires*, 34.
68. "Aimant catéchiser et à faire des prosélytes" from [Valsemey?], "Esclaves existant sur l'habitation de M. de Breda" (31 Dec. 1785), 261MIOM, ANOM (document communicated to me by Jean-Louis Donnadieu). On Louverture as a false Christian, see Pluchon, *Toussaint Louverture*, 338. On Louverture as a *vodouisant*, see Madison Smartt Bell, *Toussaint Louverture: A Biography* (New York: Pantheon Books, 2007), 288. The two religious identities are not mutually exclusive in Haiti.
69. For Kreyòl as an heir to French and regional languages, see Jules Faine, *Philologie créole: études historiques et étymologiques sur la langue créole d'Haïti* (Port-au-Prince, HT: Imprimerie de l'Etat, 1937); Albert Valdman, *Le créole: structure, statut et origine* (Paris: Klincksieck, 1978). On Kreyòl as a primarily African language, see Suzanne Sylvain, *Le créole haïtien: morphologie et syntaxe* (Port-au-Prince: Self-published, 1936); John Holm, *Pidgins and Creoles* (New York: Cambridge University Press, 1988–1989). On Kreyòl as a mixture, see Robert Hall, *Pidgin and Creole Languages* (Ithaca, NY: Cornell University Press, 1966). On Kreyòl as an embodiment of deep-rooted linguistic processes, see Derek Bickerton, *The Roots of Language* (Ann Arbor, MI: Karoma, 1981). On Kreyòl as the heir to pidgins used by slave traders, see Morris Goodman, *A Comparative Study of Creole French Dialects* (The Hague: Mouton, 1964), 130; Gwendolyn Midlo Hall, *Africans in Colonial Louisiana: The Development of Afro-Creole Culture in the Eighteenth Century* (Baton Rouge: Louisiana State University Press, 1992), 190.
70. On the demographic weight of *bossales*, see David Geggus, "The French Slave Trade: An Overview," *William and Mary Quarterly* 58:1 (Jan. 2001), 130. For a rare mention of the "langage guinéen," see Descourtilz, *Voyage*, vol. 3, 190. On *pale langaj* and Vodun, see Althéa de Puech Parham, ed., *My Odyssey: Experiences of a Young Refugee from two Revolutions* (Baton Rouge: Louisiana State University Press, 1959), 26; Joan Dayan, *Haiti, History, and the Gods* (1995; reprint, Berkeley: University of California Press, 1998), 52.
71. For a rare example of the use of a French regional language (provençal), see Jean-Baptiste Lemonnier-Delafosse, *Seconde campagne de Saint-Domingue du 1 décembre 1803 au 15 juillet 1809* (Le Havre: Brindeau, 1846), 14.
72. "Jargon" from Justin Girod-Chantrans, *Voyage d'un Suisse dans différentes colonies d'Amérique* (Neuchatel, CH: Société typographique, 1785), 191. "Finesse" and the Kreyòl song from Médéric-Louis-Elie Moreau de Saint-Méry, *Description topographique, physique, civile, politique et historique de la partie française de l'isle Saint-Domingue*, vol. 1 (Philadelphia, 1797), 64–67. For other pre-revolutionary examples of Kreyòl, see Du Simitière, "Vocabulaire créole" (c. 1770s), 968.F.9, Du Simitière Collection, Library Company of Pennsylvania; Marie-Christine Hazaël-Massieux, *Textes anciens en créole français de la Caraïbe, histoire et analyse* (Paris: Publibook, 2008).
73. For revolutionary-era Kreyòl documents, see Agence du Directoire Exécutif à Saint-Domingue, "Arrêté concernant la police des habitations" (24 juillet 1798), CC9A/19, ANOM; S. J. Ducœurjoly, *Manuel des habitans de Saint-Domingue*, vol. 1 (Paris: Arthus-Bertrand, 1803), vi and ibid. vol. 2, 283–294; Anon., *Idylles, ou essais de poësie créole* (New York: Hopkins and Seymour, 1804), Shaw-Shoemaker Fiche 6530, Massachusetts Historical Society; Paul Roussier, ed., *Lettres du Général Leclerc* (Paris: Société de l'histoire des colonies françaises, 1937), 64; Aletha Stahl, "'Enfans

de l'Amérique:' Configuring Creole Citizenship in the Press, 1793," *Journal of Haitian Studies* 15:1–2 (2009), 171; Jeremy Popkin, *You Are All Free: The Haitian Revolution and the Abolition of Slavery* (New York: Cambridge University Press, 2010), 143. For a petition by field laborers, see Mhalick Ghachem, "The Colonial Vendée," in David Geggus and Norman Fiering, eds., *The World of the Haitian Revolution* (Bloomington: Indiana University Press, 2009), 169. For speeches by Jean-François and Louverture, see P., "Mon Odyssée" (c. 1798), 85-117-L, Box 1, Historic New Orleans Collection; Pélage-Marie Duboys, *Précis historique des Annales de la Révolution à Saint Domingue*, vol. 2, p. 80, NAF 14879 (MF 5384), BNF.

74. For post-independence texts, see Juste Chanlatte, *L'entrée du roi dans sa capitale en janvier 1818* (Cap Haïtien, 1818); Albert Valdman, "Haitian Creole at the Dawn of Independence," *Yale French Studies* 107 (2005), 151, 156. On present-day Kreyòl, see Bambi Schieffelin and Rachelle Charlier Doucet, "The 'Real' Haitian Creole: Ideology, Metalinguistics, and Orthographic Choice," *American Ethnologist* 21:1 (Feb. 1994), 188.

75. On Ewe-Fon, see Antoine Métral, *Histoire de l'expédition des Français à Saint-Domingue sous le consulat de Napoléon Bonaparte (1802–1803), suivie des mémoires et notes d'Isaac l'Ouverture* (1825; reprint, Paris: Karthala, 1985), 326; Gragnon-Lacoste, *Toussaint Louverture*, 9, 126. On Latin, see Lacroix, *Mémoires*, vol. 1, 402.

76. "Je fus un jour très mal écouté" from Descourtilz, *Voyage*, vol. 3, 251. "Sa manière de narrer" from "Toussaint Louverture au Fort de Joux," 17. On Louverture's oral French, see also Sonthonax to Directoire Exécutif (30 Jan. 1798), AF/III, 210, AN.

77. For a full discussion of the linguistics of the C manuscript, see Philippe Girard, "Quelle langue parlait Toussaint Louverture? Le mémoire du Fort de Joux et les origines du kreyòl haïtien," *Annales* 68:1 (Jan. 2013), 109–132.

78. On old spellings, see Claude Buffier, *Grammaire françoise sur un plan nouveau...* (Paris: Bordelet, 1754), 329, 341; L. M. P. Favre, *"Rèflèxions intèrèssantes sur la prononciation de la langue française...* (Lyon, FR: Cizeron, 1771), 6. On old pronunciations, see also M. Viard and Luneau de Boisjermain, *Les vrais principes de la lecture, de l'orthographe, et de la prononciation françoises* (Paris: Delalain, 1773); Charles Thurot, *De la prononciation française depuis le commencement du 16ème siècle* (Paris: Imprimerie Nationale, 1882). On regional French, see Favre, *Rèflèxions intèrèssantes*; Henri Doniol, *les patois de la basse Auvergne* (Paris: Maisonneuve, 1877). On Kreyòl, see Sylvain, *Le créole haïtien*; Valdman, *Le créole*; Goodman, *A Comparative Study of Creole*; Hall, *Pidgin and Creole*; Schieffelin and Doucet, "The 'Real' Haitian Creole."

79. Louverture to Bonaparte (9 Oct. 1802), Dossier 1, AF/IV/1213, AN; Suzanne Louverture to Louverture (13 July 1794), 61J18, ADGir.

80. On the demographic weight of Gascons, see Jacques de Cauna et al., *Bordeaux au 18ème siècle: le commerce atlantique et l'esclavage* (Bordeaux: Le Festin, 2010), 117.

81. Madiou, *Histoire d'Haïti*, vol. 2, 91.

82. "It is the former variety" from Doris Y. Kadish, ed., *Slavery in the Caribbean Francophone World: Distant Voices, Forgotten Acts, Forged Identities* (Athens: University of Georgia Press, 2000), 150.

83. Saint-Rémy, *Mémoires*, 88; Jenson, *Beyond the Slave Narrative*, 304; Desormeaux, *Mémoires*, 9.

84. "Z'autres pas té connois mai ben" from Duboys, *Précis historique* vol. 2, 80.

85. For letters to/from Suzanne and Dessalines, see Suzanne Louverture to Louverture (13 July 1794), 61J18, ADGir; Louverture to Jean-Jacques Dessalines (Oct. 1798), Autograph File, T., HL-HU; Louverture to Suzanne Louverture (17 Sept. 1802), Dossier 1, EE1734, ANOM. For letters to/from his sons, see Louverture to Isaac and

Placide Louverture (10 June 1798), AF/III, 210, AN; Louverture to Placide Louverture (13 Aug. 1800), Ms. Hait. 79-3, BPL; Placide to Toussaint and Suzanne Louverture (12 Aug. 1802), Dossier 1, AF/IV/1213, AN. On the sons' fluency, see Norvins, *Souvenirs d'un historien*, vol. 2, 31.

86. On Louverture reuniting with his sons, see Jean-Baptiste Coisnon to Leclerc (11 Feb. 1802), 61J18, ADGir; Coisnon to Decrès (20 Feb. 1802), in *Moniteur Universel*, no. 212 (22 Apr. 1802).
87. On hyper-correction, see Valdman, *Le créole*, 295, 323.
88. On Kreyòl variations, see Michelson Hyppolite, *Les origines des variations du créole haïtien* (Port-au-Prince, HT: Imprimerie de l'Etat, 1949); Valdman, *Le créole*, 286–299.
89. Bonaparte, "Notes pour servir aux instructions à donner au capitaine général Leclerc" (31 Oct. 1801), in Roussier, *Lettres du général Leclerc*, 271.
90. "L'énormité du crime" from Bonaparte to Caffarelli (9 Sept. 1802), in Vaillant, *Correspondance de Napoléon*, vol. 8, 39.
91. "Il ne résulte du rapport" from Decrès to Leclerc (16 Oct. 1802), Dossier 1, EE 1734, ANOM. On the search for the treasure, see also ibid. (17 Dec. 1802).
92. "Ge ne sui pas instruire" from Louverture to Bonaparte (9 Oct. 1802), Dossier 1, AF/IV/1213, AN. On past snubs from Bonaparte, see Jean-Baptiste Michel to Pierre Forfait (26 Dec. 1800), Dossier 6, AF/IV/1213, AN. On the godfather's death, see Ramel, "Notes" (c. 1803), in Alphonse de Lamartine, *Toussaint Louverture* (Paris: Levy, 1850), xviii.
93. "Soit pour lui tenir lieu de secrétaire" from Menard to Berthier (22 Oct. 1802), B7/8, SHD-DAT.
94. On Dormoy, see Menard to Berthier (15 Oct. 1802), B7/8, SHD-DAT; Bry to Baille (15 Oct. 1802), TL-2B4a, NC-UPR. On François Pothier, see Baille, [Interrogation account] (23 Nov. 1802), Dossier 1, AF/IV/1213, AN; Gomet to Bry (18 March 1803), TL-2C1c, NC-UPR.
95. "Mes amis, l'homme ne doit jamais oublier" from Madiou, *Histoire d'Haïti*, vol. 2, 125.
96. "Une de ces horloges de bois" from [Decrès] to Baille (27 Oct. 1802), CC9B/18, ANOM.
97. "Rien n'est plus fort que l'humiliation" from Louverture to Baille (c. 18 Oct. 1802), CC9B/18, ANOM. "Lorsqu'il sortirait de prison" from Menard to Berthier (22 Oct. 1802), B7/8, SHD-DAT.
98. "Lettre supreme" from Louverture to Bonaparte (26 Oct. 1802), Dossier 1, AF/IV/1213, AN.
99. On confiscating papers (including three letters sent by Gen. Brunet before Louverture's arrest), see Baille to Decrès (6 and 18 Nov. 1802), CC9B/18, ANOM; Ménard to Berthier (27 Nov. 1802), Dossier 1, AF/IV/1213, AN. "Il m'a paru très affecté" from Baille to Decrès (14 Nov. 1802), CC9B/18, ANOM.
100. "Les choses les plus indécentes" from Baille to Decrès (6 Nov. 1802), CC9B/18, ANOM.
101. On Louverture's despondency, see Baille to Decrès (30 Oct. and 14 Nov. 1802), CC9B/18, ANOM.
102. "Une jouissance, un besoin" from [Pascal], "Mémoire secret," (c. 1801), Reel 8, Sc. Micro R-2228, SC-NYPL.
103. "Triste et sombre" from J. F. Dubois to Henri Grégoire (25 May 1823), NAF 6864, BNF.
104. On other captives, see Claude Régnier to Decrès (14 May 1803), 8Yd638, SHD-DAT; David Geggus, "Slave, Soldier, Rebel: The Strange Career of Jean Kina," *Notes d'histoire coloniale*, no. 20 (1980).
105. On the fire, see Baille to Decrès (30 Oct. 1802), CC9B/18, ANOM. On the clothes, see "Extrait des minutes déposées à la sous-préfecture de Pontarlier…" (3 May 1803), TL-2B6q, NC-UPR. On the wood, see Bry to Micaut (22 Jan. 1803), TL-2B6h, NC-UPR.

106. "Toussaint hasarde parfois des questions" from Jean Joseph Gazagnaire to Decrès (5 Dec. 1802), Dossier 1, EE 1734, ANOM. On Amiot, see Amiot to Decrès (3 Jan. 1803), CC9B/18, ANOM; Ménard to Bry (2 March 1803), TL-2B6i, NC-UPR.
107. On Louverture's health, see Ménard to Berthier (7 March 1803), B7/9, SHD-DAT; Amiot to Decrès (19 March 1803), TL-2B7g, NC-UPR.
108. On Louverture's death, see Amiot et al., "L'an onze de la république française…" (7 Apr. 1803), TL-3A1, NC-UPR; Amiot to Decrès (9 Apr. 1803), CC9B/18, ANOM. For the conspiracy theories, see Saint-Rémy, *Vie de Toussaint Louverture*, 402–406; Auguste, *Les déportés de Saint-Domingue*, 95. For evidence to the contrary, see [Amiot?], "Toussaint Louverture" (c. Apr. 1803), TL-2A1, NC-UPR; J. F. Dubois to Henri Grégoire (25 May 1823), NAF 6864, BNF.
109. Nemours, *Histoire de la captivité*, 23.
110. "Quand il se vante d'avoir été général" from [Decrès] to Baille (27 Oct. 1802), CC9B/18, ANOM.
111. "Continuum" from Kadish, ed., *Slavery in the Caribbean Francophone World*, 157.
112. On diglossia, see Valdman, *Le créole*, 314–317, 367; Michael Largey, *Vodou Nation: Haitian Art Music and Cultural Nationalism* (Chicago: University of Chicago Press, 2006), 6, 10.
113. On Louverture's distant relationship with family members, see Paul Louverture to Louverture (4 Feb. 1802), Reel 5, Sc. Micro R-2228, SC-NYPL; Charles Belair to Louverture (1 Apr. 1802), ibid. On Louverture's inscrutability, see Pascal to Louverture (12 Apr. 1799), Reel 5, Sc. Micro R-2228, SC-NYPL. On Louverture's appearance, see David Geggus, "The Changing Faces of Toussaint Louverture: Literary and Pictorial Depictions," http://www.brown.edu/Facilities/John_Carter_Brown_Library/toussaint/index.html (accessed on 4 June 2013). On the body, see John Bigelow, *Retrospections of an Active Life*, vol. 1, 1817–1863 (New York: Baker and Taylor, 1909), 238; Nemours, *Histoire de la captivité*, 18, 116, 140–164. When I visited the site of the Bréda plantation in November 2013, the last standing walls of the Bréda plantation had been razed to make way for a high school.
114. For Bonaparte's lines, see Autograph manuscript, Inv. 1153, Fondation Napoléon, Paris; Peter Hicks, "Napoleon's English lessons," at http://www.napoleon.org/en/reading_room/articles/index.asp.

PREFACE TO THE TRANSCRIPT AND ENGLISH TRANSLATION

The French version of the memoir is an exact transcript of the handwritten memoir (called "manuscript C" in the introduction) that is found in Folder 1, box AF/IV/1213 at the Archives Nationales in Paris, including passages not found in versions A, B, and D. All spelling, grammatical, and punctuation mistakes were reproduced verbatim, as well as line and page breaks (see examples 1 and 2 below).

1. D manuscript, as reproduced in the 1853 Saint-Rémy edition:

    M'arrêter arbitrairement et sans m'entendre ni me dire pourquoi, s'emparer de tous mes avoirs, piller toute ma famille en général, saisir mes papiers et les garder, m'embarquer et m'envoyer nu comme ver de terre, répandre des calomnies les plus atroces sur mon compte, et d'après cela, je suis envoyé dans le fond des cachots, n'est-ce pas couper les jambes d'un quelqu'un et lui dire: marchez; n'est-ce pas couper sa langue et lui dire: marchez; n'est-ce pas couper sa langue et lui dire: parlés; n'est-ce pas enterrer un homme vivant?
    Tout cela a été bien combiné à ma perte pour m'anéantir et me détruire. Parce que je suis noir et ignorant, je ne dois pas compter au nombre des soldats de la République, ni avoir du mérite, en conséquence point de justice.

2. Literal transcript of the C manuscript:

    arrete abitrairement sans
    mentendre ni me dire pourquoi; en parrè toute mes avoire, pillie toute la
    famille an general, saisire mes papier et les gard der, man barqué anvoier nud
    comme ver deter, répendus des calomni les plus a tros sur mon conte,, da
    précela
    je sui an voier dant le fons du cachot; nesce pas coupé la jambre dun
    quie quin et lui dire marché, nesce pas coupé sa langue et lui dire parlé
    <u>nes ce pas en teré un homme vivant</u>, tous cela a été bien conbiné a ma perte
    pour ment ne antire, et me detruire parce que je sui noire et ingnorant,
    et je nedoit pas conte au nombre des soldat de la republique ni avoire de merite,
    et point des justice pour moi

The English version is a brand-new translation based on the original C manuscript, rather than an abridged translation of the Saint-Rémy edition, as was the case with Beard's 1863 English-language edition. Whether and how to reproduce the idiosyncrasies of Louverture's creolized French were difficult editorial choices. Instead of peppering the text with misspellings and grammatical mistakes (or translating the memoir into Gullah or Jamaican Patois), I decided to translate the C manuscript into modern American English, to correct the spelling of proper nouns, and to add punctuation marks where needed to improve readability. But I followed as closely as possible the rhythm and stylistic shifts of the original (see examples 3, 4, and 5 below).

3. 1863 abridged Beard translation:

> They have sent me to France destitute of everything; they have seized my property and my papers, and have spread atrocious calumnies concerning me. Is it not like cutting off a man's legs and telling him to walk? Is it not like cutting out a man's tongue and telling him to talk? Is it not burying a man alive?

4. Literal translation of the C manuscript:

> arrest abitrarily without hearingme een general, tak my paper and ke epp them, am barkme sand nakedd like earsworm, sprad the most a trocius calumni on my acount, bazedon this I amm se end too the botom of a cell; aint that cut the legge ofa somm one and tell him wallk, aint that cutt his tongue and tell him tallk <u>ai nt that burry a man alive,</u> whole that has been well cobined four ma loss to exst ermi natme, and destroy me because I amm blak and ingnorant, and I mustnott be coumt as one of the soldier of the republic or ave any meritt, and no justices for me;

5. New translation:

> Arrested arbitrarily without
> hearing me or telling me why; took all my assets; plundered all my
> family in general; seized my papers and keep them; embarked me sent me naked
> as worm; spread the worst calumnies on my account. Based on this
> I am thrown at the bottom of a cell. Isn't it like cutting the leg of
> someone and telling him: "walk?" Isn't it like cutting his tongue and telling him: "talk?"
> <u>Isn't it like burying a man alive</u>? All of this was well thought out to lose me, to annihilate me, and to destroy me because I am black and ignorant,
> and I must not count as one of the soldiers of the Republic or have any merit, and no justice for me;

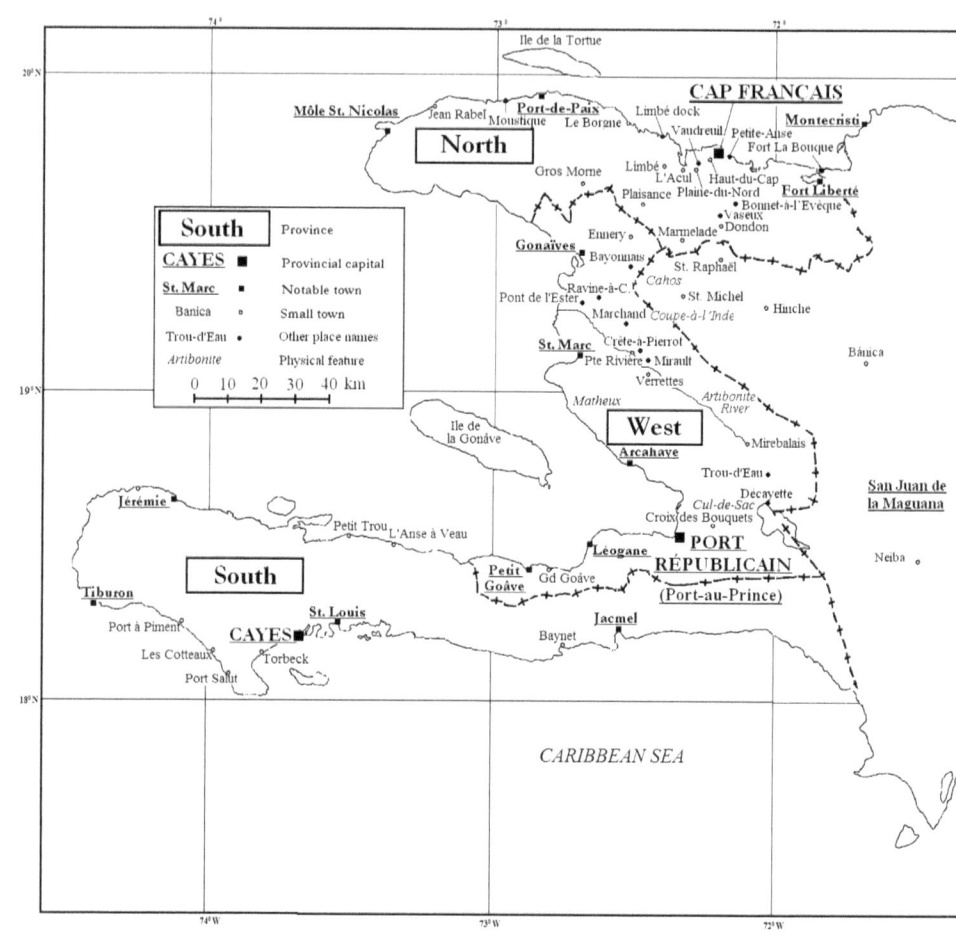

Place Names Mentioned in the Memoir of Toussaint Louverture
Map by © Philippe Girard, 2013

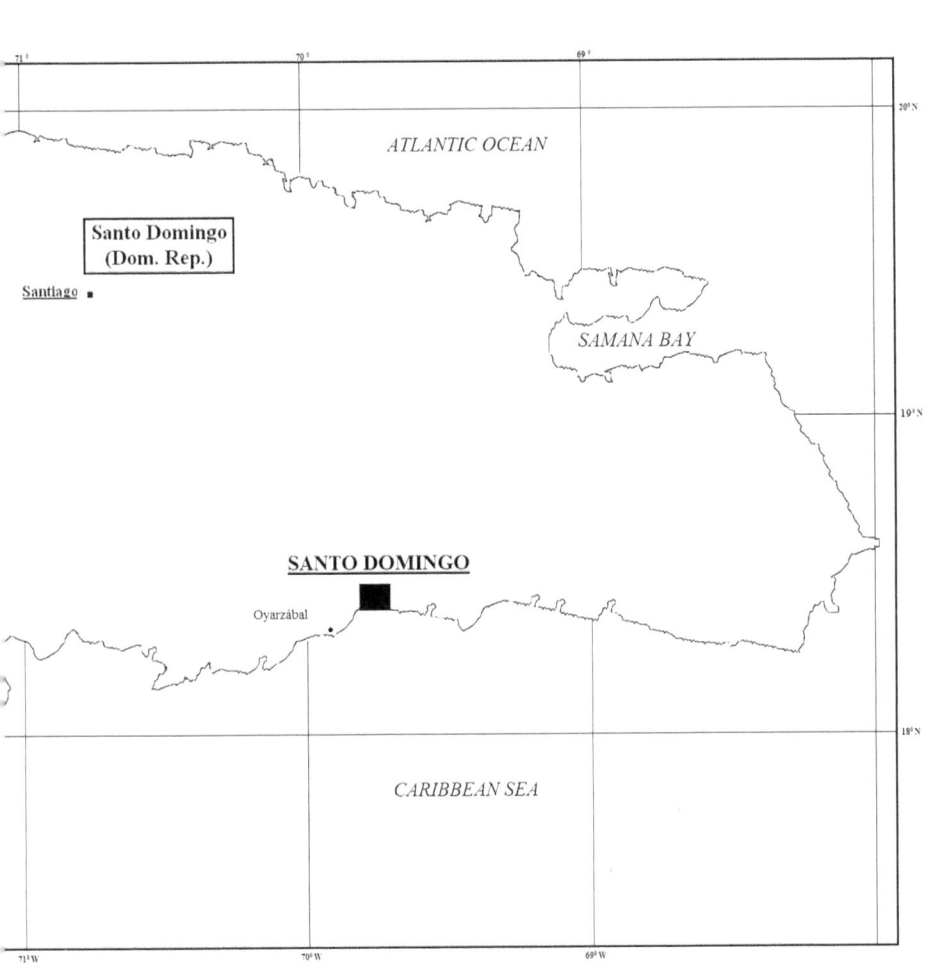

Memoire du General Toussaint Louverture

Original Transcript

The footnotes to the French transcript are editorial, linguistic, and explicatory. They indicate where the text of manuscript C differs from other versions, particularly the D manuscript reproduced by Saint-Rémy. They underline some linguistic parallels between Louverture's way of speaking and 18th-century French and modern Kreyòl. They clarify the meanings of some passages that are so badly misspelled that present-day Francophones might not understand them.

Memoir of General Toussaint Louverture

English Translation

The footnotes to the English translation are historical. They describe the main characters, events, and places mentioned in the text, discuss the accuracy of Louverture's claims, and place them in their proper context.

Notes for the transcript and translation are sequenced separately. To retain parallel lines between the two texts, some spaces were added on one page that correspond to a spillover of words on the facing page.

Memoire du General Toussaint Louverture[1]

5[2]

Il et de mon devoire de rendre au gouvernement francois
un compte éxact de ma conduite[3] je raconterait les faite[4]
avec toute la naivetet et la franchise dun anciens militaire en y a
joutant les recflecxions[5] qui se presenteront naturellement, en fin
je dirai la verite fut elle conte conte moi même.[6] la colonis de S^ت domingue
Dont j'etoits conmandant jouissoit[7] de la plus grande tranquilite la cultu[8]
et les commerce y fleurissoit, l'isle étoit parvenus a un degre des
plendeur oü on ne l avoit pas en cor vus, et tout cela joze le dire

    1. A, B, and D manuscripts: "mémoire pour" instead of "mémoire du." All versions employ the singular form "mémoire," not "mémoires."
    2. The 21-page memoir was numbered (apparently by Louverture), starting with the number 5. The last three pages were numbered 1 to 3. There is no page 4. Other numbers appear randomly, as if Louverture had used recycled paper.
    3. The passage between "ma conduite" and "je dirai la vérité" was added in the margin of manuscript A, whose opening and final segments were heavily edited.
    4. The spelling of "faite" and many other words in the memoir indicates that Louverture often pronounced a final "t" that is normally silent (see also "porte" on line 13 and "re grete," "obgete," "toute," "boulete," "interète," "cachote," and "vernette" later in the manuscript). Louverture also pronounced the final "s" and "r" in many words.
    5. This is the first of many instances of hypercorrection in the text: aware that he had a tendency to simplify consonant groups, as Kreyòl speakers often do, Louverture compensated by needlessly complicating some words to sound more French. In this case, he added two "c" to "réflexions" (see also "fics" and "vix" later in the manuscript). He also added "i," "r," and "t" to some words.
    6. The passage between "conduite" and "la commission avait rendu un arrêté" was added in the margin of manuscript A.
    7. Throughout the manuscript, Louverture used the old spelling for the past tense ("oi" instead of "ai"), which he presumably pronounced /we/ instead of /e/. Jeannin also employed "oi."
    8. Read: "culture" (the edge of the page is damaged).

Memoir of General Toussaint Louverture

5

It is my duty to give to the French government
an exact account of my conduct.[1] I will recount the facts
with all the naïveté and the frankness of a former military man, while
adding the thoughts that will arise naturally, in a word
I will tell the truth even if it were against my interests. The colony of Saint-Domingue
of which I was the commander was enjoying the greatest tranquility. Agriculture
and commerce were flourishing, the island had attained a degree of
splendor that no one had ever seen previously,[2] and all of this I dare to say

---

1. From the first sentence, Toussaint Louverture explained that his goal was to "account" for his past conduct, a word he employed 14 times in the memoir. As indicated in the title, he wrote a "memoir" (a report), not "memoirs" (an autobiography).

2. Louverture had indeed worked hard to revive the plantation sector since 1800. "Cultivation, in the colony, was at a very high degree when we arrived;" see Victoire Leclerc to Denis Decrès (9 Feb. 1802), CC9B/19, Archives Nationales d'Outremer, Aix-en-Provence (ANOM). But Louverture was exaggerating when he claimed to have exceeded previous production records, since plantations had not yet fully recovered; see Pierre Pluchon, *Toussaint Louverture* (Paris: Fayard, 1989), 400–422.

étoit mon ouvrage, cependant on y etoit sur le pied de geurre,[9]
La conmision avait rendu un arrete qui mordonnoit de prendre toute les
mesures necesaires pour en péche les ennemis de la republique de
penetrer dans lisle, en concequance je donnai lordre a tous les
conmandant des porte de mer de ne laiser entrer en rade aucuin
Batiment de geure quils ne soient reconnus et quil en naivoit[10]
obtenu de moi la permision, et si cetoit un Escadre de quelle
nation fut elle il lui etoit absolument defendus d'entrer
dans les port ni même dans le[11] rade, jus qua que je re connus par
moi nême dou elle venoit et de quel ordre elle étoit porteur
cet ordre existoit lorsque le 16 pluviose l escadre parut de

devant le cap, j'étoit a lors partis de celle ville pour faire
une tourné dans la partie Espagnole a saint domingo pour surveil[12]
le culture, chemin faisant en passant a la magouane j avoit
Expedie un de mes aide de canp au General dessaline conmandant
En chef les de partement de loueste et Sud residant[13] a S^t marc pour

---

9. Louverture almost systematically misspelled the word "guerre" as "geurre," either because he did not know how to spell it, or because he pronounced this word with a / ʒ/ instead of a hard /g/.

10. Manuscript D: "qu'ils n'en ayent" instead of "quil en naivoit."

11. As in Kreyòl, Louverture often paid no heed to the gender of French nouns (in this case, "le rade" instead of "la rade"). See also "le premiere letre," "une ordre," "un seul piece" later in the manuscript.

12. Read: "surveiller" (the edge of the page is damaged).

13. The phrase "dudit département de l'ouest et du Sud, étant alors à" was added after "en chef" in the margin of manuscript B. "Etant alors" was switched to "résidant" between manuscripts D and C.

was the result of my labors.³ And yet we were on a war footing. The commission had issued a decree that ordered me to take all the necessary measures to prevent the enemies of the Republic from penetrating the island.⁴ As a consequence, I ordered all the commanders of the seaports not to allow inside the harbors any warship unless they were known and they had been authorized by me. And if it was a squadron, no matter which nation it came from, it was absolutely forbidden to enter the ports, even the harbors, until I ascertained personally where it came from and what orders it bore.⁵
This order was still in effect when on 16 pluviôse [5 February 1802] the [French] squadron appeared
before Cap[-Français].⁶ I had at the time left the town to go on a tour of the Spanish part in Santo Domingo to check on cultivation.⁷ On my way, while passing by [San Juan de la] Maguana, I had sent one of my aides-de-camp to General Dessalines,⁸ commander in chief of the departments of the West and South, residing in Saint-Marc, to

---

3. Louverture's self-congratulatory tone is found in some of his other letters. "I had found... the colony dismembered, ruined, torn apart, and occupied by the rebels, the émigrés, the Spaniards and the Englishmen that were fighting over its remnants; I now leave the colony tranquil, purged of its foreign enemies, pacified and on its way to its restoration;" see Louverture to Etienne Laveaux (24 Sept. 1798), in Gérard M. Laurent, ed., *Toussaint l'Ouverture à travers sa correspondance, 1794–1798* ([s.n.], 1953), 451–454.

4. A commission was a group of envoys sent by France to represent its authority in the island. Louverture possibly referred to the decree by which the French agent Philippe Roume had ordered the capture of any British ship coming to a Dominguan port; see Philippe Roume, "Arrêté" (30 Aug. 1799), CC9B/9, ANOM.

5. Louverture likely referred to his decree of 3 April 1801 that put all colonial ports on high alert due to recent British raids; see Louverture, "Arrêté" (3 Apr. 1801), CO 137/105, British National Archives, Kew (BNA).

6. The squadron was part of an expedition sent by Bonaparte to unseat Louverture and perhaps restore slavery. Its first goal was the capture of Cap-Français or Le Cap (present-day Cap-Haïtien), the main commercial center on the northern coast. On the Leclerc expedition, see Philippe Girard, *The Slaves Who Defeated Napoléon: Toussaint Louverture and the Haitian War of Independence* (Tuscaloosa, AL: University of Alabama Press, 2011). See the map for the location of Cap and other place names mentioned in the memoir.

7. Louverture had invaded the Spanish part of Hispaniola (present-day Dominican Republic) in January 1801. He had indeed tried to foster agriculture in this undeveloped province, but he omitted to mention in the memoir that the main purpose of his January 1802 visit to the city of Santo Domingo was to strengthen its defenses in the event of a French invasion. According to the French commander of Bany, "Toussaint told him during his latest trip 15 or 20 days ago that he was expecting the arrival of a French army and that he was determined to combat it, and in case of setbacks to retreat to Santo Domingo with all the troops he could muster;" see François-Marie Perichou de Kerversau to Leclerc (14 Feb. 1802), 61J24, Archives Départementales de la Gironde, Bordeaux (ADGir).

8. Louverture employed Jean-Jacques Dessalines (c. 1758–1806), a former slave of his son-in-law, as division general, trusted second, and inspector of cultivation in the West; see Philippe Girard, "Jean-Jacques Dessalines and the Atlantic System: A Reappraisal," *William and Mary Quarterly* (July 2012), 549–582.

lui ordonné de venire me jondre au Gonaivé ou a Sᵗ michel pour ma
compagne dans une tourné; au moment ou l'Escadre parut je me
trouvoit a Sᵗ domingo dont je partis troi jour a pre que mes soperation
finie¹⁴ pour a le a hinche; pasant par le Banique arrivant au papaÿe
je rencontrais mon aide de camp Coupé et un officier en voier par
le General chistophte qui ma remit une lettre de ce General par
la quelle il minstruisoit de larriver de l'Escadre francois. devant
le cap et masuroit que le General conmandant en Chef cette Es
cadre ne lui avoit pas fait l'honneur de lui Ecrire; que seule
ment il lui avoit envoiér¹⁵ un officier pour lui ordonné de pre
pare le logement pour se troupe, que lui General chistophete
ayant demande a cet officie Sil n etoit pas porteur de lettre
pour lui ou de depeche pour le General Toussaint louverture

---

14. Manuscript D omits "que mes soperation finie."
15. Louverture rarely used the letter "y" in the text to replace "ii" (here: "envoiér" instead of "envoyé"), presumably because this spelling norm had recently become standard. Jeannin also wrote "envoié" in manuscript A.

order him to come join me in Gonaïves or in Saint-Michel to accompany me on a tour. When the squadron appeared I was in Santo Domingo, from which I left three days after my business was done to go to Hinche via Bánica.[9] When I arrived in Papaye, I met my aide-de-camp Coupé[10] and an officer sent by General Christophe[11] who handed over to me a letter from this general by which he informed me of the arrival of the French squadron in front of Cap and assured me that the general in chief commanding this squadron had not done him the honor of writing to him;[12] that he had only sent an officer to order him to prepare lodgings for his troops;[13] that he, General Christophe, having asked this officer if he did not carry a letter for him or dispatches for General Toussaint Louverture,

9. For an anguished letter sent from Santo Domingo that suggests that Louverture had just learned of the expedition's arrival, see Louverture to Simon Baptiste fils (27 Jan. 1802), BB4 162, Service Historique de la Défense, Département de la Marine, Vincennes (SHD-DM). For a letter from his aide-de-camp indicating that Louverture was about to pass through Hinche, see Jean-Pierre Fontaine to Louverture (3 Feb. 1802), Ms. Hait. 66-115, Boston Public Library (BPL). For a claim that Louverture actually witnessed the arrival of the French fleet in Sámana, see Pamphile de Lacroix, *Mémoires pour servir à l'histoire de la révolution de Saint-Domingue*, vol. 2 (Paris: Pillet, 1819), 63.

10. Marc Coupé was a squadron chief in Louverture's army.

11. Brigadier General Henry Christophe (c. 1767–1820), a former enslaved innkeeper, commanded Cap-Français as of 1802; see Hubert Cole, *Christophe, King of Haiti* (New York: Viking Press, 1967).

12. This letter was not in the archives consulted for this book, but as of 2 Feb., Christophe knew of the squadron's presence and was awaiting orders from Louverture; see Christophe to Louis Labelinais (2 Feb. 1802), 61J18, ADGir.

13. This officer was Lebrun, an aide-de-camp of Leclerc; see Hector Daure to Decrès (c. 3 Nov. 1802), B7/8, Service Historique de la Défense, Département de l'Armée de Terre, Vincennes (SHD-DAT).

6

en le priant de les lui remetre pour lui faire paser de suite.
cette officier lui avoit répondu quil nen etoit point charge,
quil netoit pas même quiestions[16] du General Toussaint, rende
la ville, lui avoit il ajouté vous serez bien reconpancés,
le Gouvernement francois vous envoie des presans, ici[17] ; qu'alors
lui General christophete lui avoit dit puisque vous navez pas
de lettre pour le General enchef ni pour moi, vous pous vez
vous retire z et dire a votre General quil ne connoit pas sons
de voire que ce net pas aincis quon se presente dans un paÿs
appartenante a la france, le General leclere aÿant recu cette
reponce fut sommer le General chistophte de lui livre la place,
et dans le cas de refus il le previent que dez le lendemain
matin il y debarqueront quinze mille homme, a quoi celui ci
a repondit quil le priait d attendre le General toussaint louverture,
quil lavoit deja fait a vertir, et quil alloit encor le faire une
seconde foi avec la plus Grande célerité. en effet je recu une
second letre et me hatait de me rendre au cap malgré les dé
Bordement de la riviere de hinche, Espérant a voire le plaisir
d'embraser nos freres d'armes d'Europe et recevoire en même temp
les ordres du Gouvernement francois, et pour metre plus de promp
titude dans ma marche, javois laisse toute mes Escorte;
Entre S^t michel et S^t raphael, je rencontrai le general dessaline
et lui dit, je vous avois envoier cherche pour ma conpagne dans
une tourné au porde paix et au mole, mais cela et tan[18] inutile,

16. This is the first of many instances in the memoir where Louverture added an extraneous "i" in words, either because he actually pronounced them, or as a form of hypercorrection (here: "quiestions" instead of "questions"). See also "paquiet," "Kierverceaus," "S^t domiengue," "conmuniquieraï," "lendemien," "mien vetoit," "cienq," and "flanquié" later in the manuscript. He also added "r," "t," and "c" to some words.
17. Manuscript D: "etc" instead of "ici."
18. Illegible: possibly "tan" or "tres." Manuscript D: "cela est inutile."

6

inviting him to hand them over to him so that he could pass them on at once, this officer had answered that he had not been entrusted with any; that General Toussaint had never even been mentioned;[14] "hand over the town," he had added, "and you will be well rewarded. The French government is sending you gifts, here;" that General Christophe had then said to him "since you have no letter for the general in chief or for me, you may leave and tell your general that he does not know his duty, that it is not the way one introduces oneself in a country belonging to France." General Leclerc, having received this response, demanded that General Christophe hand over the position. In case he refused, he warned him that as early as the following morning he would land fifteen thousand men, to which the latter responded that he begged him to await General Toussaint Louverture, that he had already alerted him, and that he was again going to do so a second time with the greatest haste.[15] Indeed, I received a second letter and hastened to go to Cap despite the flooding of the river of Hinche, hoping to have the pleasure of embracing our brothers in arms from Europe and of receiving at the same time the orders of the French government; and to march more rapidly I had left behind all my escorts.[16] Between Saint-Michel and Saint-Raphaël, I met General Dessalines and told him: "I had sent for you so that you could accompany me on a tour of Port-de-Paix and Môle [Saint-Nicolas], but there is no need.

---

14. Leclerc had merely sent Lebrun onshore with copies of Bonaparte's 8 Nov. 1801 proclamation, which indeed failed to mention Louverture; see Leclerc to Decrès (9 Feb. 1802), CC9B/19, ANOM. That the proclamation did not mention Louverture's name also shocked black officers in Port-Républicain; see Jean Boudet to Decrès (8 Feb. 1802), in "Extrait de la correspondance concernant Toussaint Louverture," CC9/B23, ANOM. Speaking of "general Toussaint" (as opposed to "general Toussaint Louverture") was an insulting reminder of his enslaved past; see also p. 14, line 3.

15. "I learn with indignation, citizen general, that you refuse to welcome the French squadron...under the pretext that you have no orders from the governor general....I warn you that if, today, you don't hand over Forts Picolet and Belair, and all the gun batteries of the coast, tomorrow at dawn 15,000 men will land;" see Leclerc to Christophe (2 Feb. 1802), in Christophe, "Manifeste du roi" (18 Sept. 1814), p. 20, Publications on the independence of Haiti, RG 59/MLR A1632, U.S. National Archives, College Park (NARA-CP). For Christophe's response, see ibid., p. 21, and Christophe to Leclerc (2 Feb. 1802), in A. J. B. Bouvet de Cressé, ed., *Histoire de la catastrophe de Saint-Domingue* (Paris: Peytieux, 1824), 108.

16. After first notifying Louverture around 2 Feb., Christophe updated him on the 3rd: "the squadron is still near the port and I took all the possible dispositions to repulse an attack;" see Christophe to Louverture (3 Feb. 1802), Ms. Hait. 2548 (3), BPL. Louverture's imminent arrival to Hinche in the midst of heavy rains is mentioned in Fontaine to Louverture (3 Feb. 1802), Ms. Hait. 66-115, BPL.

je vien de recevoire deux létre du General Christophete man[19]
noncant l'arrive de l'Escadre francois de vant le cap, et lui
communiquai ces letre, il me dit alors quil a voit vu lui
même de S^ت marc six Gros vaiseaux portant[20] voile du côté du port
republicuin, mais quil ignore de quelle nation ils sont, je
lui ordonnoi alors[21] de partir ~~pont~~ promptement pour se rendre
dans ce port, vus quil etoit possible que le General christopher[22]
aiant refuzé l entreré[23] du cap au General conmandant l'Es
cadre celui ci ce soit porte au port republicain dans l'Espoire
de mi trouver et dans ce cala, je lai donnois ordre de prie
ce General de mattendre en lasurant que j'alloit dabord de
de cepas au cap dans l Espérence de l'y rencontrer et dans
le cas je ne l'y trouverois pas je reviendrois de suite au port
republicains pour y confere avec lui, je partis éffectivement
pour le cap en pasant par le vaseux chemin le plu courte,
En arrivant sur les hauteur du Grand Boucans au lieu dit
a la porte S^t jaque jappercu le feu dans la ville du cap,
je pousai alors moncheval a toute bride pour me rendre
dans cette ville, y trouver le General conmandant l'Escadre
et minformé dece qui pouvoit a voire donne lieu a cette
incendie, mai en approchant je trouvai toute les route cou

---

19. Louverture added nasal sounds throughout the manuscript, here in "man noncant." See also words like "conmandant," "conmandement," "conmision," "conmis," "campangne," "pre ce dant ment," "espangne." Nasalizing words is common in rural Kreyòl. Louverture also had a distinctly nasal voice, which he attributed to a Vodou spell.

20. Manuscript D: "faisant" instead of "portant."

21. Manuscript D omits "alors."

22. Louverture often misspelled the name of his general Henry Christophe, probably in an effort to match an English pronunciation (Christophe was from Grenada). Jeannin, who had a hard time spelling unfamiliar Caribbean terms, also often misspelled Christophe's name in manuscripts A, B, and D.

23. Read: "l'entrée."

I have just received two letters from General Christophe announcing
to me the arrival of the French squadron before Cap," and
communicated these letters to him. He then told me that he had himself
seen from Saint-Marc six large ships-of-the-line sailing toward Port-
Républicain, but that he ignored to which nation they belonged.[17] I
then ordered him to leave promptly to go
to this port, since it was possible that, General Christophe
having denied entry into Cap to the general commanding the
squadron, the latter had directed himself to Port-Républicain in the hope
of finding me there. In this case, I gave him the order to invite
this general to wait for me, assuring him that I would first go
at once to Cap in the hope of meeting him there, and in
case I did not find him there I would return at once to Port-
Républicain to confer with him.[18] I indeed left
for Cap, going by Le Vaseux, the shortest route.[19]
When arriving at the heights of Grand-Boucan,[20] in the location known
as the Saint-Jacques gate, I saw a fire in the town of Cap.
I then pushed my horse at full speed to get
to this town, find the General commanding the squadron,
and determine what could have caused this
fire.[21] But as I approached I found all the roads covered

---

17. A naval squadron led by Gen. Jean Boudet passed by Saint-Marc on 2 Feb. 1802, reached Port-Républicain (formerly known as Port-au-Prince) on the 4th, and took it on the 5th after aborted negotiations. See Pamphile de Lacroix to Charles Dugua (8 Feb. 1802), B7/15, SHD-DAT.

18. This letter was not in the archives consulted for this book. Dessalines responded that he reached Croix-des-Bouquets, only to learn that Port-Républicain had already fallen to the French; see Dessalines to Louverture (6 Feb. 1802), Ms. Hait. 79-11, BPL. Louverture sent further orders to "try through force or ruse to burn this position.... What a shame that your and my orders were not implemented!" See Louverture to Dessalines (8 Feb. 1802), in Beaubrun Ardouin, *Études sur l'histoire d'Haïti*, vol. 5 (Paris: Dezobry and Magdeleine, 1854), 39.

19. Identifying place names in the memoir can be difficult since Louverture and his secretary Jeannin consistently misspelled them and many referred to a *lieu-dit*, a small location known only to locals. This place name is listed as "les Vases" in Joseph Saint-Rémy, *Mémoires du général Toussaint-L'Ouverture écrits par lui-même* (Paris: Pagnerre, 1853), 35, but it was more likely Le Vaseux, northwest of Dondon.

20. Grand-Boucan is in the region of Plaine-du-Nord, just southwest of Cap-Français.

21. Louverture is careful here and on p. 3, line 8, to point out that he arrived just after (and thus was not responsible for) the burning of Cap. His contemporary letters are ambiguous on the matter. "I was still in Hinche when news [of the fleet's arrival in Cap] reached me. I hastened to go to this town. I arrived a bit late, the enemy had already landed their troops. But they only found ashes;" see Louverture to Paul Louverture (6 Feb. 1802), 61J24, ADGir. Many contemporaries insisted that Louverture was present in Cap and masterminded all events behind the scenes, including the fire; see Dugua to Alexandre Berthier (8 Feb. 1802), B7/2, SHD-DAT; Louis-Thomas Villaret de Joyeuse to Decrès (10 Feb. 1802), in "Extrait de la correspondance concernant Toussaint Louverture," CC9/B23, ANOM; Edward Stevens to John Marshall (28 Feb. 1802), 208 MI/2, Archives Nationales, Paris (AN); Lacroix, *Mémoires*, vol. 2, 70.

verte des habitans[24] qui avoient évacuie cette malheureue ville et ne pu penetré plus loing[25] a raisons de ce que tous

---

24. Louverture occasionally used archaic French spellings, in this case for the word "habitans" (modern French: "habitants"). See also "enfans" ("enfants") and "isle" ("île") and his use of "ii" instead of "y" and "z" instead of "s."

25. This word is normally spelled "loin," not "loing." Perhaps Louverture used the archaic spelling of "loing," mentioned in L. Quicherat, *Traité de versification française*, vol. 2 (Paris: Hachette, 1850), 382. Perhaps he pronounced the word "loin" with a final /g/, as is still done in Marseille.

with inhabitants[22] who had evacuated this unfortunate
town and could go no further for the reason that all

---

22. The term "habitant" means "inhabitant" in French, but also "planters" in Saint-Domingue. Christophe had sent one thousand white civilians to Haut-du-Cap, apparently to have them massacred, but they instead headed for the Morne de la Vigie (a hill above Cap), then returned to Cap safely after the French took the town; see "Délibérations de l'administration municipale du Cap" (5 Feb. 1802), in *Moniteur Universel*, no. 212 (22 Apr. 1802).

72

les passage étoient cannonés par l artilerie des vaiseaux qui
étoient dans la rade. je pris le partix a lors de monter[26] au fort
Bellayre mais je trouvais egalement ce fort evacuie et toute les
pièce de cannon encouloue,[27] je fus enconcequance oblige de
revenire sur mes pas, apres avoire depassai l'hopitale, je rencontrai
le General christophe et lui demandai qui est cé qui avoit ordonné
quon mit le feu a la ville; il me repondit que ce tois lui, je le blamé
tres vigoureuzement da voire enploié ce moyen de rigeur, pourquoi
lui dig, na vez vous pas de fendre plutot fait des dis position
militaire pour de fendre la ville jus qua monnarivé; il me repondit
que vous lez vou, General, mon devoire, la necesite, les circonstance,
les menace reitérées du general conmandant l'Escadre, mi y ont forcé

jai fai voire a Gene ral les ordre dont j etois porteur mais
inutilement. Il ma jouta que les proclamation repandus secrete
ment dans la ville pour se duire le peuple et soule vé la troupe
ne convienoit pas a la franchie[28] dun militaire, que sivraiment
ceconmandant de l Escadre avoit des intention parcifique,[29] il ni
auroit attendu, quil n'auroit point emploié les moyens dont
il set servi pour gagner le commandant du fort la Bouque, qui et un

---

26. Manuscript D: "de monter alors" instead of "a lors de monter."
27. Louverture occasionally added /u/ sounds, in this case writing "encouloue" instead of "enclouer." See also "au goumente" instead of "augmenter."
28. As is common in Kreyòl, Louverture often simplified the end of words, in this case by dropping the /z/ sound in "franchise" (see also "quin" instead of "quinze"). He did the same with /ʁ/, /l/, and /k/.
29. This is another example of hypercorrection. In this case, Louverture added an unnecessary /ʁ/ to hide his Kreyòl-derived tendency not to pronounce this letter (see also "grandre," "jambre," "surbordonnai," "suporte," "marvertis," "mondre," "tendre," and "sourdrement"). Louverture also added "i," "t," and "c" to some words.

72

the passageways were being shelled by the artillery of the ships that
were in the harbor.[23] I then decided to go up to the fort of
Belair, but I also found that this fort had been evacuated and that all the
cannon pieces had been spiked.[24] I was consequently obliged to
retrace my steps. After passing by the hospital,[25] I encountered
General Christophe and asked him who the person was who had given the order
to set the town on fire. He responded that he had. I blamed him
very vigorously for having employed such a rigorous method.[26] "Why"
I told him, "did you not instead take military
dispositions to defend the town until my arrival?" He replied to me:
"What do you expect, General, my duty, necessity, circumstances,
and the repeated threats made by the general commanding the squadron forced me
 to do so.
I showed the general the orders I was bearing, but
to no avail." He added that the proclamations that had been distributed secretly
around town to seduce the people and rouse the troops
were not worthy of the forthrightness of a military man;[27] that if truly
this commander of the squadron had peaceful intentions, he would
have awaited me there; that he would not have employed the means that
he used to sway the commander of the fort of La Bouque, who is a

---

23. After the failure of his negotiations with Christophe, Leclerc landed his troops at the Limbé dock, west of Cap, on 4–5 February. Meanwhile, Admiral Villaret bombed the forts that defended Cap on the 5th (Belair and Picolet), and then forced his way into the harbor on the 6th.

24. Fort Belair, located just southwest of Cap-Français on the way to Haut-du-Cap, was one of several forts defending the town. The others were Fort Picolet (to the north) and Fort St. Michel (to the southeast).

25. Probably the hospital of Les Pères in Haut-du-Cap. The other hospital of Cap, La Providence, was in the town itself.

26. Louverture was actually pleased with the destruction of Cap, which was consistent with his scorched-earth strategy. "A large squadron has reached Cap and made landings, but the town was thoroughly burned.... It seems that we face a coalition against liberty, so no half-measures;" see Louverture to Augustin Clerveaux (6 Feb. 1802), 61J24, ADGir.

27. While in Cap, Lebrun had distributed a proclamation from Bonaparte to the people of Saint-Domingue that read: "The government is sending Captain General Leclerc. He brings with him great forces to protect you from your enemies and the enemies of the Republic. If you are told 'these forces have come to steal your liberty,' answer 'the Republic gave us our liberty and will not allow it to be taken from us;'" see Napoléon Bonaparte, "Proclamation du Consul" (8 Nov. 1801), F/3/202, FM, ANOM. Leclerc later issued a proclamation under his own name that also promised that he would not restore slavery; see Leclerc to the citizens of Saint-Domingue (8 Feb. 1802), CC9B/19, ANOM. The proclamations had a great impact, so to counter their influence, Louverture ordered printing presses sent to him; see Louverture to Bartalier (15 Feb. 1802), Sc. Micro R-2228 Reel 5, Schomburg Center, New York Public Library (SC-NYPL).

ivrogne, quil ne se seroit point en concequance emparé de ce fort,
quil nauroit point fait X faire de desante a la cue et quil en un mot

il nauroit point conmis dabord[30] toute les hostililite dont il set rendus
coupable. le General christophe, se rejoignit a moi et nous continuames
la route ensemble En narrivant au hau du cap, nous traverssames les habitation
de Breda jus qua le barriere de Boulard[31] la je lui donnai ordre de raliez
sa troupe; dallé camper aux bonnette jus qua nouvel ordre, et de me
donnér connoissance de toute les mouvement quil feroit, et lui dis que ja[32]
chez Dericoure et que j y receveroit peut etre des nouvelle du commanda
nt de lescadre et il me ferois pascer les ordre du Gouvernemient que peut
etre même je pouroit lui[33] rencontré, que je menformeroit alors des
raisons qui ont pu l'engager a venire dant la colonie de cette maniere
et dant le cas[34] il seroit porteur dordre du Gouvernement je le prierois de me
les conmuniquér et prendrois en concequance des arrangemens a vec lui,
le General christophe me quitta a lors pour se rendre au poste que je lui avois
indiqué, mais il rencontra un Gros de trouppe qui fit feu sur lui le forcé[35]

de se jetter a bas de son cheval de se precipite dans la riviere et de la
traverser a la nage, moi même apres la voire quitté ayant a vec moi ladjudant general fontaine et deux autre officier et mon aide de canp coupé
qui marchoit en avant de nous, ce lui ci me prevent quil decouvroit de

---

X In manuscript C, Louverture added this passage in the margin: "pascer au fil de lépés la moitie de la garnison du fort liberté, quil nauroit point fait." It was probably an initial oversight, because the passage is also in manuscript A, B, and D.

30. Manuscript D omits "d'abord."
31. Manuscript D adds "la barrière de Boular passant par les jardins."
32. Read: "j'allais."
33. The use of "lui" in manuscript C was most likely inspired by the Kreyòl pronoun "li." More generally, /y/, /œ/, and /e/ are often transcribed as /i/ in manuscript C.
34. Manuscript D omits "le cas."
35. In many passages of the memoir, Louverture used the infinitive form of verbs instead of conjugating them (here: "forcé" instead of "força"). This is common in Kreyòl.

drunkard;[28] that as a consequence he would not have seized this fort; that he would not have killed half the garrison of Fort-Liberté with a sword;[29] that he would not have landed in l'Acul;[30] and that in a word he would not have initiated all the hostilities of which he has made himself guilty.[31] General Christophe joined me and we continued our march together. When arriving in Haut-du-Cap, we went through the plantation of Bréda until the Boulard fence.[32] There, I ordered him to gather his troops, to wait in Bonnet[-à-l'Evêque][33] until further notice, and to inform me of all his future maneuvers; and told him that I was going to Héricourt[34] and that I would perhaps receive there some news from the commander of the squadron and that he would pass on to me the orders from the government; that maybe even I could meet him; that I would then learn the reasons that could have led him to arrive in the colony in such a manner; and if he had orders from the government I would bid him to communicate them to me, and I would consequently make arrangements with him. General Christophe then left me to proceed to the position I had indicated to him, but he encountered a large body of troops that opened fire on him and forced him to dismount from his horse, to rush into the river [of Haut-du-Cap], and to swim across it. As for myself, after I left him, as I was traveling with Adjutant-General Fontaine and two other officers, as well as my aide-de-camp Coupé who was marching ahead of us, the latter warned me that he was encountering

28. The commander of La Bouque was a black officer named Barthélémy; see Saint-Rémy, *Mémoires*, 36. The fort of La Bouque defended the channel leading to the city of Fort-Liberté (formerly Fort-Dauphin).

29. Fort-Liberté was taken on 3 Feb. by troops under Gen. Donatien de Rochambeau who indeed massacred the garrison to punish it for resuming the fight after surrendering; see Deseine and Courtois, "Mon premier voyage sur mer…" (c. 1809), p. 23–26, Sc. Micro R-2228 Reel 9, SC-NYPL.

30. Bonaparte had ordered Leclerc to land in Acul, a logical spot just west of Cap, but he actually landed further west at the Limbé dock; see Leclerc to Decrès (9 Feb. 1802), CC9B/19, ANOM.

31. Louverture's suspicions were correct: Leclerc's orders were indeed to employ negotiation if possible, but Leclerc was quick to resort to Bonaparte's "plan B," force, to make a name for himself; see Bonaparte, "Notes pour servir aux instructions à donner au capitaine général Leclerc" (31 Oct. 1801), in Paul Roussier, ed., *Lettres du général Leclerc* (Paris: Société de l'histoire des colonies françaises, 1937), 263–274.

32. The Breda plantation in Haut-du-Cap was the plantation on which Louverture was born and where he lived until the outbreak of the 1791 slave revolt. The Boulard plantation was in nearby Plaine-du-Nord.

33. Bonnet-à-l'Evêque was a mountain where Christophe had hidden ammunition, and where he later built the famous Laferrière citadel; see Saint-Rémy, *Mémoires*, 37.

34. Like the neighboring Breda du Haut-du-Cap plantation, the Héricourt plantation belonged to members of the Breda family. It was in Plaine-du-Nord. Louverture was leasing it as of 1802; see Jean-Louis Donnadieu, *Un grand seigneur et ses esclaves: Le comte de Noé entre Antilles et Gascogne, 1728–1816* (Toulouse, FR: Presses Universitaires du Mirail, 2009), 33, 39.

la trouppe sur le chemins, je lui ordonnais de se porter en avant on madit que cette trouppe étoit conimandér par un General je demanderoit a lors d'avoire a vec lui un conference, mai il neut pas le temps dexecuter mes ordres on nous fit feu dessus a vinct cinq pas de la Barriere de vaux dreuille,[36] mon cheval fut percé dune bal, un autre bal emporte le cha pau dun des officier qui etoient a vec moi ce qui nous a forcet da Bandonné la Grande route, de travercer la savanne et les foret pour me rendre chez Dericoure, ous je restais troi joure pour y allendre le nouvelle du conmandant de l'Escadre, mais toujour innutilement, seulement

---

36. Manuscript D omits "de vaux dreuille."

troops on the road.³⁵ I ordered him to position himself ahead of us. I was told that these troops were commanded by a general.³⁶ I then asked to have a conference with him, but he did not have time to execute my orders. We were fired upon twenty-five paces from the Vaudreuil fence.³⁷ A bullet pierced my horse. Another bullet took away the hat of one of the officers who were with me, which forced us to abandon the main road, to cross the meadows and the woods to proceed to Héricourt, where I spent three days awaiting news from the commander of the squadron, but still to no avail.

35. Jean-Pierre Fontaine was an aide-de-camp of Louverture; see Ardouin, *Etudes*, vol. 5, 177.

36. The general was Jean Hardÿ, who reported encountering "a few hundred negroes, mulattoes, and whites mixed together, commanded by Toussaint Louverture in person;" see Hardÿ to Mrs. Hardÿ (8 Feb. 1802), in Hardÿ de Périni, *Correspondance intime du général Jean Hardÿ de 1798 à 1802* (Paris: Plon, 1901), 265.

37. Vaudreuil was halfway between Haut-du-Cap and Plaine-du-Nord. The Vaudreuil family was a prominent family of absentee planters; see Comte de Vaudreuil to Elizabeth Foster (23 Apr. 1794), in Léonce Pingaud, ed., *Correspondance intime du Comte de Vaudreuil et du Comte d'Artois pendant l'émigration, 1789–1815*, vol. 2 (Paris: Plon, 1889), 200.

8

le lendemains je recu une letter du General rochambeau qui ~~me~~
mannoncoit que la colone quil commandoit sétoit empare du fort
liberté, quil avoit puni un partie[37] de la garnison qui avoit fait
réxistance en la passant au fil delépée quil nauroit pas[38] cru
que ce troupe au roit tranpé leur bayonnete dans le sang des
francoit comme heux, et il auroit cru de trouver cette garnisons
Bien disposé a leur faveur,[39] je repondis a cette letre et manifestant
mon mecontentement a ce General, je lui demandai pourquoi il avoit
ordonné le massacre de ce brave soldatx qui na voit fait que
suivre les ordres quon leur avoit donnés, qui dalieur avoient
si bien concourus au bonheur de la colonie et au triomphe de la re
publique si c étoit la la recompence que le Gouvernement leur
avait promis, et finis en lui disant que je combatroit jusqua
la mort pour vemger la mort de ces brave soldatx et ma liberté[40]
et rétablir le calme et lordre dans la colonie, cétoit éffectivement
le partit que je venois de prandre a pres avoire murement réflechie
sur les different rapport que mavoit fait le General christophe sur
le danger que je venois de courire, sur la letre du General rochanbeau
et sur la conduite en fins du General conmandant lescadre
Ces resolutions priese je me trans portois aux Gonaive je
donnois connaissance au General morepas de mes intentions je lui
ordonnois ~~B~~ Doppozèr la plus vive resistance a toux ceux qui
ce presanteront de vant le port de paix ou il commandait, et
dans le cas il ne seroit pas asez fort nayant qune demie brigade

---

37. Manuscript D: "une grande partie" instead of "un partie."
38. Manuscript D: "jamais" instead of "pas."
39. Manuscript D: "le sang des Français, et qu'au contraire il aurait cru la trouver bien disposée" instead of "le sang des francoit comme heux, et il auroit cru de trouver cette garnisons Bien disposé."
40. The phrase "et ma liberté" was added between the lines in manuscript B.

8

But the following day I received a letter from General Rochambeau who announced to me that the column that he commanded had seized Fort-Liberté; that he had punished part of the garrison that had resisted by executing them by the sword; that he would not have thought that these troops would have sullied their bayonets with the blood of fellow Frenchmen; and that he would have expected to find this garrison well disposed toward them. I answered this letter, and expressing my discontent to this general, I asked him why he had ordered the massacre of these brave soldiers who had only been following the orders that had been given to them, who by the way had so well contributed to the happiness of the colony and to the triumph of the republic, [and] if this was the reward that the government had promised to them.[38] I finished by telling him that I would combat until death to avenge the death of these brave soldiers and my liberty and to restore calm and order to the colony.[39] It was indeed the decision I had just made after having thoroughly thought about the different reports made to me by General Christophe, about the dangers I had just faced, about the letter of General Rochambeau, and finally about the conduct of the general commanding the squadron.[40] After taking these resolutions, I proceeded to Gonaïves. I informed General Maurepas[41] of my intentions. I ordered him to oppose the utmost resistance to all those who would present themselves before Port-de-Paix where he commanded, and in case he was not strong enough, having only a demi-brigade under him,

---

38. Strangely, Louverture did not mention other massacres of troops of color that took place during the campaign; see for example, R. Mends to John Duckworth (1 Apr. 1802), ADM 1/252, BNA.

39. Rochambeau's letter to Louverture and the latter's response were not in the archives consulted for this book. In his contemporary correspondence, Louverture was very concerned that the French had come to restore slavery, but he rarely mentioned these fears in his memoir, probably to avoid denouncing Bonaparte as an enemy of liberty; see, for example, "We cannot hide: die or live free," in Louverture to Clerveaux (6 Feb. 1802), 61J24, ADGir. Note that Louverture's stated willingness to die to defend his liberty is reminiscent of the motto "liberty or death" that was embraced by Dominguan rebels as their rallying cry.

40. Louverture had actually decided from the outset that he would not allow a French takeover. "The enemy will soon appear near your coast, use all your forces to prevent a landing," he wrote one general. If you have to retreat, "set the town on fire; you will also burn all the plantations you will encounter, and you will be careful not to let anything behind you that belongs to the white race;" see Louverture to Clerveaux (c. 30 Jan. 1802), in Guillaume Mauviel, "Mémoire sur Saint-Domingue" (26 June 1805), p. 40, pièce 101, AF/IV/1212, AN. For Louverture's early orders, see also Paul Louverture to Louverture (3 Feb. 1802), Sc. Micro R-2228 Reel 5, SC-NYPL; Leclerc to Decrès (9 Feb. 1802), CC9B/19, ANOM; Gingembre Trop Fort to Casimir (15 Feb. 1802), B7/2, SHD-DAT; Leclerc to Bonaparte (5 March 1802), B7/26, SHD-DAT.

41. Brigadier General Jacques Maurepas was the black commander of Port-de-Paix.

demiter l'Exemple du General christophe, de se retirér ensuite
dans la montagne emmenant a vec lui les munitions de tous
les genres et de se defendre jus qua la mort, je me transportois
ensuite a S^t marc pour y visite les fortification, je trouvois
que cette ville etoit dejas instruite des événement facheux
qui venoient da voire lieu, et que les habitant la voient deja
evacque, j ydonnois ordre de faire toute la resistance que les
munitions et les fortifications permettoient, au moment ou
jallois partie[41] de cette ville pour me rendre au port au prince
et dans la partis du Sud y donne mes ordres les capitaine jan
philippe du pain et Isaac mapporte les depeches de paul Louverture
qui commandoit dans cette partie a saint domingo[42] tous deux
mannoncerent quin dessante vénoit da voire lieu a roiale sa
Bale que les francais et les Espagnols qui habitoient dans cet
endroit, feloient[43] soulevés et a voient intercepté les chemins
de Santo domingo. je pris connaisance de ce depeche, enparcourant

la letre du General paul et copie de celle du General Kierverceau
au conmandant de place de Santo domingo qui y étoit a lors[44]
je vis linvitation que faisoit ce General au commandant et
non point au General paul comme il auroit du faire de lui
preparé le logement pour sa troupe je vis ausis le refus
qui lui avoit été faite a son invitations par le General paul
jus qua ce quil eut recu des ordre de moi. Enconceqance

---

41. Louverture often followed the practice, common in Kreyòl, of not pronouncing the final "r" of a word (here: "partie" instead of "partir"). See also "férie" instead of "férir," "remplis" instead of "remplir," "retablis" instead of "rétablir," "sortis" instead of "sortir," and "aupprob" instead of "opprobre." He also dropped /z/, /k/, and /l/ at the end of many words.

42. The phrase "à Saint Domingo" was added between the lines in manuscript B.

43. Read: "s'étaient."

44. Manuscript D: "incluse" instead of "a lors."

to imitate the example set by General Christophe, to retreat then
to the mountain, taking with him the ammunitions of
all kinds, and to defend himself to the death.[42] I proceeded
then to Saint-Marc to visit the fortifications there. I learned
that this town was already informed of the unfortunate events
that had just taken place, and that the inhabitants had already
evacuated. I gave the order to offer as much resistance as the
ammunition and the fortifications would allow. Just as I was
about to leave this town to proceed to Port-au-Prince[43]
and the southern part to give my orders there, captains Jean-
Philippe Dupin[44] and Isaac brought me the dispatches of Paul Louverture[45]
who commanded Santo Domingo. Both of them
announced to me that a landing had just taken place in Oyarzábal,[46]
that the French and the Spaniards who lived in this
area had revolted and had cut off the roads
to Santo Domingo.[47] I informed myself of the content of this dispatch. While going
through
the letter of General Paul and the copy of the letter of General Kerversau[48]
to the commander of the city of Santo Domingo that was attached,
I saw that this general was inviting the commander, and
not General Paul as he should have done, to
prepare lodgings for his troops. I also saw that
General Paul had rejected his demand
until he received orders from me.[49] Consequently

42. Maurepas mentioned receiving five letters from Louverture between 31 Jan. and 7 Feb. They must have instructed him to prepare his defenses, because he reported back that he had armed his men and stood ready to fight for liberty; see Maurepas to Louverture (6 and 8 Feb. 1802), 61J18, ADGir. Maurepas twice repulsed a French assault, then retreated after burning Port-de-Paix and inflicting heavy casualties on the French.

43. Louverture occasionally employed Port-au-Prince's old royalist name, which had been abandoned in favor of Port Républicain during the Revolution; see also p. 10, line 43, and p. 20, line 12.

44. Jean-Philippe Dupin was a black officer who had massacred partisans of André Rigaud in Port-Républicain during the War of the South; see Ardouin, *Etudes*, vol. 4, 109.

45. Brigadier General Paul Louverture was Toussaint Louverture's brother and the commander of the city of Santo Domingo. He had written on 3 Feb. to inform Louverture of the arrival of a fleet, then twice again on the 4th to ask urgently for orders. See Paul Louverture to Louverture (3 and 4 Feb. 1802), Sc. Micro R-2228 Reel 5, SC-NYPL.

46. "roiale sa Bale" in manuscript C referred to Oyarzábal, a sugar plantation near the mouth of the Nigua River, just southwest of Santo Domingo, and the site of a 1796 slave uprising.

47. No French troops had actually landed, but Spanish civilians captured a fort in Santo Domingo on 8 Feb., on which day the French came close to land; see Paul Louverture to Kerversau (9 Feb. 1802) and Kerversau to Leclerc (13 Feb. 1802), 61J24, ADGir.

48. Louverture knew Brigadier General François-Marie Perichou de Kerversau, who had served as French agent in Santo Domingo before returning to France in 1801 and urging Bonaparte to intervene against Louverture.

49. On the negotiations, see the many letters between Kerversau and Paul Louverture in 61J24, ADGir and Sc. Micro R-2228 Reel 5, SC-NYPL.

8 (Bis) 3

je repondis au General paul que japprouvois sa conduite et je lui donnois
lordre de faire tout ce qui dependeroit de lui pour se defandre en cas
Dataque, émême de faire le General Kierverceaus et toute sa trouppe
prisonnier sil le pouvoit je remis ma reponce aux capitaine dont jai
parlé et prévoiant à raison de linterception des chemins quil pouroient
etre arrété et quon leur demandéroit[45] leur dépéche, je les charjeai
dune seconde letre par la quelle jordonnois au General paul de prendre
avec le General Kierverceaus toute les moyens de conciliation possible
et les previent que si le cas prevu arrivait de caché la premiere letre et

de ne leur faire voir que la seconde, le General paul ne voiant point
arrivoi ausitot quil le desiroit des reponces a ce depeche me ren
voier un autre officier noire porteur de ces même depeche par duplicatas
a qui d je donnois seulement un recu et le renvoiai, de ce troi
officier deux etoit noire et lautre blans, ils furent arreté comme je
lavois prevus et les deux noire furent assassinés contre toute
Espèce de justice et de raisons en contre les droit de la geurre,
leur depeches furent rémize au General Kierverceau qui ayant caché
le premiere letre fit seulement voire la seconde au General paul,
cest adire celle ou je lui ordonnois dentrer en conciliations avec
lui, cest enconcequance de cette letre que Santo Domingo sest
rendu, ces depeches expédiees je pris[46] ma route ver le Sud,
apeine etoi-je en marche que je fus atteins par une ordonance
arrivant a toute bride mapportant un paquiet du General vernette[47]
et une letre de mon nepouze[48] mannonceant lun et lautre larrivé
de mes deux enfans vénant de paris et deu leur precepteure, (ce que
javois ingnoré jusqualors) en majoutant quil étoient porteur
dordre du premiere[49] consul pour moi, je retournai alors sur mes

---

45. Louverture often added extraneous /e/ sounds ("demandéroit" instead of "demanderait"). See also "epousé," "séra," "am méné," "éné," and "citéroit," among many other examples.

46. Manuscript D: "repris" instead of "pris."

47. Louverture consistently misspelled the last names of Vernet, Boudet, Fressinet, and Brunet, most likely because he pronounced the final "t" of their names, as is common in southwestern France.

48. Manuscript D: "ma femme" instead of "mon nepouze."

49. The spelling of "premiere" indicates that Louverture pronounced a final "r" that is normally silent (see also "Grenadiere," "basére," "au casionnere"). He did the same with the final "s" and "t" of many words.

8 (Bis) 3

I responded to General Paul that I approved of his conduct and I gave him
the order to do all that was within his purview to defend himself in case
of an attack, even to take General Kerversau and all his troops
prisoner if he could.[50] I handed my response to the captains whom I
mentioned and, expecting that because the roads were cut off they might
be arrested and that they would be asked to hand over their dispatch, I entrusted them
with a second letter by which I ordered General Paul to take
with General Kerversau all possible means of conciliation
and warned them that if the expected scenario took place they should hide the first
    letter and
only show the second one.[51] General Paul, not
receiving as quickly as he wished a response to his dispatches, sent me
another black officer bearing copies of the same dispatches,
to which I merely replied with a receipt and sent him back. Of these three
officers, two were black and the other white. They were arrested as I
had foreseen and the two blacks were assassinated against every
kind of justice and reason and against the laws of war.[52]
Their dispatches were handed over to General Kerversau who, having hidden
the first letter, only showed the second one to General Paul,
that is to say the one where I ordered him to seek some conciliation with
him. It is as a consequence of this letter that Santo Domingo
surrendered.[53] After sending these dispatches, I again took the road to the South.
I had barely begun my march when a courier reached me
at full speed, bringing me a packet from General Vernet[54]
and a letter from my spouse, both of which announced to me the arrival
of my two children coming from Paris and of their tutor (which
I had ignored until then), adding that they were bearing
orders from the first consul for me.[55] I then retraced my

50. For orders to resist a French landing, see Louverture to Paul Louverture (6 Feb. 1802), 61J24, ADGir.
51. For the letter in which Louverture pretended to authorize his brother to let French troops land, see Louverture to Paul Louverture (9 Feb. 1802), 61J24, ADGir.
52. This is the first of four accusations of racial discrimination in the memoir (see also p. 15, lines 40 and 57, and p. 16, line 51). Kerversau mentioned intercepting Paul Louverture's couriers, but not killing them; see Kerversau to Leclerc (7 and 17 Feb. 1802), 61J24, ADGir.
53. Paul Louverture made his submission on 21 Feb. in exchange for a promise that slavery would not be restored; see Paul Louverture to Leclerc (21 Feb. 1802), Box 1Ad./7, Rochambeau Paper, University of Florida in Gainesville (RP-UF). Louverture omitted to mention that his brother's lack of resoluteness also facilitated the French takeover of Santo Domingo.
54. Brigadier General André Vernet was the husband of Louverture's niece Justine Eléonore Chancy. As of 1802, he was commander of the Louverture region near Gonaïves; see Pierre Bardin, "Langlois de Chancy-Toussaint Louverture," *Généalogie et Histoire de la Caraïbe*, no. 92 (Apr. 1997), 1944–1947.
55. This is the first mention of Louverture's second wife Suzanne and his sons Placide and Isaac Louverture, who had been studying in Paris since 1796 under their tutor Jean-Baptiste Coisnon. Leclerc traveled to Saint-Domingue with them and sent them to Louverture c. 9 Feb.; see Leclerc to Bonaparte (9 Feb. 1802), B7/26, SHD-DAT. His sons' arrival in Ennery

pas et volai à énnery ou je trouvai effectivement mes deux enfans
et le précepteur respectable que le gouvernement avoit l eut labonte
dé leur faire donné, je les embrassai a vec la plus grande satisfaction
et boucoup[50] demprescment et leur demandoi de suite sil étoit vrai
quil fusent porteur de letre pour moi du premiere consul,[51] le precepteur
mare pondits qué oui éne remit effectivement une letre que jouvrois
et lus jus qua moitie, puis la refermai en disant que je me la reservois
de la lire dans un moment ou je serois plus tranquile, je la priai
ensuite de me faire par des intantions du Gouvernement et de me dire
le nom du commandant de l'escadre que je navois encor pu savoir
jusqualors il me repondit quil sappelloit leclerc, que lintantion
du Gouvernement a mon negard etoit tres favorable, ce qui me
fut confirmé par mes enfans et ce dont je me suite assuré
ensuite en faisant lecture de la letre du premiere consul je leur
observai cependant que si les intentions du gouvernement etoient
pacifique et bounes a mon Egard et a l'Egard deu ceux qui avoient
contribue au bonheur dont jouisoit la colonie le General ne les avoient
surement pas suivie ni executé les ordre quil avoit recu puis
quil étoit debarquie dans lisle, comme ennemis en faisant
le mal uniquement pour a voire le plaisir de le faire sans
s'etre adresé au conmandant ni lui avoire communique ses
pouvoire je de mandai ensuite au monssieur[52] coinon precepteur

---

50. As in Kreyòl, Louverture occasionally replaced the /o/ sound with /u/, in this case writing "boucoup" instead of "beaucoup" (see also "nouroiet" instead of "n'auraient," "jou rois" instead of "j'aurais," "ouquin" instead of "aucun," and "coualition" instead of "coalition"). He also replaced /œ/ and /y/ with /u/ in many words.

51. Manuscript D: "qu'ils fussent porteur d'ordre du premier Consul pour moi" instead of "quil fusent porteur de letre pour moi du premiere consul."

52. Manuscript D: "citoyen" instead of "monssieur." Louverture chose to employ the term "sieur," which was used to refer to whites in pre-revolutionary Saint-Domingue, instead of the more egalitarian "citoyen," which had emerged during the French Revolution.

steps and flew to Ennery, where I indeed found my two children
and the respectable tutor whom the government had been kind enough
to assign to them. I kissed them with the greatest satisfaction
and much haste, and asked them at once if it was true
that they were bearing letters for me from the first consul.[56] The tutor
responded to me that yes and indeed handed over to me a letter that I opened
and read half way through. Then I closed it and said that I reserved
the right to read it at a moment when I would be more tranquil.[57] I then invited
him to inform me of the intentions of the government and to give me
the name of the commander of the squadron, which I had not yet been able to learn
until then. He replied to me that his name was Leclerc,[58] that the intentions
of the government toward me were highly favorable, which was
confirmed to me by my children,[59] and which I myself verified
later when reading the letter of the first consul. I
noted to them, though, that if the intentions of the government were
pacific and good toward me and toward those who had
contributed to the happiness that the colony enjoyed, the general had
certainly not followed them or executed the orders that he had received
since he had landed in the island as an enemy, doing
evil purely for the pleasure of doing so, without
contacting the commander nor communicating to him his
powers.[60] I then asked mister[61] Coisnon, the tutor

(n55 cont.)

fulfilled Louverture's two wishes: to see his sons and to receive a personal letter from the first consul. "I again ask you for the return of my children," he had written. "I already had the honor of writing several letters to you but I have not had the joy of receiving a response from you;" see Louverture to Bonaparte (16 July 1801), Dossier 1, AF/IV/1213, AN.

56. Louverture's account of the meeting with his sons is consistent with Coisnon to Leclerc (11 Feb. 1802), 61J18, ADGir; Coisnon to Decrès (20 Feb. 1802), in *Moniteur Universel* no. 212 (22 Apr. 1802); Antoine Métral, *Histoire de l'expédition des Français à Saint-Domingue sous le consulat de Napoléon Bonaparte, suivie des mémoires et notes d'Isaac l'Ouverture* (Paris: Ainé and Renouard, 1825), 239.

57. One suspects that Louverture, who did not read well, was too proud to labor through the letter in front of his sons' teacher. In the letter, Bonaparte promised "consideration, honor, fortune" to Louverture if he subjected to Leclerc's authority; see Bonaparte to Louverture (18 Nov. 1801), in Jean-Baptiste Vaillant, ed., *Correspondance de Napoléon Ier, publiée par ordre de l'empereur Napoléon III*, vol. 7 (Paris: Plon, 1858), 410.

58. Captain General Victoire Emmanuel Leclerc (1772–1802), the husband of Bonaparte's sister Pauline, had been entrusted with the command of the expedition to Saint-Domingue; see Henri Mézière, *Le Général Leclerc et l'expédition de Saint-Domingue* (Paris: Tallandier, 1990). It is very unlikely that Louverture still did not know Leclerc's name a week after meeting Christophe near Cap. To make his claim more credible, Louverture referred to Leclerc as "the general commanding the squadron" in the early part of the memoir, slipping only once (p. 2, line 10).

59. Bonaparte had met Isaac and Placide before their departure from France to assure them of his good intentions toward their father; see Métral, *Mémoires et notes d'Isaac l'Ouverture*, 229–231.

60. Louverture was right to doubt the sincerity of Leclerc, who was expecting to launch military operations within four or five days even as he sent Louverture's sons to Ennery; see Leclerc to Bonaparte (9 Feb. 1802), B7/26, SHD-DAT.

61. The D manuscript referred to "citizen" Coisnon, which Louverture changed to "mister" in keeping with the pre-Revolutionary habit of referring to whites as "sieur" (see also

de mes enfans si le general leclerc ne lui avoit rien remis
pour moi et ne lavoit pas chargé de me dire quelque chose
il me repondit que non, en mengagnant cependent à aller
au cap pour conferre avec cegéneral, mes Enfans yjoignirent
leur sollicitations pour my déterminer, je leur representai
que da pres la conduite de ce General je ne pouvois avoire en lui
aucune confiance, quil etoit debarque comme ennemis que
malgré cela javois creu de monde voire daller audevant
de lui pour empeché le progrés dumal, qua lors il mavoit fait
Tirer[53] dessus, et que javois couru les plus grande danger, quen
fins si ses intention étoient pure comme celle du gouvernement
qui lenvoiait,, il auroit pris la peine de mecrire pour mins
truire de sa mision, que même il auroit du avant darrivé
a la rade men voier un aviso, avec vous comme se la ce
pratique ordinairement pour me faire part de ses pouvoire
et minformer de son arrivées ; que puis quil navoit renplis
aucune de ces formalite le mal étoit faite, et quincis je
refusois definitivement daller le trouver ; que cependant
pour prouver mon attachement et ma soumission au gouvernement
francais ; jécrirois une letre au general le clerc je lai envoirois
par monsieur grand ville homme respectable acompagné de mes
deux enfans et de leur precepteur que je chargerais delui[54]
quil depandoit absolument de lui de perdre entierement la colonie
ou dela conserver a la france et que jentreroit avec lui dans
tous les arrangement posibles et que j'étois prete a me soumetre
aux ordre du Gouvernement francais dez que le general leclerc
mauroit fait voire les ordres dont il étoit portuer et quil auroit
cescé toute espece d'hostilité éffectivement je fis la letre et
la deputation partis. dans lespoire que dapres mes soumision
tout seroit rentré dans lordre je restai au Gonaive jusquaus
lendemains ou jappris que deux vaisaux avoient attaquie[55]
S^t marc; je mÿ transportai et appris quil avaient de jai été

---

53. Louverture did not use modern capitalization rules. Instead, he capitalized words he wanted to emphasize, such as "tirer" here. As a general rule, he capitalized the words "gouvernement" and "general."

54. Manuscript D: "que je chargeais de lui dire" instead of "que je chargerais delui."

55. This is one of many instances where Louverture added an extra "i," perhaps as a form of hypercorrection. He did the same in "révoquier" eight lines below.

9

of my children, if General Leclerc had not given him anything for me and if he had not asked him to tell me something. He responded to me that no, while encouraging me still to go to Cap to confer with this general. My children joined their own solicitations to try to convince me. I explained to them that, judging by the conduct of this general, I could have no trust in him; that he had landed as an enemy; that despite this I had thought it my duty to go before him to prevent evil from spreading; and that he then had people shoot at me and that I had run the greatest dangers; that finally if his intentions were as pure as those of the government that was sending him, he would have taken the time to write to me to inform me of his mission; that even before his arrival in the harbor he should have sent an aviso[62] with you on board, as is done customarily, to notify me of his powers and inform me of his arrival;[63] that since he had not fulfilled any of these formalities, it was already too late, and so I definitely refused to go find him; that yet to prove my attachment and my submission to the French government I would write a letter to General Leclerc, I would send it through mister Granville,[64] a respectable man, accompanied by my two children and their tutor, whom I would ask to tell him that it was absolutely up to him to lose the colony entirely or to save it for France; and that I would make all the necessary arrangements with him; and that I was ready to submit to the orders of the French government as soon as General Leclerc showed me the orders that he was bearing and ceased any type of hostility. Indeed, I wrote the letter[65] and the deputation left. Hoping that, because of my submission, everything would go back to normal, I stayed in Gonaïves until the following day, when I learned that two ships of the line had attacked Saint-Marc. I went there and learned that they had already been

(n61 cont.)

Valtière, p. 20, line 29, and Espinville, p. 21, line 6). In contrast, people of color had traditionally been listed as "le nommé," a derogatory term that Louverture used when mentioning his black enemy Golart (p. 9, line 48). On Louverture's use of antiquated forms of address, see also Lacroix, *Mémoires*, vol. 1, 401.

    62. Small dispatch ship.

    63. According to Isaac Louverture, he and Placide were supposed to arrive two weeks before the main fleet, but Leclerc learned in Sámana that Louverture was in Santo Domingo and opted to attack Cap at once; see Métral, *Mémoires et notes d'Isaac l'Ouverture*, 232.

    64. Granville, a teacher in nearby Gonaïves, was the tutor of Louverture's youngest son Saint-Jean.

    65. In the letter, Louverture reproached Leclerc for "having come to overthrow him with cannonballs" and announced that "he needed time to make a decision;" see Lacroix, *Mémoires*, vol. 2, 124.

repouscé, je retournai alors au gonaive pour y attendre la
reponce du General leclerc enfin deux joure aprés mes doux[56] enfans
arriverent avec cette reponce tant desirez parla quelle ce
General me mandoit de me rendre prés de lui au cap; et man
noncoit quau sur plus il avoit donne l'ordre a se generaux
de marché sur tous les points, et que ses ordres étant donné,
il ne pouvoit plus les révoquier,
Il me promit cependant que le general boudette[57] sarreteroit a lartibonite
je jugai a lors quil ne connaissoit pas parfaitement le paÿ ou
quon la voit trompé, pus que pour arriver a lartibonite il
faut avoire le passage libre pas S^t marc, ce qui netoit pas
pusque les deux vaissaux qui avoient attaque cette ville avoient
été repouscé, il ma jouta encor quon attaqueroit pas les
mole que seulement on en feroit le blocus tandis que cet
endroit setoit deja rendus. Je repondis alors franchement au
General que je ne me rendrois pas aupres de lui au cap que sa

---

56. Manuscript D: "deux" instead of "doux."
57. Manuscript D omits "Boudette." Note that Louverture pronounced the final "t" in "Boudet," as he did with Vernet, Fressinet, and Brunet.

repulsed.⁶⁶ I then returned to Gonaïves to await the response from General Leclerc. Finally, two days later, my sweet children arrived with this response that I so desired, in which this general was summoning me to proceed to Cap to be with him, and announced to me that he had also ordered his generals to march on all points, [and] that since his orders were issued he could no longer revoke them.

He still promised me that General Boudet would stop on the Artibonite River.⁶⁷ I then judged that he did not know the country perfectly well, or that he had been deceived, since to reach the Artibonite one must have free passage through Saint-Marc, which was not the case since the two ships that had attacked this town had been repulsed.⁶⁸ He also added that they would not attack Môle [Saint-Nicolas], that they would only blockade it whereas this position had already surrendered.⁶⁹ I then responded frankly to the general that I would not go to meet him in Cap, that his

---

66. On 12 Feb., the French were preparing a naval attack on Saint-Marc scheduled for the 16th; see Lacroix to Bruyère (12 Feb. 1802), B7/15, SHD-DAT. Also on the 12th, Dessalines asked Louverture to come meet him in Saint-Marc because he had "plenty of things to tell you;" see Dessalines to Louverture (12 Feb. 1802), Sc. Micro R-2228 Reel 4, SC-NYPL. Louverture was in Saint-Marc as of the 15th; see Louverture to Bartalier (15 Feb. 1802), Sc. Micro R-2228 Reel 5, SC-NYPL.

67. In his letter, Leclerc invited Louverture to come to Cap, proposed to maintain him in his rank if he surrendered, promised not to restore slavery, announced that forces had been sent to all ports of the colony, and offered not to attack with his troops in Cap for four days; see Leclerc to Louverture (12 Feb. 1802), B7/26, SHD-DAT. Leclerc was certain that the negotiations would fail and planned to launch an all-out campaign on 17 Feb.; see Leclerc to Decrès (15 Feb. 1802), CC9B/19, ANOM.

68. Leclerc, who had spent his entire life in Europe, was indeed poorly informed about Saint-Domingue's politics and geography, which Louverture was pleased to underline in his memoir.

69. On 19 Feb., Maurepas reported that Bartalier, the commander of Môle Saint-Nicolas, had surrendered to a single French frigate, and that nearby Jean-Rabel and Bombarde had surrendered too; see Maurepas to Louverture (19 Feb. 1802), 61J18, ADGir.

10 4

conduite ne minspiroit pas a ses de confiance que cepandant
j étois prête a lui remetre le commandement conformement aux ordre
du premiere consul mais que je ne voulois point etre son lieutenant
General, je lengageai ensuite a me faire pascer ses intantions en
lassurant que je contribuerois par tout ce qui seroit en mon pou
voire au retabliscement de lordre et de la tranquilité, je lui
ajoutai enfin que sil persistoit toujour a marche en ~~en~~ avant
il me forceroit a la defence, malgré que je ness[58] pas de troupe,
je lui en voiai cette letre par une ordonnance tres prescé qui
me rapportoit de sapart quil navoit plus de reponce a me
faire et quil entroit en canpangne, les habitans de Gonaive mes
demanderent permision de lui envoier une deputation ce que je leur
acordai mais il reteint cette depputation, le lendemain je
fus instruitre quil setoit emparé sans coup ferie et sans tiré
un coup de fusil du dondon S^t raphael S^t michel et la mamelade[59]
et quil se disposoit a marche a ennerÿ et Gonaive. ces nou
velle hostilite me firent faire de nouvelle reflecsions, je pan
sai que la conduite du General LeClerc étoit bien contraire aux
intention du gouvernment, puis que le premiere consul dans
sa letre promettoit la paix tendis que lui faisois la geurre;
je vis quau lieu de cherche a arrete le mal il ne faisoit que
l'augmenter; ne craint-il pas me disois-je en moi même en
tenant une pareille conduite detre blamé du premiere Consul,[60]
de ce Grand homme dont léquité et limpartialite sont sibien

---

58. Read: "que je n'eusse."

59. As is the norm in Kreyòl and popular French, Louverture occasionally elided consonants and vowels to facilitate pronunciation. In this case, he dropped the "r" in "Marmelade" (see also "lattinde" instead of "l'atteindre," "re maque" instead of "remarquer," "abitrairement" instead of "arbitrairement," and "paraite" instead of "paraître"). He also elided "e," "x," "s," and "i" in some words and dropped the final letter of others.

60. Manuscript D: "d'être blâmé du Gouvernement? Peut-il espérer d'être approuvé du premier Consul?" instead of "detre blamé du premiere Consul."

10 4

conduct was not inspiring enough confidence, that nevertheless
I was ready to hand over my command to him per the orders
of the first consul, but that I did not want to be his lieutenant
general. I then encouraged him to inform me of his intentions, while
assuring him that I would do all that was within my powers to contribute
to the restoration of order and tranquility. I
added finally that if he persisted in marching forward
he would force me to defend myself, even though I had no troops.[70]
I sent him this letter via a very fast courier, who
responded on his behalf that he had no more response to
give to me and that he was beginning his campaign.[71] The inhabitants of Gonaïves
asked for my permission to send him a deputation, which I
granted, but he kept this deputation with him. The following day I
was informed that he had seized, without further ado and without firing
a single gunshot, Dondon, Saint-Raphaël, Saint-Michel, and Marmelade,
and that he was getting ready to march on Ennery and Gonaïves.[72] These
new hostilities led me to reflect again. I thought
that the conduct of General Leclerc was quite contrary to the
intentions of the government, since the first consul in
his letter promised peace whereas he was waging war.
I saw that instead of trying to stem the progress of evil he only kept
facilitating it. "Does he not fear," I was saying to myself,
"by conducting himself in such a manner, to be blamed by the first consul,
this great man, whose equity and impartiality are so well

---

70. Louverture's regular army was estimated at over 20,000 men; see Lacroix, *Mémoires*, vol. 2, 65. He had expanded it by mobilizing additional men on the eve of Leclerc's arrival so, even when accounting for defections, it is unlikely that he had no men with him by mid-February. He later said he had "few" troops (see p. 7, line 27).

71. This second set of letters was not in the archives consulted for this book.

72. Leclerc attacked on 17 Feb. The Desfourneaux division took Limbé (17th), Plaisance (19th). The Hardÿ division took Grand Boucan (17th), Dondon (18th), Marmelade (19th). The Rochambeau division took La Tannerie (17th), Saint-Raphaël (18th), Saint-Michel (19th); see Leclerc to Decrès (27 Feb. 1802), CC9B/19, ANOM. Ennery and Gonaïves, their next targets, were in the heart of the region that Louverture had captured from the Spanish and the British in the 1790s, where he had acquired many plantations, and which he had recently named after himself.

reconnus; tandis que je serois desaprouvé: je pris dont le partis
de me defendre en ca dattaque et fis malgre le peu[61] troupe
que javois, mes disposition en concéquance, Gonaive netant pas
Defensive jordonnai de la bruler en cas quon fut forcé a la
retraite, je placai le General christophe qui avoit été oblige
de se replier dans le chemin[62] deribourequi conduit à bayonnette et me re
tirai au Gonaives ou un partis de ma Garde d'honneur, qui été au port republi
cain se rendus[63] pour me rejoindre, et mi de fendre,[64] mais j appris que Gro
morne venoit de se rendre et que larmé devoit marche au gonaive sur troi

colone, quin de ces colone commande par lé General rochambeau etoit des

tine a paser par la couleuvre et desendre a la croix sur ma hatte,[65] et pour
nous couper le chemin de la ville et le pasages du pont lester, jordonnai

en concequance de bruler la ville de Gonaive et marche au de vant de la
colone qui se dirigeoit au pont lester[66] a la tete de troi cent grenadier de ma

---

61. As is common in Kreyòl, Louverture occasionally simplified French grammar, in this case by dropping the preposition "de" in "peu troupe" (see also "les cultivateur jen rabelle" instead of "les cultivateurs de Jean Rabel"). He did so repeatedly in certain passages, particularly the segment of the addendum that he wrote entirely on his own.
62. The phrase "sur les hauteurs" was replaced with "dans le chemin" in manuscript B.
63. The phrase "à St. Marc pour y recruter le plus de troupes que je pourrais" was replaced with "aux Gonaïves où une partie de ma Garde d'Honneur s'était rendue" in manuscript B.
64. Manuscript D: "une partie de ma Garde d'honneur s'était rendue" instead of "un partis de ma Garde d'honneur, qui été au port republicain se rendus pour me rejoindre."
65. Manuscript D omits "sur ma hatte."
66. "Cette ville" was crossed out and replaced with "la ville de Gonaïves" in manuscript B. "Cette colonne" was also replaced with "la colonne qui se dirigeait au pont de l'Ester."

recognized, whereas I will be approved?"[73] So I opted to defend myself in case of an attack and took my dispositions accordingly even though I had few troops. Since Gonaïves was not defensible, I gave orders to burn it in case we were forced to retreat.[74] I positioned General Christophe, who had been obliged to fall back, on the Eribourg road that leads to Bayonnet,[75] and retired to Gonaïves, where a part of my honor guard, which was in Port-Républicain, came to join me and defend me. But I learned that Gros-Morne had just surrendered and that the army was going to march on Gonaïves in three columns,[76] that one of these columns commanded by General Rochambeau was supposed to pass by the [Ravine-à-]Couleuvres and descend to La Croix on my ranch, and to cut us off from the road to the town and the passage through the Ester bridge.[77] I ordered consequently to burn the town of Gonaïves[78] and I marched ahead of the column that was heading for the Ester bridge at the head of 300 grenadiers from my

73. It is unlikely that Louverture had such a naïve view of Bonaparte's intentions, but he was careful throughout the memoir to flatter the first consul.

74. These are the whereabouts of Louverture according to the testimony of one of his guides, Barade. "On 2 ventôse [21 Feb.] Toussaint was camped on the Cocherel plantation.... On the 4th he was chased and retreated via Gonaïves to the plain of the Artibonite, where he successively stayed at various plantations, spending only a few hours on each of them before setting it on fire and leaving. On the 11th (2 March) he went to Bayonnais, recently abandoned by troops of the Republic, and burned it. On the 12th he passed by Ennery, which he burned. He then went to Marmelade, taking all cultivators with him.... On the morning of the 14th he left Marmelade [with troops]. He ordered an attack on Plaisance and marched with the left column, which was attacked and beaten on the evening of the 14th;" see Thouvenot to Dugua (28 March 1802), Dossier 2, AF/IV/1213, AN.

75. Bayonnet (or Bayonnais) was a strong position on Louverture's right flank near Ravine-à-Couleuvre; see Saint-Rémy, Mémoires, 48. According to Leclerc, Christophe retreated to the "Bayonnais plantation" on 21 Feb. after being chased from Ennery by Gen. Hardÿ, only to be attacked by Gen. Jean-Baptiste Salme and forced to retreat again; see Leclerc to Decrès (27 Feb. 1802), CC9B/19, ANOM.

76. French troops took Plaisance, Ennery, and the Bayonnais plantation on 21 Feb., Gonaïves and Ravine-à-Couleuvres on 23 Feb., Saint-Marc on 25 Feb., and Gros-Morne on 26 Feb., before heading back to Gonaïves to attack Louverture; see Leclerc to Decrès (27 Feb. 1802), CC9B/19, ANOM.

77. The Couleuvre was a mountainous area crossed by a river that passed by the La Croix plantation. The ensuing battle, mentioned in the memoir as the "affair of La Croix," is now known as the battle of Ravine-à-Couleuvre.

78. According to a white planter who was present in Gonaïves, Louverture gathered all local whites and told them "in a loud, rumbling voice while rolling his ferocious eyes" that he would destroy the planters, then sent them on to the town of Petite-Rivière; see Michel-Etienne Descourtilz, Voyage d'un naturaliste et ses observations, vol. 3 (Paris: Dufart, 1809), 288.

Garde commande par leur chef et de soisante garde a cheval ingnorait la
force du General rochanbeau, je le rencontrai dans une gorge et lattaque
conmancer a quatre[67] heur du ma tin par un feu soutenu qui dura jus qua
midis le General rochambeau commansa lattaque,[68] jai su par les priso
nier que jai faite que la colone etoit de plus de quatre mille homme;
pen dant que j etoit aux prise avec le General rochanbeau la colone
conmande par le general le clerc arriva au gonaive, laffaire de la croix
terminé, je me rendis au pont lestere pour y' prandre lartillerie qui
de fendoit cet en droit dans lintention de me rendre en suite a S^t marc ou je
contoit faire grandre resistance,[69] mai chemin faisante jappris que le
general dessaline apre etre arrive a vant mois dant cette endroit a voit
ete obligé de levaquie et se étoit retire a la petite riviere, je fus
obligé aprés cette manevre de retar der ma marche pour en voier

67. Manuscript D: "six" instead of "quatre."
68. The phrase "le Général Rochambeau commença l'attaque" was added in manuscript B.
69. The phrase "où je comptais faire grande résistance" was added in manuscript B.

guard, commanded by their chief, and sixty mounted guards. I did not know the strength of General Rochambeau. I encountered him in a gorge and the attack began at four in the morning with a sustained fire that lasted until noon. General Rochambeau began the attack. I have learned through the prisoners that I took that the column was more than four thousand men strong.[79] While I was battling General Rochambeau, the column commanded by General Leclerc arrived in Gonaïves. Once the affair of La Croix was over, I proceeded to the Ester bridge to take the artillery that defended this spot, with the intention of then heading to Saint-Marc where I planned on making a strong resistance. But on the way I learned that General Dessalines, after arriving before me at this location, had been obliged to evacuate it and had fallen back on Petite-Rivière.[80] I was obliged because of this maneuver to slow my march to send

---

79. Leclerc's account was the mirror opposite of Louverture's: Louverture entrenched himself in the Ravine-à-Couleuvre with 4,100 regular troops and 2,000 armed cultivators, but was forced to retreat to Petite-Rivière after a hard-fought battle with Gen. Rochambeau on 23 Feb.; see Leclerc to Decrès (27 Feb. 1802), B7/26, SHD-DAT.

80. Dessalines burned the town of Saint-Marc before 24 Feb., when he was pushed out of the city by Gen. Jean Boudet; see Lacroix to Dugua (1 March 1802), B7/15, SHD-DAT.

11

en avant de moi les prisonnier que ja voit faite a la croix[70] les blecé
a la petite riviere et me determinois en suite a mi rendre moi même,
arriveé che couroitte dant la plaine j y laisser me troupe et me portoit seul

en avant je trouver que toute les paÿs etoit evaque, je re cu une letre du
Géneral dessaline qui minstruisoit qua yant appris quon de voit attaquier le

cahau il s y etoit rendus avec sa troupe pour le de fendre je luis donnois
ordre de suite de venire me rejoindre je fus metre les munition de geurre et de
Bouche que ja voit a vec moi dans le fort louverture ditte[71] la crete a pieraux

j ordonnois au General vernette de se procure les vasse necessaire pour contenir
l'Eau pour la garnisons en cas de siege a larrivé du General dessaline je lui
ordonnai de prendre le commandement de ce fort de se defendre jus qua lestré
mite. je la lai sois pour cet objet la moitie de me garde avec le chef de brigade
magny et me deux Escadront je lui en joignis de ne pas laiser le general
vernette exposé au feu mai de le laisser dans une endroit retire pour
veiller au travail de cartouche, enfin je fis dire au Géneral dessaline
que pendant que le general le clerc viendroit attaque cette place, j'roit[72]
dans la partis du nord pour fere disversion et reprendre les diferante paroise[73]
dont on setoit de ja emparé, et que par cette maneuvre je forcérois

---

70. The phrase "que j'avais fait à la Croix" was added in the margin of manuscript B.
71. Manuscript D: "à" instead of "ditte."
72. Read: "j'irais."
73. Manuscript D: "places" instead of "paroises."

11

ahead of me the prisoners I had made at La Croix [and] the wounded
to Petite-Rivière, and convinced myself later to go there in person.[81]
After I arrived at the Couriotte [plantation] on the plain [of the Artibonite River],
I left my troops there and went forward
alone. I found that all the countryside had been evacuated. I received a letter from
General Dessalines informing me that, having learned that the Cahos [mountain
chain][82] was going to be
attacked, he had proceeded there with his troops to defend it.[83] I ordered him
at once to come join me. I had the ammunition and
the provisions that I had with me transferred to Fort Louverture, also known as
Crête-à-Pierrot.[84]
I ordered General Vernet to obtain the necessary vases to hold
the water for the garrison in case of a siege. When General Dessalines arrived, I
ordered him to take the command of this fort, to defend himself until the last
extremity. I left him for that purpose half of my guard with Brigadier Chief
Magny and my two squadrons.[85] I enjoined him not to let General
Vernet be exposed to enemy fire, but to leave him in a secluded spot to
oversee the making of cartridges.[86] Finally, I let General Dessalines know
that while General Leclerc would attack this position I would go
to the northern part to make a diversion and retake the various parishes
that had already been seized, and that with this maneuver I would force

81. One letter mentioned Louverture's orders that all prisoners taken in the region be sent to him; see Claude Martin to Figeac (23 Feb. 1802), Sc. Micro R-2228 Reel 1, SC-NYPL.

82. The mountain chains of Grand Cahos and Petit Cahos (Spanish: Las Caobas) were a formidable obstacle. "I have never seen anything comparable in the Alps," reported Leclerc. See Leclerc to Decrès (27 Feb. 1802), CC9B/19, ANOM.

83. A later report by Dessalines indicates that he was pushed out of the Cahos mountains, but had time to collect hidden ammunition stores and rescue the wives of Dessalines and Louverture; see Dessalines to Louverture (12 March 1802), Sc. Micro R-2228 Reel 4, SC-NYPL.

84. In his memoir, Louverture occasionally exaggerated his military role even though it made his legal situation more difficult. It was actually Dessalines who decided to fortify the fort of Crête-à-Pierrot, located on a hill near Petite-Rivière. "My desire to preserve this advantageous position convinced me to take the necessary measures. I immediately placed some of my troops in the fort and two battalions of the 4th demi-brigade on a nearby hill;" see Dessalines to Louverture (1 March 1802), Sc. Micro R-2228 Reel 4, SC-NYPL.

85. According to an account of the siege of Crête-à-Pierrot that is occasionally biased toward Dessalines, Louverture actually took troops from, rather than gave troops to, Etienne Magny, a brigadier chief in Louverture's honor guard; see Louis Boisrond-Tonnerre, "Mémoire pour servir à l'histoire d'Hayti" (22 June 1804), p. 13, CC9B/27, ANOM.

86. Vernet's presence in Crête-à-Pierrot is mentioned in Thouvenot to Dugua (16 March 1802), Dossier 2, AF/IV/1213, AN. Louverture probably wanted to protect Vernet because he was married to his niece.

ce general a revenire surce pas a prendre des arangement avec moi pour conserver au Gouvernement cette belle colonnie. Cet ordre donné je pris cix conpagnie de

Grenadiere commander par Gabard chef de la 4[74] trieme de mi Brigade et les chef de bataion pour cis lig je marchais sur ennery que je repris j'y trouvois la proclamations du général leclerc qui me metre hor de la loi, persuadé que je navoit au cune tort a me reproché, que tous ces desordre qui regne dans les pay a été aucasionné par le general le clerc, me croiant Dailleur tous jour le gitine conmandant de lisle, je refuté sa proclamation

et le irrete lai-même hor de la loi san perdre dé[75] temp je me rémite en marche et re prens sans coup férie S^t michel S^t raphael dondon et la marmelade; dans cette dernié paroisse je recu une letre du General déssaline qui minstruisoit que le General leclerc a voit marché a la petite rivierre sou troi colone que lune de ce colone, pasant par le cahau, et le grand fond setoient em paré de tous les tresors de la re publique[76] venant de Gonaive et largent que les habitant a verent déposé quelle s etoit tellement chargé de Butin, quelle navoit pu se porter a sa destination; et a voit été obligé dé retrogarder pour de posé leur riches au porrepublicain, que les deux autre colone qui avoient attaqué le fort avoient été repouse par le chef de brigade magny, que le general le clerc ayant reunit plus de force a voit ordonné une seconde attaque qui avoit egalment été répousée par liai General dessaline qui etoit arrivé a lors[77] instruit de ces fait je me portai sur plaisance et mi enparoi

---

74. Manuscript D: "40" instead of "4."
75. This is one of many instances in the memoir where Louverture added /e/ sounds, in this case in "dé," "rémite" (same line), and "dé" (line 35).
76. The phrase "de la République" was added in manuscript B.
77. The phrase "Dessalines qui y était arrivé alors" was added in manuscript B.

this general to retrace his steps [and] to make arrangements with me to preserve for the government this beautiful colony.[87] Once this order was given, I took six companies of
grenadiers commanded by Gabart, chief of the fourth demi-brigade, and Battalion Chief Pourcely.[88] I marched on Ennery, which I retook.
I found there the proclamation of General Leclerc that declared me an outlaw.[89] Convinced that I had done nothing wrong, that all this disorder
that plagued the country had been caused by General Leclerc, believing actually that I was still the legitimate commander of the island, I refuted his proclamation
and declared him an outlaw.[90] Without losing time, I resumed my march and retook without further ado Saint-Michel, Saint-Raphaël, Dondon, and Marmelade. In the latter parish, I received a letter[91] from General Dessalines that informed me
that General Leclerc had marched on Petite-Rivière with three columns; that one of these columns, while passing through the Cahos and the Grand Fonds, had seized all the treasures of the republic coming from Gonaïves and the money that the inhabitants had deposited; that it was so loaded with
loot that it had been unable to proceed to its destination and had been obliged to backtrack to deposit its riches in Port-Républicain;[92]
that the other two columns that had attacked the fort had been repulsed by brigadier chief Magny;[93] that General Leclerc after
gathering more forces had ordered a second assault that had also been repulsed by General Dessalines after his arrival.[94]
Then, informed of these events, I proceeded to Plaisance, where I first took

---

87. During the 1799–1800 War of the South, Louverture had been surprised by rebellions in the northwest and almost lost the war. His experience probably inspired this maneuver.

88. Louis Vaillant-Gabart (1776–1805) and Michel Pourcely (?–1807) were two mixed-race officers; see Daniel Desormeaux, ed., *Mémoires du général Toussaint Louverture* (Paris: Classiques Garnier, 2011), 114.

89. The proclamation declared that Louverture and Christophe were outlaws (and thus could be killed with impunity), that colonial soldiers refusing to join Leclerc would be viewed as rebels, and that cultivators assisting the revolt would be "treated like wayward children and sent back to cultivation;" see Leclerc, "Proclamation aux habitants de Saint-Domingue" (17 Feb. 1802), CC9B/19, ANOM.

90. The proclamation cited and countered every point of Louverture's 17 Feb. proclamation and declared that Leclerc, Rochambeau, Kerversau, and Edmé-Etienne Desfourneaux were outlaws; see Louverture, "Proclamation" (1 March 1802), in St. Rémy, *Mémoires*, 109–119.

91. The letter mentioned by Louverture was possibly Dessalines to Louverture (12 March 1802), Sc. Micro R-2228 Reel 4, SC-NYPL. See also Dessalines to Louverture (14 and 18 March 1802), in Jacques de Cauna, ed., *Toussaint Louverture et l'indépendance d'Haïti* (Paris: Karthala, 2004), 14.

92. On the treasure, see Isaac Louverture to M. de Saint-Anthoine (30 Apr. 1847), NAF 12409, BNF; Girard, *The Slaves Who Defeated Napoleon*, 107-109.

93. "All is well here, the enemy attacked us, but we forced them to retreat and inflicted losses;" see Magny to Louverture (8 March 1802), Sc. Micro R-2228 Reel 5, SC-NYPL.

94. After a first attack on 4 March 1802 by the French generals Jean-François Debelle and Pierre Devaux, Leclerc, Boudet, and Dugua launched on 11 March a second and equally unsuccessful assault; see Dugua to Berthier (26 March 1802), B7/3, SHD-DAT.

da bord du canp de badurette qui dominé cette place et qui etoit
au cuppé par de troupe de ligne et emportais egalment dasaut
tou les poste a vancé au moment ou jallait tonbér sur la place je
recois letre du conmandant de la marmelade qui me donne avis
quine forte colone venant d̶e̶ de la parties Espagnole dirige sur
cette place je me portai alors promptement sur cette colone qui au
lieu de se porte sur lamarmelade avoit marché sur hinche et
la pour suivé san pouvoire lattinde, a pre quoi je retournai
au Gonaive me rendis maitre de la plaine qui en vironé
cette ville, aprete a marche sur Gromorne pour aller ensuite
délivré le général morpas qui de voit etre retiré dans les montagne
de por de pais[78] ou je lui avoit ordonné de camppér[79] san savoire sil
a voit dé ja caputulé et fer sa soumisions au General le clere
je recu une troisieme letre du general dessaline qui mefaisoit
le rapport que le general le clerc ayant reunit toute se force
a voit ordonné la saut[80] et quil avoit été répoucé a vec perte
tres considerable ce qui la voit de terminé a faire cerné cette

---

78. Manuscript D: "qui devait être au Port-de-Paix, ou s'être retiré dans les montagnes" instead of "qui de voit etre retiré dans les montagne de por de pais."

79. The phrase "où je lui avais ordonné de se camper sans savoir s'il avait déjà capitulé et soumis au Général Leclerc" was added in manuscript B. Louverture probably did not use the verb "camper" in the traditional French meaning of "setting up camp for the night" but in the Kreyòl meaning of "stay there" (the term is used three times in the manuscript).

80. Manuscript D: "l'assaut général" instead of "la saut."

the camp of Bedouret[95] that overlooks this position and that was
occupied by troops of the line[96] and also captured in an assault
all the forward positions.[97] Just as I was about to descend on the position, I
received a letter from the commander of Marmelade notifying me
that a strong column coming from the Spanish part was heading toward
this position.[98] I then promptly headed toward this column, which instead
of proceeding to Marmelade had marched to Hinche, and
pursued it without being able to reach it, after which I returned
to Gonaïves, took control of the plain that surrounds
this town, [and] readied myself to march on Gros-Morne, to then go
relieve General Maurepas who had likely retired to the mountains
of Port-de-Paix, where I had ordered him to stay without knowing if he
had already capitulated and made his submission to General Leclerc.[99]
I received a third letter[100] from General Dessalines, who
reported to me that General Leclerc, after gathering all his forces,
had ordered an assault and that he had been repulsed with a very
considerable loss, which had determined him to surround this

95. Bedouret (or Bidouret) was a plantation near Plaisance.
96. Troops of the line were heavy infantry trained for pitched battles.
97. A guide of Louverture gave a far less glorious account. On the morning of 5 March, Louverture left Marmelade with two demi-brigades and various corps. "He ordered an attack on Plaisance and marched with the left column, which was attacked and beaten on the evening of the 14th.... During the retreat, someone said to a member of the honor guard 'my friends all is lost the governor was injured in his shoulder;'" see Thouvenot to Dugua (28 March 1802), Dossier 2, AF/IV/1213, AN. On Louverture's defeat in Plaisance, see also "Ordre du jour de la division Desfourneaux" (6 March 1802), B7/2, SHD-DAT.
98. After Paul Louverture's submission in Santo Domingo, Kerversau sent troops to seal off the border with Saint-Domingue to prevent rebels from fleeing to the Spanish part; see Kerversau to Leclerc (7 and 14 March 1802), 61J24, ADGir.
99. Attacked by several French columns, Maurepas had already capitulated on 26 Feb.; see Leclerc to Decrès (27 Feb. 1802), CC9B/19, ANOM; Lacroix, *Mémoires*, vol. 2, 135.
100. This letter was not in the archives consulted for this book. Other letters indicate that Dessalines fell sick and left Crête-à-Pierrot between 18 and 30 March; see Dessalines to Louverture (18 March 1802), in Cauna, *Toussaint Louverture et l'indépendance d'Haïti*, 14; Dessalines to Louverture (30 March and 4 Apr. 1802), Sc. Micro R-2228 Reel 4, SC-NYPL.

12 5

place et a la faire bonbarder, Des que jappris le dant ger dont elle
etoit menacé je me hatai d'y porter mes Troupe pour la de livré
arrivé de vant le canp, je fis ma reconnaisance pris les renseignemen
necessaire et ordonnois les dispositions necessaire pour lattaqué dapré
les quel je de oit infaiblement[81] entre dans les canp par un cote faible
que ja vois reconnus et menpare de la personne du General le Clerc
et de tous son eta major mais au moment de lexécutions j'appris que
la garnison mant quant daux a voite été obligé de vacque le forte[82]
sile projet eut reusit, mon intantion etoit de renvoient le general
le Clerc au premiere consul en leur rendant un conte exate de sa conduite
et le priant de me renvoient un autre personne digne de sa confiance
a qui je puis remetre le conmandement; le fort evaque je me retiroit
au cahau pour y reunire mes force et ya tendre la garnison. des quelle

y fut arrivé je demandai au General dessaline ou etoient les prisonnié
quil m'avoit dit precedanment etre au cahau il me repondit quine[83]
partis avoit été pris par la colone du General rochambeau quine partis

avoit été tué dans les differente attaque quil avoit esuier et que les
reste enfin setoit echapé dant les diferante marche quil avoit
été obligé de faire ; on voit par cette reponce que cet injustement quon
vou lai memputer les assasinat commis, parce que disoit on comme chef

jaurois dus les enpeche, mais sui-je responsable du mal qui se fait
an mon absance,[84] et tans au gonaive ja voit en voier mon aide de
canp coupe au pré du general dessaline pour lui dire donne ordre au conman
dant de leogane de faire sortir tous les habitan homme et fame et de les

---

81. Read: "je devais infailliblement."
82. Read: "la garnison, manquant d'eau, avait été obligée d'évacuer le fort."
83. As in Kreyòl, Louverture occasionally switched from /y/ to /i/, especially when writing "qu'une" (see "quine" in this line and the following line). He also often replaced /œ/ and /e/ with /i/.
84. Manuscript D: "en mon absence et à mon insu" instead of "an mon absance."

position and shell it.¹⁰¹ As soon as I learned the danger that was
threatening it, I hastened to bring my troops there to free it.
When I arrived before the camp, I did a reconnaissance, learned the necessary
information, and made the necessary dispositions to attack it, based
on which I was going infallibly to enter the camp from a weak side
that I had reconnoitered and seize the person of General Leclerc
and all his general staff.¹⁰² But as I was about to execute my plan, I learned that
the garrison, lacking water, had been obliged to evacuate the fort.¹⁰³
If my project had succeeded, my intention was to send General
Leclerc back to the first consul while giving [him] a precise account of his conduct,
and to solicit that he send another person worthy of his trust
to whom I could hand over my command.¹⁰⁴ After the fort was evacuated, I retired
to the Cahos to gather my forces there and await the garrison [of Crête-à-Pierrot].

As soon as it
arrived there, I asked General Dessalines where the prisoners were
who, he had told me previously, were in the Cahos. He replied to me
that some of them had been taken by the column of General Rochambeau, that some
of them
had been killed in the various attacks he had endured, and that the
rest had escaped during the various marches he had
been obliged to undertake. This response shows that it is unjustly that they
have tried to blame me for the assassinations that were committed, because, they
say, as chief
I should have prevented them. But am I responsible for the evil that is committed
in my absence?¹⁰⁵ While in Gonaïves I had sent my aide-de-camp
Coupé to General Dessalines to ask him to give orders to the commander
of Léogane to evacuate all the inhabitants (men and women) and to send
them to Port-Républicain, [and] to keep in this town as many armed

---

101. "This single day cost us 600 dead or wounded, including at least 50 officers. It was the toughest fight in my life;" in Leclerc to Decrès (26 March 1802), 416AP/1, AN; "Crête-à-Pierrot, where there were only 1,000 to 1,200 men left, had already cost us 1,500 men" in Lacroix, *Mémoires*, vol. 2, 165.

102. Leclerc learned through spies that "Toussaint Louverture was to attack that night...at the same time the garrison would make a sortie from the fort;" see Lacroix, *Mémoires*, vol. 2, 168.

103. Short on water, the garrison slipped out on 24 March. "The retreat conceived and executed by the commander of Crête-à-Pierrot was a remarkable feat. We surrounded his post with more than 12,000 men; he fled, only lost half his garrison, and only left us with his dead and wounded;" see Lacroix, *Mémoires*, vol. 2, 170.

104. Louverture had deported several French rivals in this manner, including Sonthonax (1796), Hédouville (1798), and Roume (1801).

105. Contrary to his denegation, Louverture obliquely incited his subordinates to kill whites. "Beware of whites: they will betray you if they can.... As a result I give you carte blanche: all that you do will be a good thing;" see Louverture to Dommage (9 Feb. 1802), in Ardouin, *Etudes*, vol. 5, 40. "Make sure not to leave behind you anything that may have

en voier au porrepublicain de garder[85] dant cette ville les plus d'homme
armé quil pouroit en fin de se preparé en ca d'attaque a la plus vive
resitance,[86] mon aide de canp coupé porteur de mes ordre revente et mè
dite quil na voit pas trouver le general dessaline[87] quil a voit appris
que leogane à voit étté brulé et que les habitans setoient sauvés
au porrepublicain, Tous les desatre arriver jus qua cette epoque
viennent du General le clerc pour quoi avant faire[88] debarquement ne
ma til pas fait parde se pouvoire pour quoi a telle debarqué san
mon ordre conformement a larreté de la conmision, nes ce pas lui
qui a conmi les premiere hostilete, natil pas cherche a gagné les generaux
et autre officie sou mes ordre par tous les moyent posible, natil pas
cherché a soulver les cultivateur en leur per suadant que je les
traitoit comme des Esclavere et quil venoi pour rompe leur fer,
doit on employer de telle moyent dant un pays ou regnait la
tranquilité, et qui etoit au pouvoire de la republique, si jai
fais tra vaille me samblable, cetoit pour leur faire goute le pris
de la liberté sans lixence, cetoit pour en pe che la corruptions
des meurces ; cetoit pour le bonheur general de lisle, et pour
lintéret de la republique, et javois effectivement reusire
pus que l on ne voiiot pas dant toute cette colonie au cun homme
Deseuvré et que le nombre des mendiant etoit diminué, a
parut quel quin dant les ville[89] on na voit pas un seul dant les
canpangne. Si le General le clerc avoit eu bonne intention
au roit il recu dant sont armé le nome Golard et lais aurait il
donois le conmandenant de la 9 ½ Brigade quil avoit été
de ja chef de bataion pre ce dant ment[90] et quil a voi soulvé,

---

85. Manuscript D: "réunir" instead of "garder."
86. Following the Kreyòl norm, Louverture occasionally dropped the letter "s," in this case writing "resitance" instead of "résistance" (see also "desatre" instead of "désastres" three lines below). He also often elided "r," "e," "x," and "i," along with the endings of many words.
87. The phrase "me rapporte qu'il n'avait pu pénétrer" was replaced with "me dit qu'il n'avait pas trouvé le Général Dessalines" in manuscript B. Manuscript D: "Dessalines, mais qu'il avait" instead of "dessaline quil a voit."
88. Louverture occasionally elided possessive adjectives, in this case writing "debarquement" instead of "son débarquement."
89. Manuscript D: "au point qu'à part part quelques villes" instead of "a parut quel quin dant les ville."
90. Manuscript D: "qu'il avait déja eu précédemment" instead of "quil avoit été de ja chef de bataion pre ce dant ment."

men as he could manage so as to mount the greatest possible resistance in case of
an attack. My aide-de-camp Coupé, who bore my orders, came back and told
me that he had not found General Dessalines, that he had learned
that Léogane had been burned, and that the inhabitants had escaped
to Port-Républicain.[106] All the disasters that had taken place until that time
are General Leclerc's fault. Why, before landing, did
he not inform me of his powers? Why did he land without
an order from me, in keeping with the decree of the commission? Did he not
commit the first hostilities? Did he not try to sway the generals
and the other officers under my orders by all available means? Did he not
try to incite the cultivators to rise up by persuading them that I was
treating them like slaves and that he had come to break their shackles?[107]
Should one use such means in a country where tranquility
reigned, and that was in the power of the republic? If I
made my fellows work, it was to make them appreciate the price
of liberty without license, it was to prevent the corruption
of morals; it was for the general happiness of the island, and in
the interest of the republic, and I had indeed succeeded
because you could not see in the entire colony a single man
without occupation and the number of beggars had diminished;
aside from a few in the towns there was not a single one in the
countryside.[108] If General Leclerc had had good intentions,
would he have welcomed in his army the person named Golart[109] and would he have
given to him the command of the 9th demi-brigade in which he had
already served as battalion chief previously, and which he had pushed to revolt?
This dangerous rebel, who would arrange for owners to be assassinated on

(n105 cont.)

a white skin;" see Louverture to Clerveaux (c. 30 Jan. 1802), in Mauviel, "Mémoire sur Saint-Domingue" (26 June 1805), p. 40, pièce 101, AF/IV/1212, AN. Leclerc estimated that "more than 10,000 white, black, or mulatto inhabitants" were killed on orders from Louverture and others; see Leclerc to Decrès (26 March 1802), 416AP/1, AN.

106. On Dessalines's orders, Léogane's commander Jean-Louis Diane had burned the city on 11 Feb. when the French had attacked it; see "Récit succint des événements arrivés à Léogane et Jacmel" (4–15 Feb. 1802), Box 3/114-115, RP-UF.

107. Leclerc had declared that Louverture "only saw the word 'liberty,' which he employed so often, as a means to achieve the most absolute despotism in Saint-Domingue;" see Leclerc, "Proclamation aux habitants de Saint-Domingue" (17 Feb. 1802), CC9B/19, ANOM.

108. In this important passage, Louverture justified his labor policies in terms nearly identical to those he had employed in 1800–1801. "We must devote our attention to the prosperity of Saint-Domingue, to public tranquility, and thus to the happiness of all our fellow citizens.... To ensure liberty, without which no man can be happy, all must be gainfully employed so as to cooperate to the public good and to general tranquility;" see Louverture, [Règlement des cultures] (12 Oct. 1800), in Ardouin, *Etudes*, vol. 4, 247–255.

109. Lubin Golart was the black commander of Jean-Rabel. Opposed to Louverture's policy of conciliation with England and émigrés, he had embraced André Rigaud's side during the War of the South, been defeated by Louverture, retreated to the mountains, and then joined Leclerc's side after the French landing. Note that Louverture used the expression

ce rebelle dans gereux qui fai soit assasiner les proprieter dans
leur s habitation, qui en vahis la ville du mole S^t nicola, qui
a tiré sur le General clervaux qui conmandoit la ville,
sur le General morpas et sur son chef de brigade qui a fait

their plantations; who invaded the town of Môle Saint-Nicolas; who shot on General Clerveaux[110] who commanded the town, on General Maurepas and his brigadier chief; who waged

(n109 cont.)

"the person named" before Golart's name, which was used to describe people of color prior to the Revolution, whereas he used the respectful "mister" when referring to Coisnon and Bondère, who were white (p. 5, line 49, and p. 10, line 4).

110. Brigadier General Augustin Clerveaux had served with Louverture since 1793. He had handed over Santiago to the French without a fight, yet Louverture seemed not to begrudge him in his memoir for ignoring his orders.

13

la geure dant cette partis qui a soullevé les cultivateur jen rabelle,[91] moustique
et de hauteur de port de paix qui a pousé laudace même jus qua tire
sur moi ~~tant que~~ un balle a couppé le plume mait de mon chapaux le sieur
Bonderre meid cins, qui ma conpagnie fus tué a mon coté mes aid de canp
demonte, lors que je marché contre lui pour le faire soumetre a son
chef et reprandre le teritoire et la ville qui la vé en vahis,[92] ce brigand
en fins qua pre sétre souille de tous les crime setoit caché dans une foret
jus qua larrivé de l'escadre francais, au roit il egalement recu et
élevé au rang de chef de brigade un autre rebel appellé lamour
durance qui a faite assasine tous les habitans de la plaine du cul de sace
qui a soulvé les cultivateur, qui a sacagé toute cette De lisle, contre le quel
deux moi seulenent avant larrive de lescadre javoit éte oblige demarché
sur lui et la voit force de sé retiré dant les foret, pour quoi a tons
recu amicalement ce rebelle, et dotre tendis que moi et mes surbordonnai
qui avons constamment reste fidelle au gouvernement francais, et
avons main tenire lordre et la tranquilité dans lisle nous a ton fait
la guerre, pour quoi veut-on me faire un crime da voire faite
éxecuter les ordre du gouvernement pourquoi veut-on munputer tout
les[93] mal qui a été faite ; et les desordre qui a regné les troupè qui
ce sont rendus au general leclerc en avoient-elle recu un ordre de moir,
ma voiet-elle conssulté, nont ; hé bien ceux qui ont faite les mal ne
ma voiet pas consulter non plus il ne faut dons pas apresant me donner
plus de tor que je ne mérite, je fis part de ce reflecsions a quelque prisonnier
que javois fait il me repondirent quon craignoit linfluence que
ja voit sur les peuple et quon emploit tous ces moÿens pour la de
détruire. ce la me fit faire des reflecsions ; conciderant tous les
mal heur que la colonie a voit de ja esuiéz les habitation detruite les
assasinat commis, les violations même exercés sur les femme;
joubliais tous les tore quon pouroit avoire a mon negard pour enpancer
quau bonheur de lisle, et la vantage du gouvernement, je me determinais
a obéir a lordre du premiere consul, vu sourtout[94] que le general leclerc

---

91. Manuscript D: "qui a fait la guerre aux cultivateurs de Jean Rabel" instead of "qui a fait la geure dant cette partis qui a soullevé les cultivateur jen rabelle."

92. The passage from "qui a poussé laudace" to "qui la vé en va his" is rendered in manuscript D as "qui a poussé l'audace même jusqu'à se défendre contre moi lorsque j'ai marché contre lui pour le soumettre."

93. "Les mal" is another example of Louverture's tendency to add /e/ sounds. See also "sé retiré" (line 13), "les troupè" (same line), and "les mal" (line 21).

94. Louverture occasionally replaced /y/ with /u/, in this case writing "sourtout" instead of "surtout" (see also "lous" instead of "lu"). He also pronounced some /o/ and /œ/ sounds as /u/.

13

war in this region; who incited the cultivators of Jean-Rabel, Moustique, and the heights of Port-de-Paix to rebel; who even had the audacity to shoot at me a bullet that cut off the feather in my cap (mister Bondère, a doctor who was accompanying me was killed by my side, my aides-de-camp had to dismount) as I was marching against him to get him to submit to his chief and to retake the territory and the town that he had invaded; this brigand, at last, after sullying himself with all sorts of crimes, had hidden in a forest until the arrival of the French squadron. Would he also have welcomed and promoted to the rank of brigadier chief another rebel named Lamour Derance[111] who had all the planters of the plain of Cul-de-Sac assassinated; who incited the cultivators to rise up; who ravaged all this beautiful island; against whom just two months before the arrival of the squadron I had been obliged to march to force him to retreat to the woods?[112] Why was this rebel welcomed amicably, as well as others, while I and my subordinates, who have constantly remained faithful to the French government, and maintained order and tranquility in the island, they wage war on us?[113] Why do they want to accuse me of the crime of having implemented the orders of the government? Why should I be blamed for every wrong that happened? As for the disorder that reigned, the troops who surrendered to General Leclerc, had they received their orders from me? Had they consulted me? No. Well, those who did bad things had not consulted me either, so one should not now give me more blame than I deserve. I shared these considerations with a few prisoners I had taken. They replied that some people feared the influence that I had over the people and that they employed all these means to destroy it. This led me to reflect: after considering all the misfortunes that had already befallen the colony, the plantations destroyed, the assassinations perpetrated, even the rapes perpetrated against women, I forgot the many ways I had been wronged to think only about the happiness of the island and the good of the government. I resolved to obey the order of the first consul, especially since General Leclerc

---

111. Lamour Derance was a *bossale* (African-born) leader of runaway cultivators opposed to Louverture's labor regulations. Like Golart, he had supported Rigaud during the War of the South, fled to the woods after Rigaud's defeat, then come out of hiding to join the French after the landing. He was later killed by Dessalines during a dispute over the command of the rebel army; see Ardouin, *Etudes*, vol. 4, 336, and vol. 5, 416.

112. "When going from Port-au-Prince to the Spanish part [before the French landing], [Louverture] seemed to want to try an attack on the Maniel, which is the refuge of the blacks with whom the former [colonial] government had to sign a treaty;" see Allier to Leclerc (8 Feb. 1802), in "Extrait de la correspondance concernant Toussaint Louverture," CC9/B23, ANOM.

113. Upon first learning that an expedition was on its way to Saint-Domingue, Louverture also complained about the "ungratefulness" of a French government that wanted to remove him from office even though he had defended the colony from foreign invaders and revived

venoit de se retirè lui même au cap a vec toute sa troupe, apre la faire
de la crete a pierrot,[95]...il et a re marquie que jus qua cet instans
je navoit pas encore pus trouve un seul moment pour repondre au
premier consul. je saisis avec enpresment[96] cet instent dés
tranquilite pour la faire: je lassuroit de ma soumision et de mon
entiere devoment a se sordre[97] en la surant que sil nan voient[98] un
autre officier general plus anciens[99] prandre le conmandement,
j'ai derai le General LeClerc a fer tous les mal posible par la resistance
que je lui opposerai,[100] je me rapelle que le general dessaline mavai
rendus conte que deux officier de lescadre dont un aide de canp du general
Boudete, et un officier de marine et a conpanie deux dragon, lors

quon na pris port au prince et quil avoient été en voie pour soul
ver la troup[101] jordonnai quon me les amenent a présavoire convercé
a vec eux je les renvoiet au General Boudete pour qui je leur
remis une letre a vec celle que javois ecrire au premier consul,
a lins tent ou jexpediois ces deux officier, japprendre[102] que le general

95. The phrase "après l'affaire de la Crête-à-Pierrot" was added in manuscript B.
96. Louverture omitted the letter "e" in words like"empressement" probably because he elided the sound /œ/, as is frequent in popular northern French and in Kreyòl (see also his spelling of "soulèvement," "également," "sûreté," "cordialement," and "arrondissement"). He also often elided "r," "i," "s," and "x."
97. Louverture treated the liaison, which is pronounced but not written in French, as part of the word itself, as is frequent in Kreyòl (here: "sordre" instead of "ordres"). He did the same in words like "nepouze," "savoire," "nescadre," and the stereotypically Kreyòl word "zotre" (French: "les autres").
98. Manuscript D: "en l'assurant que si jusques à présent je n'y avais déféré il avait trop de discernement et d'équité pour m'en imputer la faute; j'ai ajouté si vous n'envoyez" instead of "en la surant que sil nan voient."
99. Manuscript D omits "plus anciens."
100. The phrase "j'aiderai le Général Leclerc à faire tout le mal possible par la résistance que je lui opposerai" was added in manuscript B.
101. Manuscript D: "avaient été faits prisonniers lorsqu'on reprit le Port-au-Prince" instead of "lors quon na pris port au prince."
102. This is one of many instances where Louverture, following the Kreyòl norm, employed the infinitive form of a verb instead of conjugating it (here: "j'apprendre" instead of "j'apprends"). See also "javois ecrire" (instead of "j'avais écrit") line 46, and "lateigné" ("l'atteignis"), "sangager" (s'engagea") and "duré" (dura) line 52.

himself had just retired to Cap with all his troops after the affair of Crête-à-Pierrot.[114] Please note that until that instant I had not yet been able to find a single moment to respond to the tranquility to do so. I assured him of my submissiveness and of my first consul.[115] I hastened to use this instant of entire devotion to his orders while assuring him that unless he sent another, older[116] general officer to take over, I would help General Leclerc do as much damage as possible through the resistance that I would oppose him. I remembered that General Dessalines had recounted to me that two officers of the squadron, including an aide-de-camp of General Boudet and a naval officer accompanied by two dragoons,[117] [had been taken prisoner] when Port-au-Prince had been taken and when they had been sent to get the troops to rebel.[118] I ordered that they be brought to me. After conversing with them, I sent them back to General Boudet and handed them a letter for him along with the one I had written for the first consul.[119] Just as I was dispatching these two officers, I learned that General

(n113 cont.)

the plantations; see Louverture to Members of the Assemblée Centrale de la colonie (22 Jan. 1802), Sc. Micro R-2228 Reel 5, SC-NYPL.

114. Louverture claimed that he submitted because of his loyalty to France, but he actually called for a ceasefire at a time when his military situation had become particularly bleak because many of his subordinates had switched sides; see "Etat nominatif des chefs de la colonie qui se sont soumis aux lois de la République Française" (c. March 1802), B7/2, SHD-DAT; Girard, *The Slaves Who Defeated Napoleon*, 134.

115. It is highly unlikely that Louverture had not found the time in two months to draft a letter.

116. Louverture was about twice the age of Leclerc (60 against 30), which partly explains his instinctive hostility toward the young upstart.

117. A dragoon was a mounted infantryman.

118. Brigadier Chief Pascal Sabès and Midshipman Jean-Baptiste Gémont had been sent on shore to negotiate the takeover of Port-Républicain in Feb. 1802, only to be taken captive by the rebels; see Jean-Baptiste Gémont, *Précis des événemens arrivés à la députation envoyée par le général Boudet au Port-au-Prince, lors de la descente des Français à Saint-Domingue (Pluviôse an X)* ([s.n.], 1806), 212830/C610, Bibliothèque Municipale de Nantes.

119. Louverture's letters to Boudet and Leclerc were not in the archives consulted for this book, but they are mentioned in a dispatch by Leclerc. "Twenty times [Sabès and Gémont] were threatened with death. They witnessed all the massacres that took place, and on the 8th [29 March 1802] General Toussaint asked them to come. After talking at length with citizen Sabès, the aide-de-camp of General Boudet, and complaining about the ungratefulness of the French government…he charged him with a letter to General Boudet and another to General Bonaparte. In the letter to General Boudet, he bitterly complained about our conduct toward him. In the letter to the First Consul, he accused me of being the cause of all the woes of the colony, insisted on his obedience to the Republic, and asked for someone to be sent to replace me;" see Leclerc to Decrès (1 Apr. 1802), CC9B/19, ANOM. "General Leclerc does not want, despite the good dispositions of the government, to deal with me because I am Black;" see Louverture to Boudet (11 Apr. 1802), cited in Desormeaux, *Mémoires*, 122.

hardis ce pasé la coup a lence a vec son armé quil set porte sur mes propriété, les a ravagé quil a enlevé tous mes animaux et surtout un cheval nome Belle l'argent[103] dont je faisois le plus grand cas, san perdre de temp je me portai sur lui à vec les force que ja vois, et lateigné au pre dudondon laffaire sangager et duré avec le plus grand a charnement de pus onze heur du matin jusquà six heur du soire, a vant que de partis javois donne lordre au General dessaline da tendre la ~~garnison~~ reunion de la garnison qui avait Evaqué

---

103. The phrase "nommé Bel Argent" was added in manuscript B.

Hardÿ had passed through Coupe-à-l'Inde with his army,[120] that he had stepped on my property, ravaged it, and that he had taken away all my animals, and especially a horse named Bel Argent[121] to which I was particularly attached. Without losing any time, I headed toward him with the forces at my disposal and reached him near Dondon. The affair commenced and lasted with the utmost doggedness from eleven in the morning until six at night.[122] Before leaving, I had given the order to General Dessalines to wait until he joined up with the garrison that had evacuated

---

120. "General Hardÿ surrounded 600 blacks in Coupe-à-l'Inde. They were not spared because they still had on their bayonets the blood of 100 whites they had just killed;" see Lacroix, *Mémoires*, vol. 2, 150.

121. Louverture also mentioned "his favorite horses, which he particularly valued" when meeting Marie-François Caffarelli in Joux; see "Toussaint Louverture au Fort de Joux" (c. 17 Sept. 1802), in *Nouvelle Revue Rétrospective*, no. 94 (10 Apr. 1902), 14. "Toussaint Louverture had superb, extremely fast horses on the main plantations. It was his only luxury;" see Lacroix, *Mémoires*, vol. 1, 407. "When reviewing troops, he would mount his horse Bel Argent or Symétrie so close to the lines of soldiers that new recruits would fear for their toes;" see Isaac Louverture, "Notes historiques sur Toussaint Louverture, manuscrit d'Isaac Louverture, notes intéressantes sur Banica etc." (c. 1819), NAF 12409, BNF.

122. Concerned for the safety of Cap, Leclerc had ordered the Hardÿ division to march from Crête-à-Pierrot back to Cap. On its way, it was attacked by Louverture and Christophe near Dondon and Marmelade and lost 400 men. "In the nine years I have been waging war as a general... I never saw as cruel an action as this one;" see Hardÿ to Leclerc (2 Apr. 1802), Box 3/173, RP-UF.

14

la crètte a pierot[104] et daller se canper au canp marchand en le
prevenent qua pré les combas je me rendroit a la marmélade
arrivé dans cet endroit j y recut la reponce du General Boudete quil
mavoit envoié par mon neveux chanci quil avoit precedamment
faite prisonnie ce General ma suroit que maletre parviendroit fidellement
au premiere consul qua cet effe il lavoit de ja adresé au general leclerc
qui lui a voit promis de la faire, sur les raport de mon neveux et apre
la lecture de la letre du general boüdet je cru reconnaitre en lui un
caractere d honnetete et de franchize digne dun officie francais et
Bien faite pour conmande. en concequance je ma dressoit a lui avec
confiance pour lui prier dans gagér Le General Le clerc dant tré avec
dans des moÿens de conciliation je lassurai que lambition na voit
ja mai été mon gade guide mai bien l'honneur, quen concequance
je toit prete a rendre le conmandement pour obeire aux ordre du premiere
consul et de faire toute les sacrifice pour necesaire pour arreter le pro
gre du mal je lui en voiai ma letre par mon neveux chanci quil
reteint pres de lui, mais deus jour a pre je recu une letre par un
ordonnance preser qui man noncoit quil avoit fait par de mes
intentions au general Le clerc et masuroit que celcie etoit
prete d entre en arrangement avec moi et que je pouvois compter
sur les bonnes intention du gouvernement a mon Egard, le même jour
le General christophe ma communquie une letre quil venoit de rece
voire du citoyen vilton demerant a la petitance et un autre de
general hardiy lui demandant tous deux une antrevue et a moi la
permisions de lui acorder, ce que je luï permi en lui reconmandant

---

104. The phrase "qui avait évacué de la Crête-Pierrot" was added in manuscript B.

14

Crête-à-Pierrot and to stay in the camp of Marchand while
warning him that after the battle I would proceed to Marmelade.[123]
After I arrived there, I received the response from General Boudet that he had
sent me through my nephew Chancy whom he had previously
made prisoner.[124] This general assured me that my letter would be faithfully delivered
to the first consul, that to that effect he had already sent it to General Leclerc,
who had promised that he would do so. Based on the reports of my nephew and after
reading the letter of General Boudet, I thought I could discern in him a
character of honesty and frankness worthy of a French officer and [that he was]
fit to command.[125] Consequently, I addressed myself to him with
trust to invite him to incite General Leclerc to begin
negotiations. I assured him that ambition had
never been my guide but truly honor, that consequently
I was ready to hand over my command to obey the orders of the first
consul and to make all the necessary sacrifices to stop the progress
of evil. I sent him my letter through my nephew Chancy whom
he retained with him.[126] But two days later I received a letter from a
fast courier announcing to me that he had informed General Leclerc
of my intentions and that he assured me that the latter was
ready to conclude some arrangement with me and that I could count
on the good intentions of the government toward me. The same day
General Christophe communicated to me a letter he had just received
from citizen Vilton, a resident of Petite-Anse, and another from
General Hardÿ, both of whom asked him for a meeting and asked me to grant
him permission to do so, which I granted while enjoining him

---

123. Dessalines was in Marchand, a plantation on the plain of the Artibonite, from 9 Apr. to the end of the campaign; see Dessalines to Louverture (9 Apr. 1802), Sc. Micro R-2228 Reel 4, SC-NYPL. After Haiti's independence, Dessalines fortified Marchand extensively and made it his emergency capital.

124. Early in the campaign, Louverture had sent his nephew and aide-de-camp Bernard Chancy to the South to order local commanders to revolt, but he had been arrested on the way; see Nérette to Boudet (18 Feb. 1802), Ms. Hait. 66-184, BPL. "I ordered General Boudet to send back to him one of his nephews, who is his aide-de-camp and had been caught while carrying dispatches. I ordered him to write him a rather vague letter to allow [Louverture] to make overtures, should he want to surrender;" see Leclerc to Decrès (1 Apr. 1802), CC9B/19, ANOM.

125. Instead of handing over his command to Boudet, as Louverture had hoped, Leclerc sent him to the French island of Guadeloupe; see Leclerc to Boudet (19 Apr. 1802), Box 4/261, RP-UF.

126. Chancy was deported to France in 1802. Held in Corsica, he returned to Haiti, only to kill himself on Dessalines's orders; see Francis Arzalier, "Déportés haïtiens et guadeloupéens en Corse (1802–1814)," *Annales historiques de la Révolution française* (1993), 293–294, 479, 486.

detre tres circonspecte le Géneral christophe au lieu de serendre a lentre
vue indisquie par le General hardÿ a recu une letre du General le clerc
et[105] dont il me fit paser copie ainci que de ser reponce et me deman
dait la permision de se rendre dans lendroit qui on lui a voit in
diquie ce que je lai permis et il[106], a fon retoure il me raporta
une letre du General leclerc qui me disoit que ce seroit pour lui
une belle journé sil pouvoit mengager a me conserte a vec lui
et a me soumetre aux ordre de la republique, je repondis sur le chanp
que j avoit constamment[107] porte les arme pour lui que sis dez le
principe[108] on setoit conporté a vec moi come on devoit le faire
il ay auroit pas eu un seul coup des fusil de tiré et que la paix
n'auroit pas même ete troublé dans lisle, et que lint tention du G^t

auroit ete renplis; jai te moi te moigne tans au General Leclerc qua
christohp toute mon mecontentement de ce que ce lui la sétoit rendus
san au cune ordre de ma part[109], le lendemain je lui depechai mon
ad judant general fontaine porteur dun letre de ma par par la quel
je lui de mandoit une entre, vue a labitation dericoure a quoi
il se refuse ce pandant fontaine madis et a suré quil avoit été
tre bien recu, je ne mé rebutai point je lui depechai pour la

---

105. Manuscript B originally contained the phrase "Christophe se rendit effectivement au lieu indiqué, mais au lieu d'y trouver les citoyens Vilton et Hardy il y trouva une lettre du Général Leclerc lui-même qui l'engageait à se montrer au Haut-du-Cap." It was crossed out and replaced by "Christophe, au lieu de se rendre à l'entrevue indiquée par le Général Hardy, reçut une lettre du Général Leclerc et."
106. Manuscript D: "et il fut" instead of "et il."
107. Manuscript D: "que j'avais toujours été soumis au Gouvernement français, puisque javais constamment" instead of "que j avoit constamment."
108. Louverture probably used the word "principe" to mean "beginning" (instead of "principle") because of the influence of the Spanish word "principio." For a similar misuse of "principle," see Louverture to Laveaux (16 Sept. 1795), fr. 12103, BNF.
109. The phrase "J'ai témoigné tant au Général Leclerc qu'à Christophe tout mon mécontentement de ce que celui-ci s'était rendu sans aucun ordre de ma part" was added in manuscript B.

to be very circumspect.¹²⁷ General Christophe, instead of going to the
meeting indicated by General Hardÿ, received a letter from General Leclerc,
of which he gave me a copy as well as of his response, and asked
for my permission to proceed to the location that had been indicated
to him, which I granted, and he [went].¹²⁸ Upon his return he brought back to me
a letter from General Leclerc telling me that it would be a fine day
for him if he could convince me to confer with him
and to submit to the orders of the republic.¹²⁹ I responded at once
that I had constantly borne arms for it, that if from the
beginning people had behaved toward me the way they should have
not a single shot would have been fired and that peace
would not even have been troubled in the island, and that the intention of the government
would have been fulfilled. I personally expressed to General Leclerc as well as
Christophe how discontented I was that this one had surrendered
without any order from me.¹³⁰ The following day, I dispatched to him my
adjutant-general Fontaine bearing a letter from me in which
I asked him for a meeting on the Héricourt plantation, which
he rejected.¹³¹ Yet Fontaine told me and assured me that he had been
very well received.¹³² I did not lose heart and dispatched to him for the

127. "Abandon this errant and vagabond life that would dishonor you if you continued it any longer;" see Vilton to Christophe (11 Apr. 1802), in Christophe, "Manifeste du roi," p. 34. Hardÿ promised that the French would not restore slavery because "we have been fighting for liberty for twelve years" and offered to meet on the Vaudreuil plantation; see Hardÿ to Christophe (15 Apr. 1802), in "Manifeste du roi," p. 28.

128. Leclerc sent several letters. Christophe may not have shown Louverture one in which Leclerc asked him to kidnap Louverture. "If you intend to surrender to the Republic, you would do us a great service by giving us the means to seize the person of General Toussaint;" see Leclerc to Christophe (14 Apr. 1802), in "Manifeste du roi," p. 22. In the memoir, Louverture was probably referring instead to the letter in which Leclerc promised not to restore slavery and asked Christophe to come meet him in Cap; see Leclerc to Christophe (24 Apr. 1802), in "Manifeste du roi," p. 25.

129. Like Louverture, Leclerc was eager to negotiate because of the losses sustained during the spring campaign. "The rainy season has arrived. My troops are overwhelmed with fatigue and diseases;" see Leclerc to Decrès (9 Apr. 1802), CC9B/19, ANOM.

130. Christophe agreed to surrender when he met Leclerc in Cap on 26 April and Leclerc promised not to restore slavery, but Louverture was still not aware of his subordinate's betrayal as of the 28th; see Christophe to Leclerc (25 Apr. 1802), in Christophe, "Manifeste du roi," p. 26; Leclerc, "Le général en chef ordonne" (26 Apr. 1802), Box 4/281, RP-UF; Louverture to Christophe (28 Apr. 1802) 61J18, ADGir.

131. "Any rebel general who wants to negotiate should give his troops away and wait for me to decide on his fate. Toussaint offered me to go meet him on the Héricourt plantation, promising me safety and protection. I responded to this impertinent proposal in the appropriate manner;" see Leclerc to Rochambeau (30 Apr. 1802), lot 215, Vente Rochambeau, Philippe Rouillac auction house (VR-PR).

132. The 29 Apr. meeting between Leclerc and Fontaine is mentioned in Achille Dampierre to Pierre Thouvenot (30 Apr. 1802), B7/3, SHD-DAT.

deusieme et troisieme fois mon aide de canp coupè et mon secretaire natant pour la suré que je fairoit mai soumision et que j etoit prete a lui rendre le commandement conformement aux intantion Gouvernmet et du premiere consul, il me fit reponce quine heur de confiance versation feroit plus deffet que dix letre, en me don nant sa parolle d'honneur quil a giroit a vec toute la franchise et la loiauté quon pourait attendre d un general francais, on mappor toit en même temp une proclamation de sa part qui invitoit tous les citoyen a regarder larticle de celle du 7 plusviose qui me mettait hor de la loi comme nul et non avenue, ne cre gnez pas disoit il dant cette proclamation, vous, les generaux qui sont sou mes vos

second and third time my aide-de-camp Coupé and my secretary Nathan[133] to assure him that I would make my submission and that I was ready to hand over my command to him pursuant to the intentions of the government and the first consul. He responded to me that an hour of conversation would be more effective than ten letters, while giving me his word of honor that he would act with all the frankness and the loyalty that one could expect from a French general. I was also given a proclamation from him that invited all citizens to regard the article of the previous one dated 7 pluviôse that made me an outlaw as null and void.[134] "Don't fear," he said in this proclamation, "you, the generals who are under your

---

133. Louverture's secretary and interpreter "was an Israelite named Nathan who knew all the languages of Europe. Nathan was a landowner in Cayes, where he had once been a merchant;" see Isaac Louverture, "Notes historiques sur Toussaint Louverture," 74.

134. The date of 7 pluviôse (27 Jan. 1802) is a mistake. Louverture was actually referring to the 28 pluviôse proclamation that had made him an outlaw; see Leclerc, "Proclamation aux habitants de Saint-Domingue" (17 Feb. 1802), CC9B/19, ANOM. The proclamation was publically rescinded in *Gazette du Port-Républicain*, no. 66 (16 May 1802), CO 137/108, BNA.

15

sordre et les habitant qui sont a vec vous que je recherché
personne sur sa conduite pasér, j le rai le voil de toubles[110] les
sèvenement qui ont eu lieu a St domiengue, y ' mite en
cela lexemple que le pre miere consul a donne a la france
le 18 brumaire je ne veux voire dant lisle a la veinire que
de bon citoyens, vous de de mander du repos. quand on na
conmande comme vous et surporte au si long temp les
fardau du gouvernement le repos vous ette bien dus mais
j es per que dant votre retraite vous me conmuniquieraï vos
lumiere, dans vo moment de loisire pour la prosperite de St Domingue
a pre cette proclamation et la parol d honneur du General Leclerc
je me rendis au cap au pre de lui je lui fis mes soumisions
conformement a lintantion du premiere consul, je lui par[111]
en suite a vec toute la franchise et la cordialité dun militaire
qui aime es time son camarade il ma promi de tout ou
blier et la protection du Gouvernemet francois et il a convenus
avec moi que nous a vont eut tous deux tor, vous pouvez
General me dit il vous re tiroit che vous en toute sureté,
mai. dite moi si le General dessaline obeiai a mes ordre et si
je pourrai conte sur lui je lai repondis que oui. le General
dessaline peut avoire de de faute comme tous homme mai quil
connoit la subordination militaire. je lui observais cependent
que pour le bien publique et pour retablie les cultivateur dans leur
travaux comme a son arrive dant lisle, il etoit necesaire que

---

110. Manuscript D (citing Leclerc's proclamation): "j'ai tiré le voile de l'oubli" instead of "j le rai le voil de toubles."

111. Read: "parlai."

15

orders, and the inhabitants who are with you, that I will look
into anyone's past conduct. I will cast the veil of forgiveness on all the
events that have taken place in Saint-Domingue. Imitating in
this regard the example that the first consul set for France
on 18 brumaire,[135] I will regard everyone in the island in the future
as good citizens. You ask for rest. When one has
commanded like you and supported for so long the
burden of government, rest is owed to you, but
I hope that during your retirement you will share your knowledge
during your free time on how to ensure the prosperity of Saint-Domingue."[136]
After this proclamation and General Leclerc's word of honor,
I proceeded to meet him in Cap. I made my submission to him
in conformity with the intention of the first consul.[137] I then talked
to him with all the frankness and cordiality of a military man
who loves and appreciates his comrade. He promised me to forget
everything and offered the protection of the French government and he agreed
with me that we had both been at fault. "You can,
general," he said to me, "retire to your home in full safety,
but tell me if General Dessalines will obey my orders and if
I can rely on him." I answered him that "yes, General
Dessalines can have his faults like every man, but he
knows military subordination."[138] I pointed out to him nevertheless
that for the public good and to get the cultivators back to
work, as they were when he arrived in the island, it was necessary that

---

135. After seizing power on 18 brumaire year VIII (9 Nov. 1799), Bonaparte had followed a policy of reconciliation toward counterrevolutionary émigrés.

136. The passage cites, almost word for word, a document that Louverture had either memorized or kept with him; see Leclerc to Louverture (3 [1?] May 1802), in Roussier, *Lettres du général Leclerc*, 132–133. In keeping with the rest of the memoir, which skirts the issue of emancipation, Louverture did not mention that in order to secure Christophe's submission, Louverture had publically promised "liberty and equality for all the inhabitants of Saint-Domingue, of any color;" see Leclerc to Inhabitants of Saint-Domingue (25 Apr. 1802), Box 4/277, RP-UF.

137. Bonaparte had actually asked that all black officers be deported to France, which explains why Leclerc was negotiating in bad faith. "All rebel chiefs have made their submission. If I am not executing your instructions yet, it is because the right time has not come;" see Leclerc to Bonaparte (7 May 1802), in Roussier, *Lettres du général Leclerc*, 145. There are multiple accounts of Louverture's visit to Cap on 6 May, all of which emphasize the antipathy of the white population of Cap toward the former governor and the continued distrust between Leclerc and Louverture; see, for example, Pierre Benezech to Decrès (7 May 1802), CC9B/20, ANOM.

138. "Toussaint tried to surrender. He made proposals to me, which led to him coming to see me in Cap. It seems that his troops no longer wished to fight, and that there was a rift between him and Dessalines. I had ordered him to bring Dessalines with him. He responded that he was afraid of being deported and that he was sick, which is true, but that he would obey any order I would give him.... [Louverture] will retire to one of his

le General dessaline fut retabli dans son conmandement
a St marc, et le General charle a larcahé[112] je lui observé que je ne
pus lai ce le conmandement san ce la, parce que je neseroit ja mai
tranquille, ce quil mapromi, a onze du soire je pri conge de
lui et me tirai che dericoure ou j ai pasai la nuit avec le
General fressinette[113] et repartis lendemien ma tin pour la marmelade
le sur lend de maint je recu une letre du General le clerc qui
mien vetoit a lai renvoier me gard a pied et a cheval et men
voiai une ordre pour le General dessaline, a pre en avoire pris...
connesance je lai fus paser en langagent a si conformer et pour
remplis d autant mieux les promesse que javait faite au General le
clerc jen vitai le General dessaline a se rencontre avec moi a la
me moitie du chemin de traverce de son habitation a la miene
ce qquil fit, je lui persuadai de ce soumetre ainsi que moi que lin
terai publi[114] exigerit que je fase un sacrifice que je vouloi
bien le faire mai que pour lui il conserveroit son conmandement
j'en dis autant au General charle ainci qua tous les officier qui
toient avec eux et je vien a bout de les persansuadér
malgre toute la re pu gance et le re grete et les larme[115] quil
me te moignerent de me qui te et de se pare de moi, apré cette
entrevue chaquin se ren dit a leur poste respective ; ladjudant
General perrens que le General Leclerc avait en voier a dessaline
pour lui porte ses ordre le trouva tre bien disposé a les renplis
pus que je lui avoit engagé precedemment par mon an

---

112. Manuscript D omits "je lui observé que je ne pus lai ce le conmandement san ce la, parce que je neseroit ja mai Tranquille."
113. The phrase "à Marmelade" was crossed out and replaced with "chez d'Héricourt où je passai la nuit chez le Général Fressinet" in manuscript B. The phrase "et repartis lendemien ma tin pour la marmelade," which does not appear in manuscript D, was added in manuscript C. Note that Louverture pronounced the final "t" in "Fressinet," which he also did for Vernet, Voudet, and Brunet.
114. Louverture omitted the final "c" in "public" in the memoir, possibly because he did not pronounce the /k/ (he spelled "république" correctly, however). He also simplified the ending of other words by dropping the final /z/, /ʀ/, and /l/.
115. The phrase "et les larmes" was added in manuscript B.

General Dessalines be restored to his command
in Saint-Marc and General Charles [Belair][139] in Arcahaye. I pointed out to him that I
could not abandon my command without this, because I would never be
tranquil, which he promised.[140] At eleven at night I bade him
goodbye and retired to Héricourt, where I spent the night with
General Fressinet[141] and left the following morning for Marmelade.
The next day I received a letter from General Leclerc that
invited me to send back to him my guard, both on foot and mounted, and
sent me an order for General Dessalines.[142] After I informed myself of its
content, I passed it on while encouraging him to conform to it; and to
better fulfill the promises I had made to General
Leclerc, I invited General Dessalines to meet me
on the service road half way between his plantation and mine,
which he did. I convinced him to submit as I had done, that
public interest demanded that I make a sacrifice, that I was willing
to make it, but as for him he would keep his command.[143]
I said the same thing to General Charles [Belair], as well as to all the officers who
were with them, and I finally managed to persuade them
despite all the repugnance and the regrets and the tears that they
displayed for leaving me and separating from me.[144] After this
meeting, each proceeded to his own post. Adjutant-
General Perrin, whom General Leclerc had sent to Dessalines
to pass on his orders, found him well disposed to fulfill them
because I had incited him to do so previously during our

(n138 cont.)

plantations, from which he will not be able to leave without my authorization;" see Leclerc to Rochambeau (7 May 1802), lot 215, VR-PR. For longer transcripts of the conversation, see Jacques de Norvins, *Souvenirs d'un historien de Napoléon: mémorial de J. de Norvins* vol. 2 (Paris: Plon, 1896), 395–396; Métral, *Mémoires et notes d'Isaac l'Ouverture*, 287–290.

139. Brigadier General Charles Belair was Louverture's nephew. The French had tried to get him to defect since early April, but unsuccessfully; see Belair to Rochambeau (4 Apr. 1802), Sc. Micro R-2228 Reel 1, SC-NYPL.

140. According to Leclerc, Louverture asked to remain in active service, which Leclerc refused; see Leclerc to Decrès (6 May 1802), CC9B/19, ANOM.

141. Louverture knew Gen. Philibert Fressinet, who had served in Saint-Domingue previously, most notably during the March 1796 Villatte incident; see Pluchon, *Toussaint Louverture*, 122–129.

142. The letter from Leclerc to Louverture was not in the archives consulted for this book. The letter to Dessalines delineated the area under his command and placed him under the French general Rochambeau; see Leclerc to Dessalines (7 May 1802), Ms. Hait. 66-159, BPL.

143. Dessalines was indeed eager to continue fighting. "My heart is disgusted at the thought of starting negotiations with the enemy.... The first person who hesitates or dares to make observations will serve as an example to the rest of the army;" see Dessalines to Louverture (5 May 1802), Folder 23C, Kurt Fisher Collection, Howard University, Washington, DC (KFC-HU). He backed down after receiving orders from Louverture. "I only know obedience.... I have always thought it my duty to obey oral and written orders;" see Dessalines to Leclerc (12 May 1802), Sc. Micro R-2228 Reel 4, SC-NYPL.

144. To anxious cultivators from Ennery, Louverture responded not to worry because "all your brothers are still under arms, and the officers have all kept their rank;" see Métral, *Mémoires et notes d'Isaac l'Ouverture*, 295.

trevue, comme on me la voit promis de placer le General charle a larcahé ce pendant on ne la pas faite. il etoit inutile qu jordonnaisce aux habitans de dondon de St rapha êle St michel et de la marmelade de ren tre dans leur habitations pus quil la voient fait dez[116] que je me toi enpare de ces commune[117] je leur en joingnier selemet de re prandre leur travaux acoutumé, jordonnai a ceux de plaisance et des endroit ce con voisin[118] de rentre et de reprendre également leur travaux, il me témoi gnerent les crainte quil avoient quon' ne les inquita, je crevis

---

116. Louverture and Jeannin occasionally employed "z" instead of "s," a spelling norm that was archaic in 1802.

117. The word "places" was crossed out in manuscript B and replaced with "coutumes," which also appears in manuscript D. Louverture corrected Jeannin's mistake in manuscript C, writing "communes" instead.

118. Read: "circonvoisins."

meeting.¹⁴⁵ I had been promised that General Charles [Belair] would be assigned to Arcahaye, yet it was not done.¹⁴⁶ It was no use ordering the inhabitants of Dondon, Saint-Raphaël, Saint-Michel, and Marmelade to return to their plantations since they had done it as soon as I had taken over these towns. I only enjoined them to resume their customary work. I ordered those of Plaisance and of the surrounding areas to return home and to go back to work as well. They expressed to me their fears of being threatened.¹⁴⁷ I wrote

145. "In the presence of adjutant-commandant Perrin, I gathered all the officers of the National Guard under my orders, as well as cultivators, to reassure them...that your intentions were pure regarding liberty;" see Dessalines to Leclerc (12 May 1802), Sc. Micro R-2228 Reel 4, SC-NYPL. Perrin died of yellow fever in early June.

146. Belair was actually re-integrated into the French army, only to revolt once more in Aug. 1802 and be executed. Note that Louverture was unaware that Belair and Dessalines were denouncing him to the French at the time. According to a French general, "I had dinner with those two gentlemen, mellowed them, and made them chat. They say that they do not like Toussaint much.... In the end Dessalines opened his heart to me and told me that Toussaint had only used him as a workhorse;" see Jean-Baptiste Brunet to Rochambeau (20 May 1802), lot 224, VR-PR.

147. After the end of the campaign, Leclerc encouraged cultivators to resume working under the cultivator system designed by Louverture, but popular resistance was strong. One of the persons most concerned about the surrender was a black commander from the area of Ennery named Sylla: "Since you were planning to surrender, why then did you put weapons in my hands to defend myself? Many people want riches, but I desire my liberty;" see Sylla to Vernet (c. 25 Apr. 1802), 61J18, ADGir.

16

en concequance au General le Clere pour lui rapellain se promes et le prier de
tenire la main a leur execution, il me fit reponce que si se ordre etoit de jadonné a ce sugé
cepandant ce lui qui conmandoit en se place avoit de ja divercé[119] sa troupe et en
voier de détachement dant toute les habitation ce qui avoit effraié les cultivateur et
les avoit force de fuire dans les montagne je mi etoit retire a ennery et en avoit don
ne connesance au General leclerc comme je lui a voit promis en arrivant dans ce commune
j'y trouvais grand nonbre de cultivateur de gonaive que j an ga geai de rentre, avan

mon depar de la marmelade j avoit donne lordre au conmmandant de cette place de remetre
lartilleris et le munition au conmandant de plaisance conformement aux intention du general
leclerc jai egalment donne lordre du conmandant ennery de rendre un seul piece qui étoit
ainci que les munition au conmandant dé Gonaive, ces ordre donne je ne me sui plus

ocuppé qua retablis mes habitation qui avoient éte insandiees, jai fais faire un
logement commode dans un des maisons de la montagne qui ma voit echappé aux
flames pour mon epousé qui étoit en cor dans les boi ou elle a voit éte obligée
de se refuger ; pendant que je etoit ocuppé a ce travaux jai appris quil etoit
arriver cienq cent homme de trouppe pour loger a d'ennery pétite bouque[120] que jus qua lors

---

119. Manuscript D: "divisé" instead of "divercé."
120. Throughout the manuscript, Louverture rendered the word "bourg" as "bouque" or "bourque" (see, for example, p. 13, lines 16, 18, 33, 39). This probably reflected the old pronunciation of the letter "g" as a /k/ in a liaison, which has only survived in present-day French in the pronunciation of "Bourg-en-Bresse" but has remained in Kreyòl.

16

consequently to General Leclerc to remind him of his promises and to invite him to ensure their execution. He responded to me that he had already issued orders on this subject.[148]
Yet the person who commanded this position had already divided his troops and sent detachments on all the plantations, which had frightened the cultivators and had forced them to flee to the mountains.[149] I had retired to Ennery and had informed General Leclerc of this, as I had promised to him. When arriving in this town,

I found a large number of cultivators from Gonaïves, whom I encouraged to return home. Before
my departure from Marmelade, I had issued an order to the commander of this position[150] to hand over
the artillery and the ammunition to the commander of Plaisance.[151] Agreeably to the intentions of General
Leclerc, I also gave the order to the commander of Ennery to give back the one gun that was there
and the ammunition to the commander of Gonaïves. Once these orders were issued, I only
busied myself with restoring my plantations that had been burned. I had a convenient home made in one of the houses of the mountains that had been spared by the flames for my spouse who was still in the woods, where she had been forced to seek refuge.[152] While I occupied myself with this work, I learned that five hundred regular troops had arrived to take quarters in Ennery, a small town that until then

---

148. These two letters were not in the archives consulted for this book. The "orders" probably referred to the proclamation asking cultivators to return to their plantations under the army's supervision; see Leclerc "Proclamation aux habitants de Saint-Domingue" (12 May 1802), CC9/B22, ANOM.

149. Leclerc had asked Rochambeau, who commanded the western province, to "keep a particularly close watch on Mr. Toussaint, Dessalines, and all the posse;" see Leclerc to Rochambeau (16 May 1802), lot 215, VR-PR. Rochambeau delegated this task to General Jean-Baptiste Brunet, who commanded the area of Gonaïves. Brunet's subordinate in Ennery, Battalion Chief Pesquidous (or Pesquidoux, d'Esquidoux) was to spy on Louverture while Battalion Chief Margeret did the same with Dessalines in Saint-Marc; see Andrieu to Brunet (c. 14 May 1802), BN08268/lot 1, RP-UF.

150. Laurent Désir was commander of Marmelade; see Hardÿ to Bertrand Clauzel (14 May 1802), B7/4, SHD-DAT.

151. Jean-Pierre Dumesnil was commander of Plaisance; see "Etat nominatif des chefs de la colonie qui se sont soumis aux lois de la République Française" (c. March 1802), B7/2, SHD-DAT.

152. Suzanne Louverture had spent the spring campaign on the Vincidière plantation in the Cahos Mountains. She moved to the Sancey plantation in the hills above Ennery after the ceasefire, while Louverture moved to the Descahaux plantation nearby. He later moved again to the Beaumont plantation, immediately near the village of Ennery; see Saint-Rémy, *Mémoires*, 73.

na voit pas plus conprendre plus des cinquante jandarme pour la police ; quon navoit en voier egalment un tre gros detachement a S^t michel, je metrans porte de suite au bouque

j'y vis que toute mes habitation a voint éte pillé et connavoit enlevé jus queaux coffre de me cultivateur ; a lins tan même je portoit mes plainte au conmandant je lui fis appercevoire des soldat qui etoient chargé de fruit de toute es pece qui ne toient même pas encore muris, je lui fis ausivoire des cultivateur con voïnat[121] ce pillages se sauvoit dans deautre habitation de la mon ta gne, jai rendu conpte au general le clerc de ce qui se passoit je lui ai observé que les mesure quon prenoit loing

d'ens piré la confiance ne faisoit que d au goumente la mefiance que le nombre des troupe quil a voit en voié etoit bocoup trop conciderable et ne pouvoient que nuire a la culture, et eux habitant, jere montai en suite dans mons habitation de la montagne, le len demain j y recy la visite du conmandant dennery, et mapperçu

fort bien que ce militaire loing de me rendre un visite d honnêteté ce netoit venuz che moi que pour reconnaitre mon nabitation ët se fase[122] da voire plus de facïlite de sampare de moi lors quon lui en donneroit lordre pen dant que je causoit avec lui on vien marvertis que plusieur sol dat se toient rendu a vec de chevaux et autre bete de charge dans une de mes habitation pré du bourque ou restoit un de me filleule enlevoit le caffé et autre danrée quil ja voient trouvé ; je lui

en fait mes plainte, il me promit de reprime ce brigandage et depunire sèver

ment ceux qui san rendroit coupables, craignant que ma de meur dans la mon tagne inpiré de la mefiance je mé determinai avenire dans cette même habi

---

121. Read: "qui voyant."
122. Illegible in manuscript C. Manuscript D: "afin" instead of "ët se fase."

must never have housed more than fifty gendarmes for the police,[153] [and] that a very large detachment had also been sent to Saint-Michel. I immediately proceeded to the town.

I saw there that all my plantations had been looted and that they had even taken my cultivators' chests. I immediately went to complain to the commander [Pesquidous]. I showed him soldiers who were loaded with fruits of all kinds that were not even ripe yet. I also showed him cultivators who, upon seeing this looting, were fleeing to other plantations in the mountain. I informed General Leclerc of what was going on. I pointed out to him that the measures that were being taken, far from inspiring confidence, were only feeding distrust, that the number of troops that he had sent was far too considerable and could only be bad for cultivation and the planters. I then returned to my plantation in the mountain. The following day, I received the visit of the commander of Ennery [Pesquidous] and realized quite well that this military man, far from paying me an honest visit, had only come to my home to reconnoiter my plantation so as to make it easier to seize me when he would receive the order. While I was talking with him, someone came to warn me that several soldiers had come with horses and other draft animals to one of my plantations near the town where resided one of my goddaughters[154] to take away the coffee and other crops that they had found there. I complained to him. He promised me that he would repress this thievery and severely punish those who would be guilty of it.[155] Concerned that my stay in the mountains was inspiring distrust,[156] I decided to come to this same [Beaumont] plantation

---

153. Pesquidous, who had been sent with an entire battalion to Ennery, was to report on Louverture's every move and to treat him with "deference" but also "circumspection;" see Andrieu to Pesquidous (14 May 1802), BN08268/lot 1, RP-UF.

154. A goddaughter of Louverture is mentioned in "Acte de baptême" (19 Jan. 1784), 1DPPC 2324, ANOM; there were probably others.

155. According to a coded transcript of this conversation (or the previous day's), Louverture complained that "[The general in chief had not told me] that they would put [a garrison here]. I would only get 25 [men]. I was told you [have] 700, I won't hide from you [I am suspicious; my wife is] still in the [woods she was supposed to] return home these days; I cannot make [her] come today. [My] cultivators had begun to work, now they have fled. I lost everything, my belongings were stolen;" see Pesquidous to Brunet (20 May 1802), 135AP/6, AN.

156. The French were growing suspicious because Dessalines accused Louverture of inciting Sylla to reject the recent ceasefire; see Dessalines to Leclerc (22 May 1802), Sc. Micro R-2228 Reel 4, SC-NYPL. Pesquidous was also almost killed in a suspicious fire in Ennery; see Pesquidoux to Brunet (26 May 1802), 135AP/6, AN.

tation qui venoit detre pille et qui avoit été presque totalement detruite et tout pret de bourque qui et éloigne que de deux cens pas.[123] je lai sai ma famme dant lappartement que je lui avoit fai preparé, je ne mau cupais plus qua faire des nouvelle plantation pour en placé celle qu'on navoit totalement detruit et a faire preparé les materiaux nese saire pour la reconstruction des mes ha bitation, mais tous les jour jen nai éprouvé que de nouvelle vexation et de nouvaux pillage, les soldat qui se portoient chemoi étoient sis grand nombre[124] que je nosoit, même pas les faire arreter en vain j en portoit mes plainte a leur conmandant je ne en recevoire aucune satisfaction, je me deter minais enfin quoique le General le clerc ne meut pas fait l honneur deme repondre aux deux premiere letre que je lui avoit ecris a ce suget de lui en Ecris une troisieme que je lui en voiai au cap par un des fit plaside[125] pour plus de surté, je nai pas plus de reponce a celle ci quaux precedante, seulement le chef de le tat ma jore me fit fire quil feroit son rapport, quel que temp après le conmandant étant venus de nouvaux me voire un a premidis et me trouvas a la tete de mes cultivateur au cupé a conduire mes travaux de reconstruction, il fut temoins lui même que mon fist Isaac repousait plus sieur soldat qui étoient venue jusqua la porte de ma maison coupés des bananne et des figue bananne[126] et les en porter, je lui en reiterais les plainte les plus grave et me promit tou jour quil empecheroit ces desordre, pandant troi semainne que jai reste[127] dans cette habitations, chaque joure jai été temoin de nouvaux piallige et chaque joure jai recu de visite des personne qui venoient mes pionné mais qui tous furent temoint que je maucupais uniquement des travaux domestiques, le general Brunette[128] etois venus lui même et ma trouvé dans les meme au cu pation

---

123. The phrase "et tout près du bourg qui n'en est éloigné que de deux cents pas" was added in manuscript B.

124. This is one of several instances in the second half of the manuscript where Louverture simplified French grammar in a manner typical of Kreyòl, in this case by dropping the preposition "en." This passage would normally be "étaient en si grand nombre" in standard French.

125. The name "Placide" was added in manuscript B.

126. The phrase "et des figues bananes" was added in manuscript B. "Figues bananes" (also: "bacoves") are a type of small, very sweet bananas common in the Caribbean.

127. One says "je suis resté" instead of "j'ai resté" in standard French, but the confusion between "avoir" and "être" is common in popular French.

128. Louverture pronounced the final "t" in "Brunet," which he also did for Vernet, Boudet, and Fressinet.

that had just been looted and that had been almost totally destroyed and was very near the town [of Ennery] that is only two hundred paces away. I left my wife in the apartment that I had had prepared for her. I only spent my time planting new crops to replace those that had been totally destroyed and preparing the materials necessary for the reconstruction of my plantations, but every day I only experienced new vexations and more looting. The soldiers who were coming to my home were in such large numbers that I did not even dare to put them under arrest. I vainly complained to their commander; I received no satisfaction from him. I finally decided, even though General Leclerc had not done me the honor of responding to the first two letters I had written to him on this subject, to write him a third one that I sent to him in Cap with one of my sons, Placide,[157] for greater safety. I received no more response to this one than to the previous ones. The chief of the general staff only said that he would write a report.[158] Some time later, the commander [Pesquidous] having again come to see me one afternoon, he found me at the head of my cultivators in the process of leading my reconstruction work. He himself witnessed that my son Isaac was pushing away several soldiers who had come all the way to the door of my house to cut plantains and small bananas and take them away. I reiterated to him the sternest complaints and he promised as always that he would prevent these disorders. For three weeks[159] that I spent in this plantation, every day I witnessed more looting, and every day I was visited by people who had come to spy on me, but all witnessed that I was only occupying myself with domestic work. General Brunet had come in person and found me occupying myself in the same manner.[160]

---

157. Louverture referred to Placide as his son, even though he was actually Suzanne's child from a previous union; see Thomas Gragnon-Lacoste, *Toussaint Louverture* (Paris: Durand, 1877), 15.

158. Division General Charles Dugua was Leclerc's chief of staff. He died of yellow fever in Oct. 1802.

159. Louverture agreed to a ceasefire in Cap on 6 May 1802 and then left for Ennery the following day. He was arrested on 7 June.

160. The account by Brunet (the French commander of Gonaïves) of his conversation with Louverture actually emphasized his disloyalty. Louverture allegedly said that "if people continued to bother him, he would flee to the woods and fight again for his liberty, he even repeated several times this threat.... For a man who so desires tranquility, he seldom rests, he is always on the go and I still don't know for sure on which plantation he has established his residence.... Spite could be seen beneath a veil of hypocrisy, and I believe he is willing to act on his threats;" see Brunet to Rochambeau (26 May 1802), lot 224, VR-PR.

17

malgré cela je recu une letre du general leclerc quau lieu de me donner satisfaction

sur le plaintes que je lui avois porté macusoit davoire garder des homme armes dans les
environs[129], et mordonnoit de les renvoier, persuadé de mon innocence et que surement
de gens mal intentionne la voient tromper je lui ai repondu que ja vois trop
d honneur pour ne pas tenire les promes que ja vois faite et quan lui rendant le conmandement
je ne la vois pas faite sans avoire bien reflechis et quiencis mon intention netoit
point de cherche a le reprendre, je lasurois au sur plus que je ne connaisois point d'homme
armes dans les environs d ennery et que depui troi semaine jetois constamment res te dans
mon habitations a y faire travaille, je lui envoier enfins mon fils Isaac pour lui rendre
conpte de toute lès vaixation que je suiois et Les prevenire sil ni mettois pas fins je seroit
obligé dabandonner le lieu ou je demeurais pour me restois dans ma hatte[130] sur la partie
Espagnole, un jour a vant que de recevoire aucuint reponce du general Le clerc, je fus
instruit quin de se aide canp pasant par ennery a voit dit au conmandant quil étoit

porteur dordre pour me faire arretér a dresé au general Brunette, le general Leclerc maÿant
d̶h̶o̶n̶ donné sa parole d honneur et promit la protection du gouvernement françois, je ne veu[131] a
da joute fois a ce propos ; je dis même a la personne qui me conseilloit de quiter mon habitation
que javoit promis dy rester tranquil et d'y travailler a réparer les degat qui avoient

été conmis, que je navois point cede le conmandement et renvoié me troup pour
faire de sotise, et quian ci je ne voulais pas sortis de che moi et que si lon venoit pour

marreter on metrouveroit, que je ne voulais point prete matiere a la calomnie ;

le lendemains je recus une seconde lettre du general leclerc par mon fits que je lui

---

129. Manuscript D adds "les environs d'Ennery."
130. Jeannin wrote "hutte" (hut) in manuscript D. Louverture corrected it in manuscript C to "hatte," a Dominguan term for a cattle ranch that Jeannin probably did not know.
131. Manuscript D: "je refusais" instead of "je ne veu."

17

Despite this, I received a letter from General Leclerc that, instead of satisfactorily addressing
the complaints I had made to him, accused me of having kept armed men in the

area [and] ordered me to demobilize them. Convinced of my innocence and that surely

ill-intentioned people had deceived him, I responded that I had too much
honor not to keep the promises that I had made, and that when handing over my command to him
I had not acted without careful deliberation, and thus my intention was
not to try to reclaim it. I assured him further that I was not aware of any armed

men in the area of Ennery and that for three weeks I had constantly stayed on

my plantation getting people to work.[161] I finally sent my son Isaac to give him
an account of all the vexations I was enduring and to warn him that if he did not bring an end to them I would
be obliged to abandon the home where I resided to retire to my ranch in the Spanish

part.[162] One day, before I received any response from General Leclerc, I was
told that one of his aides-de-camp [Ferrari] passing through Ennery had told the commander that he was
bearing orders to put me under arrest that were addressed to General Brunet. Since General Leclerc had
given me his word of honor and promised me the protection of the French government, I did not want
to believe this allegation.[163] I even told the person who was advising me to leave my plantation
that I had promised to stay there quietly and to work on repairing the damages that had
been made, that I had not yielded my command and demobilized my troops to
do something stupid, and thus I did not want to leave my home, and that if they came to
arrest me they would find me there, that I did not want to give any grounds for calumny.
The following day I received a second letter from General Leclerc through my son I had

---

161. These letters were not in the archives consulted for this book, but Brunet mentioned them in another dispatch. "I sent to General Toussaint the proclamation of the general in chief dated 22 floréal [12 May]; I am attaching a copy of his response;" see Brunet to Rochambeau (26 May 1802), lot 224, VR-PR.

162. On Isaac's mission to Cap, see Métral, *Mémoires et notes d'Isaac l'Ouverture*, 298.

163. "For the past two days he seems in deep thoughts.... He says he heard from Cap that he would soon be arrested with all his partisans;" see Brunet to Rochambeau (26 May 1802), lot 224, VR-PR. This was the second warning that Louverture ignored (see also p. 13, line 31). On Louverture's premonitions, see also Descourtiz, *Voyages*, vol. 3, 186; Métral, *Mémoires et notes d'Isaac l'Ouverture*, 302.

avois envoiér ; concu en ces terme armé de St Domingue au quartier General du cap.
francois; le 16 prairail an dix; le general en chef au general Toussaint puisque vous

persister citoyen general a penser que le grand nombre de troupe qui se trouve a
plaisance, +[132] effraige les cultivateur de cette paroise, je charge le general Brunette
de se conserte avec vous pour le plascement dune partis de ces troupe en arrierre de
Gonaive et dun detachement a plaisance, preven venez bien les cultivateur
que cette mesure une fois prie, je ferai punire ceux qui aban donneront leur habitation
pour aller dans la montagne faite moi connoitre au sitot que cette mesure séra
éxécuté les resúltat quillle au ra produit par ceque si les moÿens de persuasion
que vous enploirez ne reusissoient pas, j em ploirois lés moÿen militaire,
je vous salu, signe Leclerc;) il are maque que cet sandoute par erreur que le
secretaire a Ecris, plaisance et quil doit y a voire Ennery;) le meme jour je
recu une autre letre du general Brunette dont suit un Estrait;[133] armé de S^t

domingue; au quartie general de la habitation George le 18 praiial en 10 Brunette

General de divisions au General de division Toussaint Louvertur, voici le moment
citoyen general de faire connoitre dune maniere incontestable au general en
chef que ceux qui pouvent le tronpé sur votre conte[134] et votre bonne fois sont des
mal heureux calomniateur et que vos sentiment ne ten dent qua ramener
lordre et la tranquilite dans les quartié que vous habite, il faut me secondér
pour a surér la libre conmunication de la route du cap qui de puis hier ne tet
pas pus que troi personne ont éte égorgé parcin quantainne de brigand entre
Ennery et la coupe à pientade en voiez aù pre de ces homme sanguinaire
des gens digne de votre confiance que vous pairez bien je vous tien drai conpte
de votre de bour ce, nous avon mon cher General des arrangement a prandre en
samble quil et imposible de traité en letre mais quine conference dune heur

---

132. The cross symbol in the manuscript refers to the comment, a few lines below, that Leclerc must have meant "Ennery" instead of "Plaisance." That comment was added in the margin of manuscripts A and B.

133. As is the norm in Kreyòl and popular French, Louverture occasionally elided some consonants and vowels to facilitate pronunciation. In this case, he rendered /ks/ as /s/ in "extrait." He also elided "e," "i," "s," and "r" in some words.

134. Manuscript D omits "sur votre conte."

sent to him. It was worded as such: "Army of Saint-Domingue headquarters of Cap-Français 16 prairial year ten [5 June 1802] the general in chief to General Toussaint Since you persist, citizen general, in thinking that the large number of troops that are in Plaisance are frightening the cultivators of this parish, I am asking General Brunet to confer with you about locating some of these troops behind Gonaïves and a detachment in Plaisance. Make sure to inform the cultivators that once this measure is taken, I will punish those who abandon their plantation to go to the mountains. As soon as this measure is implemented, let me know what results it has produced, because if the means of persuasion that you employ fail to succeed, I will employ military means. I salute you, signed Leclerc." (Note that it is surely by mistake that the secretary wrote Plaisance and that it should be Ennery.) The same day I received another letter from General Brunet, of which here is an excerpt: "Army of Saint Domingue Georges plantation headquarters 18 prairial year 10 [7 June 1802] Division General Brunet to Division General Toussaint Louverture. Here is the moment, citizen general, to prove to the general in chief in an unequivocal way that those who may deceive him on your account and your good faith are hopeless slanderers and that your sentiments only tend toward bringing back order and tranquility to the areas that you inhabit. You must help me ensure the free circulation on the road of Cap, which is no longer [safe] since yesterday, because three people had their throat cut by fifty brigands between Ennery and Coupe-à-Pintade. Dispatch against these sanguinary men people worthy of your trust and whom you will pay well. I will reimburse you for your expenses. We have, my dear general, to make arrangements together that cannot be dealt with by mail, but that a one-hour meeting

termineras, si jai ètois pas exedé de tavaille et tracas munitieux
jou rois été au jour dhuit porteur de ma reponce mai ne pou vant pas ces jour
ci sortis vou même si vous etes retablis de votre andispositions que ce soit
de main quand sagit de faire le bien on ne doit ja mais retarder; vous
ne trouverez pas dans mon habitation champetre tous les agrement que
jai désiré reunir pour vous recevoire mais vous trou verèz la franchie
dun galant home qui na fait dotre veux que pour la prosperite de lacolonie
et [vo]tre bonheur personnel, si ma dame Toussaint dont je desiré infinement
faire sa connaisance vous loit etre du voiage je seroit trop content, si elle
a besoin de chevaux je lui en verrais les mien,, ces je vous le répete
General jamais vous ne trouverez damis plus siencer que moi, de la
confiance dans le capitaine general, de lamitie pour tous ce qui lui et
subordonnoit et vous jouirez de la tranquilité, je vous salut cor
dialment Signé Brunette.)[135] daprè ces deux letre quoique indisposé je me

---

135. Manuscript C omits the following paragraphs, possibly because Louverture concluded that they digressed from the account of his arrest. Manuscript A included the first two sentences of this passage; the rest appeared in full in manuscripts B and D.

"'P.S. Votre domestique qui va au Port-Républicain a passé ici ce matin, il est parti avec son passe en règle.' Ce même domestique, porteur de son passe en règle, a été arrêté; c'est celui qui est dans les prisons avec moi.

Il est bon d'observer que j'étais instruit par le nommé La Fortune, qui a été arrêté avec les 3 personnes qu'on a assassiné, a eu le bonheur de se sauver, il m'a rapporté cet assassinat, lui ayant demandé s'il avait parlé au commandant des troupes à d'Ennery, il m'a répondu qu'oui, de fait j'envoyai chercher Justin commandant, qui commande à présent la Garde Nationale et trois autres personnes raisonnables, je leur ai fait sentir combien il était dangereux de laisser commettre dans leurs quartiers de semblables désordres, ils m'ont répondu l'avoir senti et en être très fâchés, tous les quatre m'ont assuré qu'ils feraient des recherches, je leur ai conseillé en les engageant à découvrir les auteurs, ils ont tous instruit leurs camarades, et ont aperçu les malfaiteurs cachés dans la lisière de Plaisance et d'Ennery. Le lendemain matin j'en ai été instruit et l'on m'a observé qu'il fallait des mesures sages pour les arrêter. Le commandant Néron m'a demandé un ordre, j'ai cru devoir donner cet ordre, et une lettre pour le commandant de d'Ennery, d'après la lettre du Gal Brunet ci joint en copie.

'Il est ordonné au Commandant Néron, de partir de suite, avec un détachement de la Garde Nationale, qui sera partagé en trois portions. Premièrement, passera dans le carrefour de [Pierrot?] et l'autre dans les montagnes de d'Ennery et la troisième avec le commandant pour aller vers Plaisance, pour arrêter le C[en] Léveillé, avec ses complices, qui a commis un assassinat. Le commandant passera auprès du commandant Pesquidoux pour lui donner un ordre pour si au cas il se trouve quelque détachement à Plaisance, pour que les commanda[nts] de ces places lui portent des secours.

A d'Ennery le 18 prairial an 10, dix heures du matin. Le Général pour copie conforme.'

D'après mes lettres le commandant a refusé le passage à la Garde Nationale et moi allant aux Gonaïves d'après la lettre du Gal Leclerc l'on m'a remis en chemin la lettre dont copie suit.

A d'Ennery le 18 prairial an 10.

Le chef de bataillon commandant le quartier d'Ennery.

Au général de division Toussaint Louverture.

'Je ne puis, citoyen Général, permettre dans le quartier que je commande aucun mouvement de troupes sons les ordres exprès du général commandant la division.

Je m'empresse de lui donner connaissance de celui que vous projetez en attendant sa réponse, je vous prie d'ordonner aux Citoyens de la Garde Nationale de rentrer chez eux.

J'ai l'honneur de vous saluer, signé Pesquidoux.'"

will finalize. If I were not so overwhelmed with work and minute annoyances, I would have handed over my response in person, but as I cannot leave these days, if you have recovered from your illness, come tomorrow. When it comes to do good one should never delay. You will not find in my rural abode all the comforts with which I would have liked to greet you, but you will find the frankness of a gallant man who has no other wish but the prosperity of the colony and your personal happiness. If Mrs. Toussaint, whom I infinitely want to meet, wished to accompany you, I would be very pleased. If she needs horses I will send her mine. I repeat this to you, general, you will never find a more sincere friend than me. Trust the captain general, show friendliness toward all those who are his subordinates, and you will enjoy tranquility. I salute you cordially, signed Brunet."[164] Based on these two letters, even though I was ill I

---

164. The memoir reproduced word for word letters from Leclerc to Louverture on 5 June and from Brunet to Louverture on 7 June (another letter from Pesquidous to Louverture on 7 June was reproduced in manuscript D but was omitted in manuscript C). Louverture had the originals of the three letters with him during his captivity until he had to hand them over during a search of his cell; see Baille to Decrès (18 Nov. 1802), CC9B/18, ANOM.

rendie aux sollicitation de mes fics et dautre personne,[136] et partis pandant
   lanuit même
pour me rendre au pres du General Brunette; àconpagné de deux officie[137] seulement,
a huit heure du soir arrivé che lui aprés ma voire introduit dans sachambre,
je lui dis que javois recu sa letre aincis que celle du General leclerc qui mienvitoit

a me conserte avec lui et que je venois pour cet obgete, que je navois pas am
méné mon Epouse suivant se desire, parcequelle ne sortoit jamais, ne voioiet
au cuins société éné socupoit uniquement que des ses affaire domestique, que si
lors quil feroit sa tourné il vouslait lui faire l'honneur de la voire elle le
recevroit avec plaisir; je lui observais quie tant malade je ne pouvois rester
longtenps a vec lui que je le priais en concequance determiner le plutot
posible nosafaire a fien que je pussier men retourné et lui communiquai la
letre du General le clerc, après en avoire prit lecture il me dit quil na voit

---

136. The word "famille" was crossed out and replaced with "fils et d'autres personnes" in manuscript A.

137. The word "personnes" was crossed out and replaced with "officiers" in manuscript A.

followed the urgings of my sons and other persons and left that very night

to meet General Brunet. Accompanied by only two officers,
I arrived at his home at eight at night.[165] After entering his bedroom,
I told him that I had received his letter as well as that of General Leclerc in which he invited me
to confer with him and that I was coming for this purpose; that I had not
brought my spouse despite his wishes, because she never went out, never saw
other people, and only busied herself with her domestic affairs; that if, when
he toured the area, he wished to do her the honor of seeing her, she
would host him with pleasure.[166] I pointed out to him that, being sick, I could not stay
very long with him, that I invited him consequently to finish our affairs
as soon as possible so that I could depart, and showed him the
letter of General Leclerc. After reading it he told me that he had not

---

165. The two officers were Squadron Chief César and Placide Louverture; see Saint-Rémy, *Mémoires*, 80.

166. This description of a homebound, matronly Suzanne Louverture is consistent with an account of the Louvertures' domestic life in *Moniteur Universel* (9 Jan. 1799).

18

en cor recu au cune ordre de se conserte avec moi sur lobget de cette letre, me fit ensuite excuse, sur ce quil étoit obligé de sortir un instent et sortir en effet après avoire appellé un officier pour me tenir conpagnie, a peine etoit il sortire quin aide de canp du General leclerc entra a conpagnie dun tres grand nombre de grenadier qui m environnait

sen parent de moi me garoterait comme un criminel et me coinduisirent a bord de la frégate la créole, je reclamais la parol du General Brunette et les promeses quil ma voit fait mais inutilement je ne le revis plus,, il sétoit probablement caché pour se soustraire aux reproche bien merite que je pouvoi lui faire, jai même appris de puis quil

setoit rendu coupable de plus grande vexations en ver ma famille que setoit aprés mon arrestations,, il avoit ordonné a un detachement de se porter sur l habitation ou je demeurois avec un grande partis de ma famille, pour la plus par femme et en fans ou cultivateur[138] quil avoit ordonné de faire feu desus, ce qui avoit forcé ces mal heureux victime de fuire a demi nud dans le boi, quetout avoit été pillé et sacagé, que l aide de canp du general Brunette même[139] avoient enlevé de che moi cent dix portugaise qui m appartenoiet, et soixante et quinze a une

de mes niece, a vec tou mon linge et ce lui de mes gence,[140] ces horreure commis dans ma demeure le conmandant d Ennery ser porta a la tete de cent homme sur labitations ou etoit de ma famme et mes niece[141] les arreta sans leur don

ner même le temp deprandre du lange ni au cune de leur éffet ni des miens qui etoient en leur pouvoir, on les aconduit comme des coupable au Gonaive et de la abord de la frégate la geurriere,[142] lors que je fut arreté je navoit dautre

---

138. The phrase "pour la plupart femmes et enfants et cultivateurs" was added in the margin of manuscript A.
139. The phrase "qu'on avait" was replaced by "que l'aide de camp du Général Brunet avait" in the margin of manuscript A.
140. The spelling of "gence" and other words indicates that Louverture occasionally pronounced a final "s" that is normally silent. He did the same with the final "t" and "r" of many words.
141. "Mes deux enfants et mes nièces" was added in the margin of manuscript A. "Mes deux fils" was crossed out in manuscript B.
142. "On les a conduit à Gonaïves et de là à bord de la frégate la Guerrière" was added in the margin of manuscript A.

18

yet received any order to confer with me regarding the object of this letter.[167] He then excused himself because he had to leave for a moment and he left indeed after having summoned an officer to keep me company. No sooner had he left that an aide-de-camp of General Leclerc[168] entered accompanied by a very large number of grenadiers who surrounded me,
seized me, tied me up like a criminal, and led me on board the
frigate *Créole*. I invoked General Brunet's word and the promises he had
made to me, but to no avail. I never saw him again. He was probably hiding to avoid the well-deserved reproaches that I could have made to him.[169] I have even learned since then that he
had been guilty of the greatest vexations toward my family; that after
I was arrested he had ordered a detachment to proceed to the plantation
where I resided with a large part of my family, most of them women and children
or cultivators; that he had ordered his men to open fire, which had forced
these poor victims to flee half-naked into the woods; that everything had been
pillaged and vandalized; that the aide-de-camp of General Brunet[170] had taken from
my house one hundred and ten portugaises[171] that belonged to me, and seventy-five from one
of my nieces,[172] along with all my linen and those of my people. After these horrors were committed in my residence, the commander of Ennery went with one hundred men to the plantation where my wife and my nieces were, arrested them without even giving
them the time to take their linen or any of their belongings or mine that
were in their possession. They were taken like guilty people to Gonaïves and from there on board the frigate *Guerrière*.[173] When I was arrested I had no other

---

167. In reality, "since the 14th [3 June] I had orders [from Leclerc] to nab him;" see Brunet to Rochambeau (8 June 1802) lot 224, VR-PR.

168. Leclerc's aide-de-camp was Squadron Chief Ferrari; see Brunet to Leclerc (19 June 1802), Box 2:4, John Kobler/ Haitian Revolution Collection, MG 140, SC-NYPL.

169. According to Brunet's version of Louverture's arrest, "Toussaint was arrested in my home last night at 9:30 with a battalion chief and a servant.... My officers behaved admirably, with the greatest calm, and at a glance seized the ex-governor. At the same time in a nearby room they seized the battalion chief and Toussaint's servant; the former tried to resist and grabbed a dagger, but the rifleman on guard disarmed him with his bayonet;" see Brunet to Rochambeau (8 June 1802) lot 224, VR-PR.

170. The aide-de-camp of Brunet was Battalion Chief Hypolite Grandsaigne; see Grandsaigne to Brunet (12 Sept. 1802), B7/7, SHD-DAT; Saint-Rémy, *Mémoires*, 82.

171. A *portugaise* was a Brazilian gold coin worth 11 Spanish piastres or 66 French Caribbean livres; see [Du Simitière?], "Des manières de compter et des monnayes des Isles du Vent et sous le Vent" (c. 1758), 968.F.2, Du Simitière Collection, Library Company of Philadelphia.

172. Presumably Louverture's niece Louise Chancy, who was deported with him.

173. According to another account by Louverture, the day after his arrest "Commandant Pesquidoux came to my plantation with 100 riflemen.... From there my house was attacked from all sides; they shot at the women and men who fled to the woods; my papers were

vetement que ceux qui[143] je portoit sur moi, je crivis en concequance a mon epouse pour la prier de menvoier les chose dont javoit le plus present besoins au cap ou jesperoit quon alloit me conduire,[144] cet letre[145] avoit été remis a laide de camp du General le clerc pour le priier de le faire pascer mai il net pus parvenus a sa destination et je nai rien recu. des que je fus abord de la frégate la créole a mi a la voile on me conduient a quatre lieux du cap ou se trouvoit le vaiseaus le héros a bord duquel on me fit monter le lendemain mon Epouse ainci que mes enfans[146] qui a voient été arrete avec elle y arriverent ausis, on mit desuite a la voile pour france appres une traversce de trente deux jour dans laquelle jai ésuié non seulement les plus grande fatigue mais des desagrement tel quil et imposible de les imaginer au moint que des avoire été temoint ma femme même et mes enfans ont eprouver un traitement que leur séxe et leur rang auroit du leur rendre meillieur, et au lieu de nou faire debarque pour nous procurer des soulagement on nous a[147] garde a bord soixante sept jour: apré une pareil traitement ne pui-je pas a juste titre demander[148] ou

---

143. As is common in modern Kreyòl, Louverture often replaced /œ/ with /i/, in this case writing "qui" instead of "que" (see also "regitter" instead of "rejeter," "tinire" instead of "tenir," "soutinire" instead of "soutenir"). He also pronounced some /e/ and /y/ sounds as /i/.
144. The phrase "au Cap où j'espérais qu'on allait me conduire" was added in manuscript B.
145. Manuscript D: "ce billet" instead of "cet letre."
146. The phrase "les personnes" was replaced with "mes enfants" in manuscript B.
147. Manuscript D: "on nous a encore gardé" instead of "on nous a garde."
148. Manuscript D omits "demander."

clothes beside those I was wearing. I wrote consequently to my spouse
to send me the things that I most urgently needed to Cap, where
I hoped to be sent. This letter was given to the aide-de-camp of
General Leclerc who was asked to deliver it, but it never reached its destination
and I received nothing.[174] As soon as I was aboard the frigate, the *Créole* set
sail. They took me four leagues from Cap to the ship of the line
Héros, where they took me the following day.[175] My spouse, as well as
my children who had been arrested with her, arrived as well. We set
sail at once for France.[176] After a thirty-two day crossing during
which I endured not only the greatest fatigues but also unpleasantness
such as it would be impossible to imagine unless having witnessed it,[177]
even my wife and my children endured a treatment that their sex
and their rank should have made better, and instead of having us disembark
to relieve us, they kept us on board sixty-seven
days.[178] After such a treatment, am I not justified to ask: where

(n173 cont.)

seized; 75 portugaises were taken by the aide-de-camp that General Brunet had sent to Ennery, and my linen was looted. Then they went to look for my spouse: commander Pesquidoux behaved well toward her and treated her with all the attentions owed to her sex;" see Louverture to Leclerc (18 July 1802), Folder 3C, KFC-HU. For Isaac Louverture's account of French depradations, see Métral, *Mémoires et notes d'Isaac l'Ouverture*, 304–307. According to Brunet's account, "the ex-governor, his wife, his two sons, the chiefs of his guards Morisset and Maupoin and his closest accomplices are in our hands.... No less important was the capture of the correspondence and all the papers of Toussaint.... I ordered that Mrs. Toussaint and the women be treated with all the attentions owed to their sex; nothing was taken from them, money, jewels, linen, belongings;" see Brunet to Rochambeau (10 June 1802), lot 224, VR-PR. A decree by Leclerc stated that all of Louverture's assets would be confiscated; see Leclerc, "Arrêté" (13 June 1802), Dossier 1, EE1734, ANOM.

174. This letter was not in the archives consulted for this book.

175. Louverture did not mention in his memoir the famous quote that is usually attributed to him. "He was led to Gonaïves and taken aboard the *Héros*: it is there that he told Division Chief Savari, the captain of this vessel, these memorable words: 'By toppling me, you have only struck down in Saint-Domingue the trunk of the tree of the liberty of the blacks; it will grow back from its roots, because they are deep and numerous;'" see Lacroix, *Mémoires*, vol. 2, 203–204.

176. Louverture was deported with his wife Suzanne, his sons Placide, Isaac, and Saint-Jean, his nieces Louise Chancy and Victorine Tussac, and two servants, Mars Plaisir and Justine; see Auguste Nemours, *Histoire de la famille et de la descendance de Toussaint Louverture* (Port-au-Prince, HT: Imprimerie de l'Etat, 1941), 27.

177. Instead of dining at the officers' table, Louverture was put "among the seamen, allowing him no other rations but such as the ship's crew;" see W. L. Whitfield to Nugent (26 July 1802), CO 137/108, BNA. Louverture was kept incommunicado and could not talk to his own children; see Philippe d'Auvergne to Robert Hobart (2 Aug. 1802), WO 1/924, BNA.

178. Louverture left Cap around 12 June and reached Brest around 14 July, dates that are consistent with Louverture's account of a fast 32-day crossing of the Atlantic; see Leclerc to Decrès (11 June 1802), CC9B/19, ANOM; Decrès to Berthier (15 July 1802), CC9/B24, ANOM. Louverture probably included both the time spent crossing the Atlantic and the time spent waiting in Brest when claiming that he spent 67 days on board, since he disembarked on 13 Aug.; see Joseph Caffarelli to Decrès (13 Aug. 1802), in Victor Schoelcher, *Vie de Toussaint Louverture* (Paris: Ollendorf, 1889), 351.

sont les effet des promesse qui mi ont été faite par le general leclerc, sur sa
parole d honneur aincis que de la protections du gouvernement francois, si on avoi
plus[149] Besoin de mes service et quon eit voulus me renplacer n'auroit on
pas du a gir avec moi comme on a agit dans tous les temp a legard de generaux
Blans francois, on les previent avant que de les saisire de leur autorite,
on envoier un personne charge par le Gouvernement de leur intention l ordre
de remetre le commandement a tel ou tel que le gouvernement indique, et
dans les cas il refuzent dobeire on prend a lors avec justice de grande
mesurre contre eux et on peut alors avec justice les traiter de rebel, et
les embar que pour france, jai vus même quelque fois des officie generaux
criminel pour avoire gravement manque a leur de voire, mais en concédera
tion[150] du caractere dont il etoit revetus on les menagoit, on les respectoit jus
qua cequil soient de vant lotorité superieure; le General le clerc nouroiet
il pas dus menvoier cherche et me prevenire lui même quon lui avoit fait des
rapport contre mois sur tel ou obget tel obget vrai ou non, mau roit il pas dus
me dire je vous avoit donne ma parole et promis la protection du gouvernement,

au jour dhuit pusque[151] vous vous ete rendu coupable je vais vous en voier au
pre du Gouvernement pour rendre conpte de votre conduite, ou bien le Gouvernement vous
vous ordonne de vous rendre au pré de lui, je vous transmetre cet ordres, mais point
du tous il en agit avec moi avec de moÿent quon a jamais emploiié même
a le gard des plus grand criminels, sans doute je doit cette meprise[152] a ma cou
leur, mais ma couleur ma tele enpéché des servis ma patrie a vec zele
et fidelité, la couleur de mon corp nuit elle a mon honneur et a mon
courage, asuppozés même que je fus criminel et quil ÿ eut des ordre du
gouvernement pour mé arreter étoit il besoin d'employer cent carabinier

pour arracher ma femme mes enfans de leur proprieté sans respecte[153] et
sans égard pour leur range[154] et pour leur séxe, sans humanite et sans charité
falloit-il faire feu sur mes habitations et sur ma famille et faire pille et
sacager toute mes propriete; (non)[155] ma femme mes enfans et ma famille ne
sont chargé dau cune responsabilité, et na voit au cune conpte a rendre

---

149. As is common in popular French and in Kreyòl, Louverture simplified the negative form "ne...pas" (or, in this case, "ne...plus") by dropping the correlative conjunction "ne."
150. Read: "considération."
151. Louverture often simplified /yi/ as /y/, especially in the word "puisque" (see also "de pus" for "depuis"). He also occasionally replaced /œ/ with /y/.
152. Manuscript D: "ce traitement" instead of "cette meprise." Manuscript B: "cette maniere de se conduire a mon egard" instead of "cette meprise."
153. Louverture pronounced the final consonants in "respect," as is the case in old and regional French (see also "circonspecte").
154. Read: "rang" or "âge." The former, found in manuscript D, is more likely.
155. Manuscript B: "oui" instead of "non."

are the results of the promises made to me by General Leclerc based on his
word of honor as well as the protection of the French government?[179] If my
services were not needed anymore and they wanted to replace me, should they
not have proceeded with me just as was done every time with white
French generals? They were warned before their authority was taken away,
they sent a person charged with the government's intentions [and] the order
to hand over the command to this or that person listed by the government, and
in case they refuse to obey one can then take great
measures against them and one can then with justice label them as rebels, and
embark them for France.[180] I have even sometimes seen general officers
who were criminals for having gravely faltered in their duty, but in light
of the character that was theirs they were treated cautiously, they were respected
until they appeared before superior authorities. Shouldn't General Leclerc have
sent for me and warned me himself that he had received
reports against me on this or that object true or not? Shouldn't he
have told me "I gave you my word of honor and promised the protection of the
government,
today since you have made yourself guilty I am going to send you to
the government to account for your conduct," or "the government

orders you to appear by its side, I am passing on these orders to you?" But not
at all, he used against me means that were never employed, not even
against the greatest criminals. Surely I owe this misunderstanding to my color,
but did my color ever prevent me from serving my fatherland with zeal
and fidelity? Does the color of my body demean my honor and my
courage?[181] Supposing even that I were a criminal and that there were orders from
the government to put me under arrest, was it necessary to employ one hundred riflemen
to tear my wife and my children from their property without respect and
deference to their rank and their sex, without humanity and without charity?
Was it necessary to open fire on my plantations and on my family, and to have all our
estates looted and vandalized? No: my wife, my children, and my family
have no responsibilities and had no account to give

---

179. This sentence ends Louverture's account of the Leclerc expedition and opens the less orderly second section, in which he covered a variety of topics in a more lively tone.

180. Louverture had not followed this procedure when deporting rivals like Sonthonax (1796), Hédouville (1798), and Roume (1801); but he had not deported them as prisoners.

181. This complaint about racial discrimination, the third in the memoir, was likely based on Othello's comment in act I, scene 5 in a French translation by Jean-François Ducis (whose brother lived in Saint-Domingue). "Does the color of my face demean my courage?;" see Jean-François Ducis, Œuvres, vol. 2 (Paris: Nepveu, 1813), 160, 174.

19

au gouvernement,[156] on na voit même pas le droit de les faire arrete;
le general le clerc doit etre fran. au roitil craint da voire un rival? je le compare
dapré sa conduite au Senat romain qui pour suite anibal jus queau fons
de sa retraite; a larrivé de lescadre dans la colonie on a profite de mon
absance momantanée pour san parrér les plus grand partis[157] de mas correspondance
qui etoit au port republicain et tous ce que je posede dans cet partis.[158] une
autre partis qui etoit dans une des mes habitation egalement été saisire
apré mon arrestation. pour quoi ne ma ton pas en voÿer avec cette
correspondance auprés du gouvernement, pour rendre conpte, on na dont
saisire tous mes papier pour men pute des faute que je nai pas commis mais
je nai rien a redouter cette correspondance seule suffit pour me justifie aux
yeux du gouvernement Equitable qui doit me juge;[159] arrete abitrairement sans

mentendre ni me dire pourquoi; en parrè toute mes avoire, pillie toute la[160]
famille an general, saisire mes papier et les gard der, man barqué anvoier nud
comme ver deter, répendus des calomni les plus a tros sur mon conte,, da précela
je sui an voier dant le fons du cachot; nesce pas coupé la jambre dun
quie quin et lui dire marché, nesce pas coupè sa langue et lui dire parlé[161]

---

156. Manuscript D omits "et na voit au cune conpte a rendre au gouvernement."
157. Manuscript D: "d'une partie" instead of "les plus grand partis."
158. "et tous ce que je po sede dant cet partis" was added in Louverture's hand in the margin of manuscript B.
159. The long passage that follows, from "arrete abitrairement" to "<u>mal heure mau rait pas arrivé</u>," does not appear in manuscript B (there was only a short paragraph that was crossed out by Louverture) and was added as one long paragraph in manuscript D. That it was added so late in the writing process probably explains why it is one of the passages in manuscript C whose grammar differs most markedly from standard French. Personal pronouns are dropped before each verb. Verbs are not conjugated. Prepositions are dropped (such as "de" in "em parrè toute mes avoire"). Some articles are dropped (such as "un" in "comme un ver").
160. Manuscript D: "ma" instead of "la."
161. The sentence "nes ce pa couper sa langue et loui dire parlés" was added in Louverture's hand in the margin of Manuscript D. Note that he pronounced /y/ as /u/ in "lui."

19

to the government. They did not even have the right to put them under arrest.[182] General Leclerc must be frank: was he afraid of having a rival? Based on his conduct, I compare him to the Roman Senate that pursued Hannibal all the way into his lair.[183] When the squadron arrived in the colony, they used my momentary absence to seize the greatest part of my correspondence that was in Port-Républicain and all that I possess in this region. Another part that was on one of my plantations was also seized.[184] After I was arrested, why was I not sent with this correspondence to the government to account for my deeds?[185] They have thus seized all my papers to blame me for faults that I did not commit. But I have nothing to fear, this correspondence alone is enough to justify myself in the eyes of the equitable government that must judge me.[186] Arrested arbitrarily without hearing me or telling me why; took all my assets; plundered all my family in general; seized my papers and kept them; embarked me sent me naked as worm; spread the worst calumnies on my account. Based on this I am thrown at the bottom of a cell. Isn't it like cutting the leg of someone and telling him: "walk?"[187] Isn't it like cutting his tongue and telling him: "talk?"

---

182. Protecting his family was Louverture's abiding concern from the moment he arrived in Brest. "A 53-year-old mother deserves the indulgence of a generous and liberal nation. She has no account to give. I am solely responsible for my conduct;" see Louverture to Bonaparte (20 July 1802), Dossier 1, AF/IV/1213, AN. "If I faltered in my duty, I alone must be responsible for my conduct before the government;" see Louverture to Leclerc (18 July 1802), Folder 3C, KFC-HU. Louverture's son Placide had actually served with his father during the campaign.

183. Like French officers of his time, Louverture liked to make references to classical antiquity. Instead of Spartacus, the rebel slave to whom he was usually compared, Louverture chose in his memoir to invoke Hannibal, the valorous victim of European imperialism run amok. On Louverture's library (which contained works on ancient history), see Marcus Rainsford, *An Historical Account of the Black Empire of Hayti* (London: Albion Press, 1805), 244.

184. On the capture of Louverture's papers in Port-Républicain and Ennery, see Brunet to Rochambeau (10 June 1802), lot 224, VR-PR; Lacroix, *Mémoires*, vol. 2, 104.

185. Much to the French government's exasperation, most of the people deported from Saint-Domingue in 1802, including Louverture, were not accompanied by documentary evidence. The government accordingly prepared a dossier summarizing Louverture's faults; see "Rapport aux consuls concernant Toussaint Louverture" (23 July 1802), CC9/B23, ANOM.

186. This is the first mention in the memoir of Louverture's ultimate goal: a public trial (see also p. 17, line 32, p. 18, line 55, p. 21, line 28). But the French government eventually decided to hold Louverture without trial because Leclerc feared that "in the current situation his trial and execution would only sour the spirit of the blacks;" see Leclerc to Decrès (26 Sept. 1802), Box 12/1098, RP-UF.

187. Desormeaux, *Mémoires*, 142, claims that the metaphor was inspired by Marie-François Caffarelli, but it was Caffarelli's brother who was one-legged.

nes ce pas en teré un homme vivant,[162] tous cela a été bien conbiné a ma perte
pour ment ne antire, et me detruire parce que je sui noire et ingnorant,
et je nedoit pas conte au nombre des soldat de la republique ni avoire de merite,
et point des justice pour moi;[163] et ci jane pas dant ce mondre jorré dant lautre,
jai cé con va cherché et payer dans toute les diapasons[164] de la colonie et partous
pour trouver ou faire des mensonge conpte moi, mais l'homme propose et dieu
an dispose, pans dant que la france faisait la geurre et combatre avec
sé senemis nepouvant pas venire dant ces colonie nous portait des soucoure[165]
jai tous faite pour la lui conservé jus qua larrivé du general leclerc;
san force, sans munitions, sans arme, sans auquin Batiment de guerre,
sans argent et sans commerce, mais jai en ploier couprage, sageste,[166] et
prudance, sécond der par mes camarade darme et par la permitions de dieu
je réucire de metre toute en ne tate, et en bon nordre, et faire fleuris le paÿ
confier a mon conmandement, en nespérant qua la paix les Gouvernement au
roit declaré que larmé de S^t domingue a bien servis leur patri, et ce toute

que nous demandont ou espéront,[167] et celle action nous aurait bien flaté,
particulierement moi qui a tous dirigé mais au contraire le General le clerc nous
sa en voier les boulete. 36. et 24, pour toute reconpance, un paÿe partien[168] à
la france qui la trouvé tranquille et paisible; il étoit dependre de lui a
vec un peu de sageste et franchise, de prandre le conmandement et rendre
conpte au gouvernement dant quel et ta quil a trouvé cet paÿe, ce ne pas a la

paix qui[169] doit venire faire la geurre,[170] forcé un peuple soumis a sons gouvernement
de prandre les arme, forcé francois ce battre contre francois, et tronppé ma
Bonne fois, ci le General leclerc ai toit vraiment un militaire frant, et loÿalle
il mauroit pas traité de cet manière, da pre que je lui et remi le commandement

162. This passage was underlined in the C manuscript, presumably by Louverture.
163. Manuscript D: "en conséquence point de justice" instead of "et point des justice pour moi."
164. Manuscript D: "je sais que mes ennemis cherchés et payés dans tous les dispazons de la colonie pour trouver de faire des mensonges sur moi" instead of "jai cé con va cherché et payer dans toute les diapasons de la colonie et partous pour trouver ou faire des mensonge conpte moi." Either sentence is unclear because of the odd use of the word "diapason."
165. Louverture occasionally replaced /œ/ with /u/ ("soucoure" instead of "secours"). He also often replaced /o/ and /y/ with /u/.
166. Louverture added an extra "t" in "sageste" twice on the same page. This is probably an instance of hypercorrection. He also added "i," "r," and "c" to some words.
167. Manuscript D: "et c'était toute notre espérance" instead of "et ce toute que nous demandont ou espéront."
168. Louverture often detached the first syllable when writing a word or, in this case, elided it altogether, writing "partien" instead of "appartient" (see also "joute" instead of "ajouté"). This is typical of Kreyòl.
169. Louverture occasionally dropped the final "l" (in this case, "qui" instead of "qu'il"), as is common in popular French and Kreyòl. He did the same with the final /z/, /ʁ/, and /k/ in many words.
170. Manuscript D: "ce n'est pas la paix qui doit faire la guerre" instead of "ce ne pas a la paix qui doit venire faire la geurre." Louverture corrected Jeannin's nonsensical phrasing.

<u>Isn't it like burying a man alive?</u> All of this was well thought out to lose me, to annihilate me, and to destroy me because I am black and ignorant,[188] and I must not count as one of the soldiers of the Republic or have any merit, and no justice for me; and if I have none in this world I will have some in the next. I know that they will look and pay in all the corners of the colony and everywhere to find or manufacture lies against me, but man proposes and God[189] disposes of him. While France was waging war and combating her enemies, and was unable to come to the colony and bring us any help, I did everything to conserve it for her until the arrival of General Leclerc, without forces, without ammunition, without weapons, without any ship of war, without money and without commerce, but I employed courage, wisdom, and prudence.[190] Seconded by my comrades in arms and by God's will, I managed to put everything back in good order and to make the country entrusted to my command flourish, hoping that when peace came the government would have declared that the army of Saint-Domingue had served the fatherland well, and that is all that we ask for or hope for, and this action would have flattered us, me in particular, who directed everything.[191] But to the contrary, General Leclerc sent us cannonballs of 36 and 24 [pounds] as our only reward. The country belonged to France, which found it tranquil and peaceful: it only depended on him, with a bit of wisdom and frankness, to take command and give an account to the government of the state in which he found this country. It is not in a time of peace that he should come to wage war,[192] to force a people loyal to its government to take up arms, to force Frenchmen to fight Frenchmen, and deceive my good faith. If General Leclerc were truly a frank military man, and loyal, he would not have treated me in this manner, considering that I handed my command over to him.

188. This is the first of three instances in the memoir in which Louverture mentioned his lack of education, which clearly bothered him (see also p. 19, line 33, and p. 21, line 22).
189. Note the divine references on p. 16, lines 21, 23, and 29.
190. Louverture referred to his successful war against Spain and Britain in 1793–1798, which he had conducted with minimal material assistance from France. For obvious reasons, he hid his diplomatic ties to Britain and the United States in ensuing years, which could be seen as treasonous.
191. Until the spring of 1801, Bonaparte had actually thought of using Louverture as a strategic ally, only to change his mind and send an expedition (which he regretted later); see Philippe Girard, "Napoléon Bonaparte and the Emancipation Issue in Saint-Domingue, 1799–1803," *French Historical Studies* 32:4 (Fall 2009), 587–618.
192. As Louverture probably understood, Bonaparte had sent an expedition precisely because the London peace preliminaries of Oct. 1801 had left him free to ship a fleet past the British navy.

cil ave vus conmant je mesuis Exposé dans plusieur foit, a la prise de forti
fications lacudusaux, maitre piétater pacer a la tete des grenadié[171] enlevé
cet fort malgré la mitraille et fusilliade, plus sieur demes camarade ont été
Blaicé, et moi[172] recu plus sieur blaisure dant la jambre, sans conte ceux qui ont
resté sur les caro, et plus sieur d'autre a faire que je citéroit apré ci le General
Leclerc et tai presant, et ésuiér comme moi tendre misere, et pené pour chasé

les senemis de la france, il noré pas travaille sourdrement a me perdre, il auré
peuttre connai la valeur d un militaire qui a servis sa patris a veccourage et

fidelite, et si jai été un blan[173] a pré savoir servis comme jai servis toute cette
mal heure mau rait pas arrivé[174] ; au suget de la constitutions on na voulus ma

cusér, ma justifications et bien facile, apprès avoire chase les enemis de
la republique hor de la colonie, calmé toute les faction et reunit tous les partis
apres avoire pris posesions de Santo domingo, voiant que le Gouvernement
d'envoioit ni lois ni arrete, santant lurgence dé tablir la police dans cépaÿez

pour la sureté et la tranquilité de chaque individus et pour les bien du gouvernement
je fit une invitations a toute les commune de convoquie un nasamblé pour
non mer des depute et choisire des homme sages et eclairés pour former une
asanblés centrale, a léffet de leur confier le soins de ce travaille, cette
assenbléé formée par des homme de bien, sage et de probité en fins des honnet
gence,[175] je fis conte connoitre a ce membre quil avoient une tache penible
et honorable a renplis, quil devoient faire les lois propres au paÿes, a van
taguere pour le gouvernement, et utile au interête de tous: des lois basére
sur les moeurs, et les caractere des habitans de la colonie, et sur les localité.

---

171. Manuscript D adds "avec les officiers de ma suite."
172. Louverture used the reflexive form "moi" instead of the nominative "je" as a personal pronoun, which is typical of Kreyòl ("mwe").
173. Manuscript D: "un officier blanc" instead of "un blan."
174. This is one of two passages that were underlined in manuscript C, presumably by Louverture.
175. Manuscript D omits "par des homme de bien, sage et de probité en fins des honnet Gence."

If he had seen how I risked my life on several occasions when taking the fortifications of l'Acul-du-Saut, how I dismounted, led the grenadiers, [and] took the fort despite the grapeshot and musket volleys. Several of my comrades were injured and I received several wounds to my leg, without counting those who were killed outright, and several other affairs that I will cite later. If General Leclerc were present, and if he had endured as much misery as me, and struggled to chase the enemies of France, he would not have secretly labored to lose me, he would perhaps have recognized the valor of a military man who served his fatherland with courage and fidelity, and if I were a white man, after serving like I served, all these <u>misfortunes would not have happened to me</u>. As for the constitution they tried to blame on me, it is easy to justify myself.[193] After I chased the enemies of the republic from the colony, quieted all factions and gathered all the parties, after I took possession of Santo Domingo, seeing that the government was not sending laws or decrees,[194] feeling the urgency of establishing a police in this country for the security and tranquility of each individual and for the good of the government, I invited all the city councils to summon an assembly to appoint deputies and select wise and enlightened men to form a central assembly, so as to entrust them with this work.[195] This assembly was composed of good men, wise and upright, in a word honest people. I informed its members that they had an arduous and honorable task to fulfill, that they had to make laws specific to the country, advantageous for the government, and useful to everyone's interests: laws based on customs, and the character of the inhabitants of the colony, and the areas

193. Louverture referred to the constitution he presented to the public on 7 July 1801 and that enraged Bonaparte when he learned of its content in October 1801. To Caffarelli, Louverture admitted "yes it is true I made a mistake, but my intentions were pure;" see "Toussaint Louverture au Fort de Joux," 10.

194. Contrary to the Directory's 1795 constitution, which stated that colonies were within the French legal sphere, Bonaparte's 1799 constitution had stated that they would be governed by later, unspecified clauses. It is this legal vacuum, widely seen as a first step toward a restoration of slavery, that the 1801 constitution was intended to address.

195. Louverture summoned a constitutional assembly in a 5 Feb. 1801 proclamation; see Louverture to Pierre Forfait (12 Feb. 1801), 61J18, ADGir; Ardouin, *Etudes*, vol. 4, 314.

20

Du payz: la constitution a chevé devoit etre soumie a la sancetions du Gouvernement qui seul avoit le droit de la dopter ou de la regitter, ainci dez que les bases de cette constitutions furent établie, et les lois organique rendus je me sui empresé d envoier le tout par un membre de la semblé sentralle, au Gouvernement pour en obtenir la Sanction; on ne peut don pas men puter a aucune les erreurs prétendue ou les faute que cette constitution pouvoit con tenir, jus qua larrivé du general leclerc je nai recu aucune nouvelle du Gouvernement sur cet obget;[176] pour quoi don au jour d'hui veut on me faire un crime de ce qui ne peut pas en etre; pourquoi veut on que la vérité soit un mensonge, et que les mensonge devienne la verité; pourquoi veut-on que les tenebre soient la lumiere, et la lumiere soient les tenebre; dans une con versation que jai eu au cap avec le general leclerc il ma dit qui étant a Sanmanna a la tete de lisle, il avoit envoié un Espion a Santo domiengo[177] pour voir si j y etoit, que cet Espion lui avoit rapporté que effectivemant j y étoit, dans cette ville; pour quois don net il pas venue my trouver pour me me Transmetre les ordre du premiere consul avant de commancer les hostilité, il au roit vus lemprescement que jauroit mis a y souscrir: au contaire contraire il a profite de mon se jour a Santo domiengo pour se rendre au cap et en voier des disvision sur tous les point de la colonie. cela prouve quil na voit pas lin tention de me rien communique; si le General le clerc et

176. Louverture added a sentence in his hand in the margin of manuscript B, then crossed it out (the sentence is illegible).
177. Manuscript D omits "a Santo domiengo." Louverture probably added these words not to contradict the claim he made earlier in the manuscript that he was not present in Sámana when the French arrived.

20

of the country.[196] Once finished, the constitution was to be sent for approval to the government, which alone had the right to adopt or reject it.[197] Thus, as soon as the bases of the constitution were established and organic laws were passed, I hastened to send all of them with a member of the central assembly to the government to obtain its approval.[198] One cannot then blame me for any of the so-called errors or faults that this constitution possibly contained. Until the arrival of General Leclerc I had received no news from the government on this subject. So why today do they want to make a crime of what cannot be a crime? Why do they want truth to be a lie, and lies to become truth? Why do they want darkness to be light, and light to be darkness?[199] In a conversation I had in Cap with General Leclerc, he told me that when he was in Samaná at the tip of the island, he had sent a spy to Santo Domingo to see if I was there, that this spy had reported to him that indeed I was there, in this town.[200] Why then did he not come to meet me there to give me the orders of the first consul before beginning the hostilities? He would have seen the haste with which I would have fulfilled them. To the contrary, he used the fact that I was in Santo Domingo to proceed to Cap and send divisions to all points of the colony. This proves that he had no intention to communicate anything to me. If General Leclerc went

---

196. The deputies were Bernard Borgella and Etienne Viart (from the West), Julien Raimond and Jean-Baptiste Lacourt (North), Philippe Collet and Gaston Nogerée (South), and four deputies from Santo Domingo who played a limited role (Juan Monceybo, Francis Morillas, Carlos Roxas, André Mugnoz). For Louverture's instructions to the delegates, see "Extrait des registres de l'Assemblée centrale de Saint-Domingue" (28 March 1801), CO 137/106, BNA.

197. Art. 77 allowed Louverture to provisionally implement the constitution until he received France's approval.

198. Louverture referred to the constitutional delegate Gaston Nogerée, whom he sent to France in Sept. 1801 with a letter to Bonaparte. Louverture had actually sent Charles Humbert de Vincent a month earlier with a copy of the constitution, but Louverture likely preferred not to mention his name because he had heard that Vincent had criticized his conduct; see Nogerée to Louverture (17 Oct. 1801), Box 1:5, John Kobler/Haitian Revolution Collection, MG 140, SC-NYPL.

199. Louverture used the same analogy in a 1798 letter: "de homme pour leur interé particulier... veul fer pacé lé mal pour le bien et le bien pour mal, on faite pacé les tenebre pour la lumier et la lumier, pour les tenebre;" see Louverture to Hédouville (c. 1798), AF/III, 210, AN. This was likely a reference to Genesis 4 ("God saw that the light was good, and he separated the light from the darkness") or Isaiah 5:20 ("Woe to those... who put darkness for light and light for darkness").

200. On 6 May 1802, while Louverture and Leclerc were discussing a ceasefire in Cap, Leclerc allegedly "confessed that the pilots embarked near Sámana had assured him that Toussaint Louverture was in Santo Domingo;" see Métral, *Mémoires et notes d'Isaac l'Ouverture*, 289. Leclerc's account does not mention this piece of intelligence; see Leclerc to Decrès (9 Feb. 1802), CC9B/19, ANOM.

allé dans la colonie pour faire du mal on ne doit pas me linputer; il et vrai
quon ne doit sen prendre qua un de nous deux, mais pour peu quon veille
me rendre justice on vaira que cet lui qui et lauteure de tous les maux que
lisle a ésiuié, pus que sans me prevenire il et entre dans la colonie quil a
trouvé intacte quil et tonbé sur les habitans qui travail loient et surtous
ceux qui ont contribuée a la conservation de la colonie en versant leur sang
pour la merre patris: voila precisement la source du mal: si deux enfans
se battent ensemble leur per ou leur mere ne doivent il pas les empeché et sien
former le quel et lagresseur et le punire ou les tous deux, en ca quil en fust
tore[178] tous deux de même; le General Leclerc na voiet pas les droit de me faire arrete
le Gouvernement seul pouvoit nous faire arreté tous deux nous en tendre et nous
jugé, cepandant le General leclerc jouit de la liberté, et je sui dans le fond
Duns cachot; aprés avoire rendus conpte de ma conduite depuis larrivé de
l'Escadre a S^t domingue. j entrerais dans quel que detaille sur celle que jai tenus
avant le debarquement, depuis que je sui entre au service de la republique
je nai ja mais recu un sol dappointement, le General la vaux et tous les sagant
du Gouvernement et les personne contablé[179] qui a voient linspection sur[180] la caisce
publique peuvent me rendre cette justice, personne na jamais été plus de
licat ni plus désinteresé que moi, jai seulement recu quel que foit le traitement
de table qui metoit acordé encor tres souvent ne lai-je pas de mandé, si jai
donne des ordre de prendre quel que somme[181] a la caisce cé ètoit tous jour pour le bien
du service publique, lordonnateur les fasoit pàsai ou le bien du service lexigeoit
jai connaisance quine seule fois seulement étai eloigné de che moi jai em
prunte six mille frant du citoyen cimite[182] qui étoit ordonateur au de par
tement du sud.; voici en deux mot ma conduite et le résultat de mons administration;. a le vacuation des anglois il n y a voit pas un sol au tresor
publique; on étoit aublige de faire des emprunte pour paÿer la troup et les
salaries de la republique; a larrivé de General Leclerc il a trouvè trois millions
cinq cent mille livre, en caisce, quand je rentrait au caÿe après le depart du
General rigaud le caisce étoit vinde, le General leclerc y a trouvé trois millions
il en na trouvé de même et a pro portion dant toute les autre caisce particuli[183]

---

178. Manuscript D: "en cas qu'ils eussent tort tous deux" instead of "en ca quil en fust tore tous deux."
179. Manuscript D omits "contablé" (French: "comptables").
180. Louverture added "sargant du Gouvernement et" in his hand in the margin of manuscript B, but the revision was not incorporated into later drafts.
181. The phrase "un sol" was replaced with "quelque somme" in manuscript A.
182. Manuscript D: "Smith" instead of "cimite."
183. Read: "particulières" (the edge of the page is missing).

to the colony to do wrong I should not be blamed for it. It is true that only one of the two of us should be reproved, but if one takes the time to do me justice, one will see that it is he who is the cause of all the woes that the island has endured, since without notifying me he entered the colony which he found intact, that he pounced on the inhabitants who were working, and especially those who had contributed to the conservation of the colony by shedding their blood for the motherland.[201] Here is precisely the source of evil. If two children are fighting, isn't their father or their mother supposed to prevent them, and enquire as to who is the aggressor and punish him or both of them, in case they are both wrong?[202] General Leclerc did not have the right to put me under arrest. The government alone could arrest the two of us, give us a hearing, and judge us. Yet General Leclerc enjoys his liberty, and I am at the bottom of a cell. After having given an account of my conduct since the arrival of the squadron in Saint-Domingue, I will give details about my conduct before the landing.[203] Ever since I started serving the republic,[204] I have never received a dime as salary. General Laveaux and all the agents of the government and the accountants who were charged with inspecting the public treasury can vouch for me: no one was ever more delicate or disinterested. I only received sometimes the meal allowance that was owed to me, and even then very often I did not ask for it. If I gave orders to take some sum in the treasury, it was always for the public good. The paymaster would send it wherever the good of the service required it. I only know of one instance, when I was far from my home, when I borrowed six thousand francs from citizen Smith who was paymaster in the department of the South.[205] Here, in two words, is my conduct and the result of my administration. When the English evacuated, there was not a dime in the public treasury; we were obliged to issue loans to pay the troops and the salaries of the republic. When General Leclerc arrived he found three million five hundred thousand livres in the coffers. When I entered Cayes after the departure of General Rigaud,[206] the treasury was empty; General Leclerc found three million there. He found money in the same proportion in all the various treasuries

---

201. Throughout the manuscript, Louverture used terms like "Frenchman," "colony," and "motherland" to reject accusations that he was on a path to independence; see also, for example, p. 16, line 40.
202. Louverture occasionally used the parent-child bond as an analogy for the colonial bond; see Louverture, "Proclamation" (20 Dec. 1801), in Nugent to Hobart (19 Jan. 1802), CO 137/106, BNA.
203. This sentence marks the beginning of the memoir's third section, in which Louverture retraced his record prior to 1802.
204. Louverture switched from the Spanish to the French army around May 1794.
205. L. L. Smith, the scion of a family of planters, became paymaster in Cayes in 1800 and died in Oct. 1802; see Desormeaux, *Mémoires*, 148.
206. The mixed-race general André Rigaud commanded the southern province until Louverture defeated him in the 1799–1800 War of the South and captured the southern capital of Cayes in August 1800. Rigaud returned to Saint-Domingue with the Leclerc expedition, only to be deported by Leclerc back to France.

de lisle, da près ce la on peut voire que je nai pas servis ma patrix pour lin
térét; mai au contraire que je lai servis a vec honneur et fidélité et probite;
dans lespoire de recevoire un jour des Temoignage flateurs de la reconnaisance
des Gouvernement, Toute les personne qui mon connait me rendront justice,
jai éte Esclave[184] joze la vancer; mais je nai jamais ésuié même de repro
che de la part de mé maitre, je nai jamais rien negligé a S^t domingue pour
le bonheur de lisle, jai pris sur moi[185] repos pour y contribué; je faisais
    tout sacrifié
je me faisoit un de voire et un plaisir de contribuer a la prosperite
decett belle colonie, zèle, activite, courage, jai tout emploiier;
lisle avoite ètè envahie par les ennemis. de la republique, je na voit alo
quine quarantaine de mille homne arme de pique, je les renvoier toute a la
culture, et organisé quel regiment da prè lotorisation du general lavau[186]
la partis Espagnole sè toit joute aux anglois pour faire la geurre au francois

---

184. This is one of only two times that the word "slave" is employed in the manuscript. Note that the word is capitalized, like all the words that Louverture wished to emphasize. In manuscript A, the passage went "n'est-ce pas pour moi un crèvecoeur j'ai été esclave je ne le cache pas mais je n'ai jamais été réprimandé."

185. Louverture probably spelled the French "mon" as "moi" to approximate the Kreyòl possessive determiner "mwen."

186. The phrase "je les renvoÿer toute a la cul ture, et organisé quelque regiment dapre lo torisation du Ge neral lavaux" was added in Louverture's hand in the margin of manuscript B. He also added "au francais" and "il na pa pu la prendre" in the two following sentences.

of the island.²⁰⁷ Based on this one can see that I did not serve my fatherland for personal interest, but that to the contrary I served it with honor and fidelity and probity, in the hope of receiving one day flattering displays of the gratefulness of the government.²⁰⁸ All the people who know me will do me justice. I was a slave, I dare to announce it, but I never had to endure even a reproach on the part of my master.²⁰⁹ I never neglected anything in Saint-Domingue for the happiness of the island. I used my time of rest to contribute to it.

I sacrificed everything. I made it my duty and my pleasure to contribute to the prosperity of this beautiful colony. Zeal, activity, courage: I employed everything. The island had been invaded by the enemies of the republic. At the time, I only had forty thousand men armed with pikes. I sent them all back to the fields and organized a regiment with the authorization of General Laveaux.²¹⁰ The Spanish part had allied itself to the English to wage war on the French.

---

207. A French general indeed reported finding "millions" in Cayes; see Lacroix to Dugua (15 Feb. 1802), B7/15, SHD-DAT. Leclerc also mentioned finding one million in Santo Domingo; see Leclerc to Bonaparte (1 Apr. 1802), B7/26, SHD-DAT. Embezzlement was endemic in the French officer corps, so many other finds went unreported.

208. Louverture's ambitions were both financial and political. He enriched himself considerably during the Revolution by using his political clout to lease public lands, but he also longed for recognition, particularly from Bonaparte; see Pluchon, *Toussaint Louverture*, 352, 425.

209. This is the only instance in the memoir in which Louverture mentions his past enslavement. On his life as a slave, see Jean-Louis Donnadieu and Philippe Girard, "Toussaint Before Louverture: New Archival Findings on the Early Life of Toussaint Louverture," *William and Mary Quarterly* 70:1 (Jan. 2013).

210. Louverture referred to his 1794 switch from the Spanish army to the French army, which helped Etienne Laveaux, the governor of Saint-Domingue, defeat a joint British and Spanish invasion. The reference to "40,000 men armed with pikes" is less clear. Perhaps Louverture gave an inflated account of the forces at his disposal, generally estimated at 4,000 soldiers, or perhaps he was referring to armed cultivators and other irregular troops; see David Geggus, "The 'Volte-Face' of Toussaint Louverture," in Geggus, *Haitian Revolutionary Studies (Blacks in the Diaspora)* (Bloomington, IN: Indiana University Press, 2002), 119–136.

21

le General desfournaux fut envoyer pour attaque S.t michel avec de la troupe
de ligne bien disipliné, il na pas pus. la prendre, le General lavaux mordonné
dattaque cette place, je lan porter, il et a remarquer que lors de lattaque
du general desfournaux sé place n'étoit pas fortieé et que lors que je men
fus emparé elle ètoit fortifié et flanquié des bastions dans tous le coins[187]
j ai egalement pris S.t raphael, hinche, et en ai rendu conpte au general la
vaux, les anglois etoient retranché au pont lestere je les en ai chascé,
ils étoient en poscesions de la petite riviere, ja vois pour toute munitions
une caisce de cartouche qui étoit tombér dans laux en nallant attaque,
cela ne ma pas rebute jai emporte d'assaut cette place a vant le jour a vec mes
dragond et jai faite toute la garnison prisonnie que jai envoiez au General
lavaux, et pris neuf piece de canon, avec un seul piece canon au nombre de ceux
que je pris a la petite riviere,[188] jai attaqué emporté dassaut un fortifications
de fendus par sept piece de canon dont je me suis emparé, je me suis egalement
emenparé sur les Espagnole des camp retrancher miraux et de la bourque verrette,
jai livré et gagnè aus anglois une fameuzè bataille, qui a du ré de pus six
heure du matin jus qua la nui, cette bataille a èté si sanglante que les chemin
etoient couverte. de morte et quon voient de toute part couler des ruiseaux
de sang, je me suis emparé de tous les bagage et munition de lenemis, leur a
faite un Grand nombre de prisonnier et jai envoier les tous[189] au general la
vaux, et lui rendre conpte de laction, tous les poste des anglois sur le hauteur
de S.t marc ont été re poussé par moi, les fortifications en meme dant
les montagne de fonbatiste et de lisce, le canp doite dans la montagne de
mateux que les anglois regardoient comme ien prenable, les citadelle de
mirbalais appallé le gil braltarred[190] de lisle, aucuppé par onze cent homme,[191]
le fameux canp de la cu du saut,[192] le fortifications a troi étages en ma
connage du trou d eau, celle du camp de caiete, et du bau bien en un maut
toute les fortifications que les anglois[193] avoient dant cette partie nont pa me resitaiz

---

187. Manuscript D: "angles" instead of "coins."

188. The phrase read "avec une seule pièce de canon que j'avais prise" in the original version of manuscript B. Louverture added "je marché avec une piesce, mai je vé pris neufe a la petiterie vier" in the margin of manuscript B. The phrase became "et pris neuf pièces de canon avec une seule pièce de canon et neuf que j'avais prises a la Petite Rivière" in manuscript D.

189. Using the word order of standard French, the passage would read "je les ai tous envoyés."

190. Read: "Gibraltar."

191. The phrase "onze cents hommes de garnison anglaise" was added in the margin of manuscript A.

192. Manuscript A adds "retranché par des fossés, je l'ai emporté d'assaut à la tête de mes grenadiers. Après y avoir reçu sept blessures je me suis de même emparé de."

193. From this point forward, Manuscript C is written in a thinner, lighter ink. Louverture's handwriting also gets progressively tinier as the memoir progresses. The first full page (page 2) contains 47 lines and 2,500 characters. There are 72 lines and almost 5,000 characters on page 14.

21

General Desfourneaux[211] was sent to attack Saint-Michel with well-disciplined troops of the line, [but] he could not take it. General Laveaux ordered me to attack this position, I carried it (it is worth noting that during the attack of General Defourneaux this position was not fortified, whereas when I captured it it was fortified and all its corners were flanked by bastions). I also took Saint-Raphaël [and] Hinche and gave an account to General Laveaux. The English were entrenched at the Ester bridge, I chased them from it. They were in possession of Petite-Rivière, my only ammunition was a box of cartridges that had fallen in the water during the attack, this did not discourage me: I carried this position before daybreak with my dragoons and captured the entire garrison, which I sent to General Laveaux, and I took nine cannons, using only one cannon from the ones I had taken in Petite Rivière. I attacked and overwhelmed a fortification defended by seven cannons that I captured. I also seized from the Spanish the fortified camp of Miraut and the town of Verrettes. I waged and won against the English a famous battle that lasted from six in the morning until nighttime. This battle was so bloody that the trails were covered with the dead and that one could see rivulets of blood flowing everywhere. I seized all the baggage and ammunition of the enemy, took a large number of prisoners, and I sent the lot to General Laveaux, and gave him an account of the encounter.[212] All the posts of the English in the heights of Saint-Marc were pushed back by me, as well as the fortifications in the mountains of Fond-Baptiste and Délices, the camp of Droët in the mountain of Matheux, which the English regarded as impregnable, the citadel of Mirebalais, known as the Gibraltar of the island, occupied by eleven hundred men, the famous camp of l'Acul-du-Saut, the three-story fortifications in masonry of Trou-d'Eau, those of the camp of Décayette and of Baubin. In a word, none of the fortifications that the English had in this part could resist me,

---

211. Division General Edmé-Etienne Desfourneaux had spent much of the 1790s as a French envoy in Saint-Domingue and Guadeloupe; he served in the Leclerc expedition until Leclerc deported him in Aug. 1802.

212. Louverture fought many battles against the English in the neighborhood of Verrettes, so authors disagree on whether this anecdote referred to a battle fought in Dec. 1794, Aug. 1795, or 1797; see Desormeaux, *Mémoires*, 151. The most likely candidate was a March 1797 campaign related in Louverture, "Procès Verbal de l'expédition...sur le Mirebalais et sa descendance" (9 Apr. 1797), 61J18, ADGir.

nontplus que celle de Neibre de S^t jan de la magoinne de la matte Banique et autre
lieux au cupé par les Espagnolle; tout a été remis par moi au pouvoir de la republique
jai courus les plus grande danger, faïlli plusieure fois detre prisonnie; évercér mon sang
pour ma patrie, jai recu une bale dans la hanche droite que jai encor dans les corp, jai eu
une constuvion violante a la tete au casionnere par un boulete qui matellement ebranlé
la machoire que les plus grande partie de mes dant sont tombé et que les peux qui mes
restent sont encorre tre vacillante, enfins jai recu dans deferene[194] aucasion dix
sept blesure, dont il me reste encore de cicatrices honorable; le general lavaux a
été temonit de plusieur aucation il et trop juste pour ne pas me rendre justice, dir
si jai jamais hésite a sacrifié ma vi lors quil sagisait de prouver un bien
etre à mon paÿ, et au triomphe a la republique, si je voulois conpter tous les service

que jai rendu dans tou les geure au gouvernement il me faux droit plusieure volume
et ne finiroit jamais; et pour me reconpance de tou ces services on marrété
arbitrairement a S^t domingue comme un criminel,[195] on me garote et me conduit a
Bord sans egard pour mon rang, et pour ce que jai fais sans aucune menagement;

et ce la la reconpance due a mes Travaux, daprè ma conduite pouvois-je mattendre
a un pareille traite ment, ja vois de la fortune depuis longtemp, la revolutions
ma trouver a vec en viron six cent qua rante hui mille frans, je les ai
épuizér, en servant ma patrie, ja vois seulement a che té une petite propriete
pour y ètablis mon Épouse et sa famille, au jour dhuit apré une pareille conduite
on cherché a me couvrire d'aupprob, dinfamie,[196] et on ne me rend les plus, mal

---

194. Read: "différentes."
195. The following passage from "on me garote" to "de ma vix" does not appear in manuscript A.
196. Louverture often treated prepositions and articles as if they were part of the word itself, writing here "dinfamie" instead of "d'infamie" (see also "dun" instead of "d'un" on line 51). This is common in Kreyòl ("dlo" for "de l'eau").

nor those of Neiba, San Juan de la Maguana, Bánica and other
spots occupied by the Spanish. All these I handed over to the republic.²¹³
I faced the greatest dangers, was almost taken prisoner several times, and spilled my blood
for my fatherland. I received a bullet in my right hip that is still in my body. I had
a violent concussion to the head caused by a cannonball that so shook
my jaw that most of my teeth fell off and that the few that remain
are still very wobbly.²¹⁴ Finally, I suffered on different occasions seventeen
wounds, of which I still bear honorable scars. General Laveaux
witnessed several engagements. He is too just not to do me justice, not to say
if I ever hesitated to sacrifice my life when it came to contributing to the
well-being of my country and the triumph of the republic.²¹⁵ If I wanted to count all the services
I have rendered to the government in all the wars, I would need several volumes
and would never end. And to reward me for all these services they arrest me
arbitrarily in Saint-Domingue like a criminal, they tie me up and bring me
on board without any regards for my rank and for what I have done, without any attention
Is this the reward worthy of my labors? Based on my conduct, could I expect
such treatment? I had some wealth for a long time. The revolution
found me with about six hundred and forty-eight thousand francs. I exhausted
it all serving my fatherland. I had only bought a small property
to settle my spouse and her family.²¹⁶ Today, after such a conduct,
they try to cover me with opprobrium, infamy, and they make me the unhappiest

---

213. Louverture was understandably eager to emphasize his proud military record against the Spanish and the British, which would likely please Bonaparte and allowed him to relive his past.

214. Louverture had "no teeth on his upper jaw; the lower one juts forward and is lined with long, salient teeth;" see "Toussaint Louverture au Fort de Joux," 1. Louverture had several of his remaining teeth pulled out during his captivity; see Baille to Decrès (18 Oct. 1802), TL-2B3a, Nemours Collection, University of Puerto Rico.

215. Laveaux was the only one of several French envoys to Saint-Domingue who left the island on good terms with Louverture, which explains why he cited him repeatedly as a character witness in the memoir. "As for me, my friend, I can never repeat enough that I love you for life;" see Laveaux to Louverture (29 Dec. 1799), Sc. Micro R-2228 Reel 1, SC-NYPL.

216. Louverture's claim that he was worth 648,000 francs at the outbreak of the Revolution is puzzling since documents indicate that he only became rich during the course of the Revolution; see Gabriel Debien, "Les biens de Toussaint Louverture," *Revue de la Société Haïtienne d'Histoire et de Géographie*, no. 139 (June 1983), 5–75; Donnadieu and Girard, "Toussaint Before Louverture." When pressed by Caffarelli on the matter, Louverture backtracked, saying that "I have never been rich in cash.... My wife was rich;" see "Toussaint Louverture au Fort de Joux," 12. Perhaps Louverture, who referred to the "revolution of 10 August 1790 [1792]" in another letter, did not use the Aug. 1791 slave revolt as the starting point of the Revolution but rather Louis XVIII's overthrow a year later; see Louverture to Bonaparte (9 Oct. 1802), Dossier 1, AF/IV/1213, AN.

heureux des homme, en me privant de la liberté, et en me separant de ce que
jai de plus cher au monde, dun pere respectable agé de cent cienq ans qui a
besoin de mes secours; dun famme adorèe qui ne poura san doute supporte les maux
Dont elle séra a câblé, loin de moi; et dune famille cherix qui faisoit le bonheur
de ma vix,[197] en dessandant de vaiseau on ma faite mon ter en voiture, j Esperois
a lors quon alloit me traiduire de vant un tribunal pour y rendre conpte de mas
conduite et y etre jugé; mai au lieu on ma conduit sans me donner un instent
de repopos dans un fort sur les frontiere de la republique, ou lon man
fermé dans un affreux cachot, cet du fond de cett prison que je recoure a
la justice et a la magnanimitè du premiere consul; il et trop genereux et trop bon
General pour lai ser un ancien militaire couvert de blesure au service de sa
patrie mourire dans un cachot sans lui donner même la satisfaction de sé
justifié et de faire prononcer sur son sort,[198] je demande dont detre Traduit
De vant un tribunal ou conseil de geurre ou lon féra paraite ausis le general
leclerc et que lon nouguge apré nous a voire enten dus lun et lautre, lequité,
la raison, les lois, tout massure, quon ne peut me refusere cette justice.

---

197. Manuscripts A, B, and D include the following passage: "En arrivant en France j'ai écrit au premier consul et au ministre de la marine pour leur rendre compte de ma position et leur demander des secours pour moi et ma famille. Sans doute ils ont senti la justice de ma demande, et ont ordonné qu'on m'accordât ce que je demandais, mais au lieu d'exécuter leurs ordres on m'a envoyé de vieux haillons de soldats déjà à moitié pourris et des souliers de même. Avais-je besoin qu'on ajoute cette humiliation à mon malheur." Louverture may have deleted this passage after Caffarelli confiscated his uniform during the visit and he realized that such humiliations were the French government's official policy.

198. The first draft of manuscript A originally stopped here. Sentences added in the margin brought manuscript A all the way to "une pareille absurdité" (before the addendum).

man in the world[217] by denying me my liberty and by separating me from what is dearest to me in the world, from a respectable father aged one hundred and five who needs my help,[218] from a beloved wife who will probably not be able to bear the woes that will burden her, far from me, and from a cherished family that made my life happy.[219] When I disembarked from the ship they made me climb in a car. I was hoping that I would be brought before a tribunal to account for my conduct and to be judged, but instead I was taken, without allowing me an instant of rest, to a fort at the frontiers of the republic, where I was locked in an awful cell.[220] It is from the depths of this prison that I invoke the justice and the magnanimity of the first consul. He is too generous and too good a general to let a former military man who suffered many wounds in the service of his fatherland die in a cell without giving him even the satisfaction of justifying himself and obtaining a ruling on his fate. I thus ask to be brought before a tribunal or court martial, where General Leclerc will also be made to appear, and that we be judged after being both heard. Equity, reason, laws: all convinces me that this justice cannot be denied to me.

217. "Toussaint, the most unhappy man of men! /. .. Though fallen thyself, never to rise again, / Live, and take comfort;" poem by William Wordsworth in *Red-Letter Poems by English Men and Women* (New York: Thomas Y. Crowell, 1884), 287–288. According to a guard in Joux, "the poor man thought of his country, his children! He had so much sorrow;" see J. F. Dubois to [abbé?] Grégoire (25 May 1823), NAF 6864, BNF.

218. In captivity, Louverture also mentioned "my father who is currently blind;" see Louverture to Bonaparte (9 Oct. 1802), Dossier 1, AF/IV/1213, AN. Louverture's biological father had died in 1774; see François Bayon de Libertat to Pantaléon II de Breda (30 Apr. 1774), Dossier 12, 18AP/3, AN. According to Isaac, "the 105 years old elder mentioned in the manuscript of Joux attributed to my father is the virtuous Pierre Baptiste his godfather;" see Isaac Louverture to M. de Saint-Anthoine (8 March 1842), NAF 6864, BNF.

219. Suzanne Louverture was allowed to live with her sons and other relatives in Agen, where she died in 1816; see Nemours, *Histoire de la famille*, 240.

220. According to a French general who met Louverture as he passed through Tours, Louverture was convinced that he was on his way to defend himself before Bonaparte in Paris; see Fernand Clamettes, ed., *Mémoires du général Baron Thiébault*, vol. 3 (Paris: Plon, 1893–1895), 301, 303.

1

entraversant la france jai lous sure les papie publi un article qui me consernez, on macuze
d etre un rebel et un traitre, et pour justifié cette acusation on dite avoire entercepte

une letre par la quelle jengageois les cultivateur de S^t domingue a se soulever, je nai jamais Ecris de pareille letre, et inetre en de fit[199] qui que ce soit de la produitre de me citer a qui je lai a drescé et de faire paroite cette personne, au reste cette calomnie

Tombre d'elle même; sis javoit eu lin tantion de prendrandre[200] les armes les auroi-je de pozé et auroi je fais ma soumision, un homme raisonnable encormoin un militaire ne peut pas suppozè une pareile absurdite.[201]

aDi dition au presante memoire; sis le gouvernemenet a voit en voié un homme plus sage, il n y auroit eu aucune male ni un seul coup de fusil de tiré, pourquoi la peure a telle aucasionne tant d injustice de la par du General leclerc[202] ; pour quoi a til man que a sa parol; pour quoi a larrivé dela fregate la Guerriere qui conduisoit mon nepouse ai-je vus plusieur personne qui avoient été arrete a vec elle, de[203] ces personne a avoient jamais tiré un coup de fusil, étoient des innosante, des pere de famille, quon a arraché des bras de leur famme et de leur enfans. cesont autant de bras oté a la culture, Toute les personne qui avoient vercé leur sang pour conservé la colonie

---

199. Read: "je mets en défi."
200. Read: "prendre." This is one of a few typos in the text (see also "gouvernemenet" on line 9). These are relatively few, a sign that Louverture carefully proofread the manuscript and that most misspellings reflect his lack of schooling and his way of speaking, rather than lack of attention on his part.
201. Manuscript A ends with this sentence. Manuscripts B and D include a short version of the following addendum.
202. Manuscript D omits "leclerc."
203. Manuscript D: "plusieurs de" instead of "de."

1

While crossing France I read in public papers an article that concerned me. I am accused
of being a rebel and a traitor, and to justify this accusation they claim to have intercepted
a letter in which I was inciting the cultivators of Saint-Domingue to revolt.[221] I
never wrote such a letter, and I defy anyone to produce it, to
tell me to whom it was addressed and to bring this person in public. At any rate, this calumny
falls on its own. If it had been my intention to take up arms, why would I have laid
them down and made my submission? A reasonable man, and even more so
a military man, cannot believe such an absurdity.[222]

Addendum to this memoir. If the government had sent a
wiser man, nothing bad would have happened, nor a single shot
fired. Why did fear lead General Leclerc to commit so many
injustices? Why did he not keep his word? Why, at the arrival of the
frigate *Guerrière* that was bringing my wife, did I see several persons
who had been arrested with her? Some of these persons had never shot
a rifle and were innocent people, heads of family who were torn
from the arms of their wife and their children.[223] These are so many arms lost to
cultivation. All the persons who had spilled their blood to save the colony

---

221. The letter mentioned here was a letter to Louverture's aide-de-camp Fontaine dated 27 May 1802, in which he plotted a new uprising for the summer of 1802; it was described as genuine in Leclerc to Decrès (11 June 1802), CC9B/19, ANOM. Louverture was supposed to cross France in an enclosed carriage but evidently managed to obtain some information on the way; see Berthier, "Rapport fait au premier consul" (1 Aug. 1802), B7/6, SHD-DAT. The "public papers" referred either to the *Gazette officielle de Saint-Domingue* (23 June 1802) or more likely the *Gazette des Débats* (29 July 1802), both of which reproduced the letter to Fontaine.

222. Manuscript A ends with this appeal. The addendum that constitutes the memoir's fourth and final section was added in the B and D versions and considerably expanded in the C version.

223. Leclerc ordered 50 supporters of Louverture deported to Corsica and 20 to Cayenne in the aftermath of Louverture's arrest; see Leclerc to Decrès (11 June 1802), B7/26, SHD-DAT. The group sent to Corsica on the frigate *Muiron* included Louverture's aide-de-camp Fontaine, to whom he had sent his infamous 27 May 1802 letter, and Gingembre Trop Fort, who had been cited in it; see "Etat des officiers, soldats, et individus quelconques partant pour France sur l'escadre du contre-amiral Magon" (6 June 1802), Box 6/464, RP-UF. The other group arrived in Guyana in Aug. 1802; see Jean Destrem, *Les déportations du consulat et de l'empire (d'après des documents inédits)* (Paris: Jeanmaire, 1885), 279.

a la france les officier de mon éta major, mes sécretaire non jamais rien
fait que par mon ordre tous ont don été arreté sans motife; En me de bar
quant a brest mes enfans ont été envoier a une destination a moi inconnu
et mon nepouse dans une autre que jignore, que le gouvernement me rendre plu de
justice ma femme et mes enfans nont rien faite et nont aucune conpte
a rendre, elle doivent dont etre renvoier chez elle pour surveiller nos in
tèret et porter soins a notre malheureuse famillle,[204] le General le clerc qui a ocasion
né toute le mal[205], et moi je sui au fond dun cachote, sans pouvoire mes
justifié, le gouvernement et trop juste pour me laiscer aincis les bras liès et
me laisaire frapper pare le general le clerc sans men tendre; en arrivant en
france tout le monde ma dite que le gouvernement etoit juste, ne doi-je pas
participée a sa justice et a se bien faite; le general le clerc dite dans sa letre
au ministre que jai vus dans les gazette que jattand la maladie des se troup

pour lui faire la geure et reprendre le conmandement; cet un mensonge a
Troce et abominable, cet tun lacheté de sa part, mal gré que jai peu de con
naisance et que jai ne pas d'Education jai aser de Bonsan pour menpeché de
luter contre la volonté de mon gouvernement; je nÿ ai jamais pancér; le
gouvernement francois et trop fort trop presant pour que le general le clerc prescie lé[206]
comparent a vec moi qui sui son subalterne: a la verité quant il a marché
contre moi jai dis plussieur fois que je nattaquerois pas que je me de
fendrois seulement jus quau moi de juillet ou aout que je commencerois a m[207]
toure, mai depuis jai reflechis sur les malheur de la colonie, et sur la letre du
premiere consul, et jai fais masoumisions; je de mande daprés ce la les preuve
de chosse dont le General Le clerc macuse, on verras les mensonge et les calomnie
quil a vomy contre moi, on verras que le general dessaline set soumis dapres me

ordre tandis que les general leclerc a dite que jemaitois soumis que dapres la
soumisions du general dessaline;[208] pour quoi que le General Le clerc na pas suivis la
marche qui étoit etablis deu puis lontans, que tous les generaux ou chef descadre
on tou jour suivis, un Escadre na jamais arrivé dans la colonie sans avoir en

204. Manuscript D omits "et porter soins a notre malheureuse famillle."
205. Manuscript D adds "est libre."
206. Read: "puisse le."
207. Illegible (the edge of the page is missing). The passage ends with "à mon tour" in manuscript B.
208. The following extended passage, from "pour quoi que le General Le clerc" to "je les repete encor je demande que le General leclerc et moi paroisions en sanble de vant un tribunal" (p. 21, line 27) does not appear in Manuscripts A, B, or D. Louverture must have written it entirely on his own.

for France, the officers of my staff, [and] my secretaries never did
anything except under my order: all were thus arrested without cause.[224] When I
disembarked in Brest my children were sent to a destination unknown to me,
and my spouse to another that I ignore.[225] May the government give me more
justice: my wife and my children have done nothing and have no account
to give. They must thus be sent back home to look after our interests
and care for our unhappy family. [It is] General Leclerc who caused
all this evil, and I am at the bottom of a cell, without being able to
justify myself. The government is too just to leave me like this with my arms tied and
allow me to be slapped by General Leclerc without hearing me. When I arrived in
France, everyone told me that the government was just. Should I not
partake of its justice and its blessings? General Leclerc says in his letter
to the minister [of the navy] that I saw in the gazettes that I am waiting for his troops
   to get sick
to wage war on him and retake my command. It is an atrocious and
abominable lie, it is an act of cowardice on his part.[226] Even though I have little
knowledge and I have no education, I have enough good sense to hold back from
fighting against the will of the government; I never thought of it. The
French government is too strong, too overwhelming for General Leclerc to
compare it to me who is its subaltern. In truth, when he marched
against me I said several times that I would not attack, that I would only defend
myself until the month of July or August when I would also start to [fight].[227]
But later I thought about the colony's woes, and the letter of the
first consul, and I made my submission. So I demand the evidence
for the things of which General Leclerc is accusing me. We will see the lies and calumny
that he vomited against me. We will see that General Dessalines made his submission
   on my
orders, whereas General Leclerc said I only submitted after
the submission of General Dessalines.[228] Why did General Leclerc not follow the
procedure established for a long time, which all generals or squadron leaders
have always followed? A squadron never arrived in the colony without having

---

224. Contrary to his earlier stance on the burning of Cap (p. 3, line 7) and civilian massacres (p. 9, line 21), Louverture courageously took full responsibility for his subordinates' actions.

225. Placide Louverture was sent to captivity in Belle-Ile while the rest of the family was placed under house arrest in Agen; see Berthier to Decrès (26 July 1802), B7/5, SHD-DAT.

226. "This ambitious man has never ceased to conspire since being pardoned.... He was trying to organize an insurrection among the cultivators;" see Leclerc to Decrès (11 June 1802), CC9B/19, ANOM. Note that the passage from line 22 to line 32 repeats earlier passages of the memoir, notably page 15, line 65, page 17, line 32, and page 19, line 1.

227. This incriminating sentence, which supports Leclerc's accusation that Louverture was awaiting the summer's fevers to fight back (p. 19, line 31), was underlined in manuscript B by an unknown hand.

228. Dessalines had indeed surrendered at Louverture's demand; see Dessalines to Louverture (5 May 1802), Folder 23C, KFC-HU. Note that Louverture must have ignored Dessalines's role in his arrest because he was consistently positive about him in the memoir; see Philippe Girard, "Jean-Jacques Dessalines et l'arrestation de Toussaint Louverture," *Journal of Haitian Studies* 17:1 (Spring 2011), 123–138. The ensuing passage, which includes anecdotes that illustrate the concepts of preparedness and forgiveness, is unique to manuscript C.

voié un naviso un moi ou quin jour das vance pour prevenire son narivé, a fin con
pus préparé a les recevoire, et on observe cet mesure plus dans les tans de geure,
pour invite toute inconvoinien qui pouroit y arrivé au quin des ceformalité
na pas été renplis, il faut observé au ci les desante qui ces faisoit dans les
dis férente en droit. il na pas un de ces Generaux conmandant an chef les de
partement ou les conmandant des arondisment qui a faite un grand resitance,
ce lui qui a navélordre et ceux qui en navoit un peu du de connaisance
dans les tamilitaire, tous disoit a ten de les general Toussaint louverture, qui
conmande chef lisle. a son narrive vous rentréroit, les zotre voiens que

ce sons des francois et il ce sont rendus sans même atendre au quin ordre,
et on vera deprece la que toute a na voit de bone emeieur intantion[209]
et les mal qui a été faite et conmis provien par les fol mésure du general
leclerc: jobserve ancore peu destans a vant larrivé de lescadre un frega[210]
angloi vint de vans sanmanna pour rentré dans la bais prendre un not

---

209. Read: "tous avaient les meilleures intentions."
210. Read: "frégate" (the edge of the page is missing).

sent an aviso one month or fifteen days ahead to warn of its arrival, so that one could prepare to receive it, and this measure is even more followed in times of war, to avoid any of the inconveniences that might occur. None of these formalities was fulfilled. One should also note the landings that were being made in various spots. There was not a single general commanding the departments or a county commander who opposed a great resistance.[229]

Those who had such an order and all those who knew a bit about military matters, all were saying "wait for General Toussaint Louverture, the commander in chief of the island, when he arrives you may come in." The others saw that
these were Frenchmen and they surrendered without even waiting for any order, and one will see, based on this, that all had the good and best intentions and that all the bad things that were done come from the foolish measures of General Leclerc. I also observe that, not long before the arrival of the squadron, an English frigate came before Samaná to enter the bay to capture another

---

229. Louverture's claim is contradicted by his previous account of the burning of Cap and the difficult French landings in Port-de-Paix, Saint-Marc, Port-Républicain, and Léogane.

2

Batiment qui et toit mouie dant la rade ne sa chan pas cil avoit un garnisont
dans cet endroit, on le voire venire et on croiiet que se toit un batiment
francois on les ses aborder da ja a la pas.²¹¹ heureuse ment que le conmandant a vus
les contraire ordonna de tiré dussus, et ils fus contrin de san retourné a pré nous

savoire tue sept homme et blecé plussieure, nous etions antans de geurer;
et jai navoit pas connaisance ci un nescadre doit venire dant la colonie, seulement
par voi indirecte jai en tan dus dire qua la pais il viendra un flote et bocoup

des batiment marchans pour les conmerce dans la colonie; poure-je a joutoit
foi a ce la, sans en recevoire les nouvelle de la pais officielle de mon gouvernement
ni les prochienne arrivé de lescadre; et san etre prevenux par le General leclerc

qui et toit chargé les ordres du Gouvernement, et ci y étoit au cap, ou porto au
portoprince:²¹² que le general Leclerc arrivé de cet maniere dant la colonie:
faire des de sante dans tous les point comme ennemis san me donné connaisance
porteur dordre²¹³ pour moi le caché sans vouloire me le remaitre qua presavoire

conmis les sotilité,²¹⁴ qui ore-je faire suivant la raisons et la justice, sui

vans le reglement militaire et la hierarchie des pouvoire; je loroit faire
prisonnie, ou les forcer de partire et rendre conte au gouvernement sa conduite,

on moré peu taitre blamé, mai tous cés malheure qui étarrivé norepas
eu lieu, et joroit faire mon devoire, par ce que au quin officier né doit
pas remetre sonposte a qui que ce soit sans les zodre de son supeuriere, ni sou
frire au quin de zordre se face²¹⁵ dant len droit confiié a son conmandement.
et je croi quant un homme rentrai dans un poste comme ennemis et on doit
les recevoire de même, jai vus monsieur de vinsans qui et toit Gouverneur
au cap a été pour sur prandre un poste et voire ci la garnison fait sait²¹⁶ bien
leur devoire, et il a pacer par un notre chemin pour y rentre a cet poste,

 211. Read: "on le laissait déjà aborder à la passe."
 212. Louverture treated "Port-au-Prince" as if it were a single word, as is the case in modern Kreyòl.
 213. Louverture's grammar differs markedly from standard French in the segment of the addendum that he wrote entirely on his own. By writing "porteur dordre" (standard French: "qu'il était porteur d'ordre"), he omitted the subordinating conjunction, the personal pronoun, and the verb. His handwriting is also more rushed and less legible, especially at the end of long words.
 214. The placement of the letter "s" in the word "sotilité" (French: "hostilités") is an example of three characteristics of Louverture's writing style and of Kreyòl: (1) writing the liaison as if it were part of the word itself ("sotilité"); (2) simplifiying pronunciation by dropping some consonants ("hostilités"); (3) not indicating the plural form ("hostilités"). See also "zodre," five lines below.
 215. Read: "souffrir qu'aucun désordre ne se fasse."
 216. Judging by his spelling, Louverture pronounced the French word "faisait" /fese/ instead of /fœze/, as would be the norm in modern French. See also "fait sait" on line 45.

2

ship that had cast anchor in the harbor, not knowing if there was a garrison in this spot. They saw it coming and they believed that it was a French ship, [so] they let it enter the pass. Luckily, the commander saw that it was the opposite and ordered to open fire, and they were forced to turn back after having
killed seven of our men and wounded several.[230] We were in a state of war, and I was not aware that a squadron was going to come to the colony. Only through indirect means did I hear that when the peace comes a fleet will come along with many
merchant ships for the commerce of the colony.[231] Could I believe this without receiving word of the official peace from my government, or of the impending arrival of the squadron, and without being forewarned by General Leclerc
who was bearing the orders of the government, and if he was in Cap or in Port-au-Prince? General Leclerc arrived in this manner in the colony: he ordered landings in all the spots like an enemy without informing me [that he was] bearing orders for me, hid them and would not hand them over until after
he had begun the hostilities. What would have I done according to reason and to justice,
following military regulations and the hierarchy of powers? I would have made him prisoner, or forced him to leave and to give an account of his conduct to the government.
Maybe I would have been blamed, but all this misfortune that took place would never have happened, and I would have done my duty, because an officer cannot hand over his command to anyone without orders from his superior, or suffer that any disorder occur in the area entrusted to his command.
And I believe that when a man enters a position like an enemy he must be received the same way. I once saw Mr de Vincent,[232] who was governor in Cap, go to surprise a position and see if the garrison was doing its duty, and he used a different route to return to this position.

---

230. Louverture frequently complained in the spring of 1801 of incidents involving British ships; see Louverture to Edward Corbet (1 Apr. 1801), CO 137/105, BNA.

231. Louverture had known of French military preparations since the spring of 1801: "The rumor I had mentioned to you in Santo Domingo about a French expedition was not inaccurate;" see Pascal to [Louverture] (31 March 1801), Folder 9C, KFC-HU. Louverture learned of the peace with Britain in Dec. 1801 and immediately suspected that "the British government had engaged to join with the Republic in offensive measures against" Saint-Domingue; see W. L. Whitfield to Nugent (9 Dec. 1801), CO 137/106, BNA.

232. Louverture probably referred to Charles Humbert de Vincent, who was not governor but director of Saint-Domingue's fortifications, and whom he had employed extensively when negotiating with France; see Christian Schneider, "Le colonel Vincent, officier du génie à Saint-Domingue," in Annales historiques de la révolution française, no. 329 (July 2002), 101–122.

l'officie de garde fut tiré dusus et tué un homme de sa suite et on lui
consigné au cordegarde jus qua quil fus reconnus, bien loin de punire
cet officier il étoit capitaine on la faite chef de bataion, monssieur la
valtiere a été de même pour visité un poste la santinelle a tiré dusus,
balle a raflé un des officie qui la conpagné, et bien,[217] cet santinelle qui
étoit sinple sol dat, on la faite soulieutenent, et moi pour avoire defande
mon poste qui a été supris pandant mon napsans moment enné, jai étoit
arreté san ouquin consideration ni la justice, et la raison, dapre une
proclamation que le General le clerc a proclamétion a la fas de la colonie
da pre sa parolle d honneur, et la protection du gouvernement quil ma promis
je fait ma soumisoin remetre mes troupe et les armes, cepandant dant
Tous les tans la parolle d honneur et tem gage: et les protection d un gouv;
ment a été tou jour sacré; ou et dont la promes du General leClerc,
ce dont pour me tronpé et cil a ve voulus me tronpé pour quoi natil pas
servis les ruse, et la fines seullement: et non sa parolle et la protections
du gouvernement francois; an me don n'ant sa parolle, et ne pas la tinire
cet man quié a l honneur; promi la protections du gouvernement, et a gire
d un notre maniere; ce violé les lois; et manqué au gouvernement même;
et la parol d honneur a été Tout jour suivis par tous les homme sancé
et les fran militaire; et pan dant que jai fait sait la geurre avec
Tous les enemis de la re publique je ne jamais tronpé qui que ce soit an
donnant ma parolle, ni même au cuin des enemis qui me faisoit
la geurre; a servis cette moien[218] pour me tronppé il on enploié tous sorte
des ruse et les fines; a lors je faite de même de mon coté,
voisi un fait notoire, les marqui des pinville étoit conmandant
a mirballai pour le roi d espangne, et il avoit souce zordre cint
mill homme dinfantérie des ligne, et 18 cens homme dragond bien monte
et il a mar ché plus sieur fois sur le verrette et lartibonite, dans les
tans de la coualitions conte la republique, et quante jai été maitre des
toute[219] cet partis jus quo verrette; jai attaque le mirbalai et je eu les
Bonheur de prandre cet place et toute les autre endroit voisine,
et il fus mon prisonnie, et cet a qui voulai lui faire de la pene
comme il et chevallié S^t lui; jai le pris sur la protection de la répu
blique, an lor et lui donné ma parolle que rien lui féras, et je la

---

217. Note the use of the interjection "et bien," typical of the oral style of this passage.
218. Read: "il s'est servi de ce moyen."
219. The word "toute" was added by Louverture in the margin, indicating that he proof-read manuscript C.

The officer on guard ordered to open fire and killed a man of his escort and he was consigned in the guardhouse until he was recognized. Far from punishing him, this officer, who was a captain, he promoted to battalion chief. Mr. la Valtière went similarly to visit a position. The sentry shot at him. The bullet scratched one of the officers who was accompanying him, well, this sentry who was a mere private was promoted to sub-lieutenant, whereas I, for defending my position that was surprised during my temporary absence, I was arrested without any consideration, nor justice, and reason. Based on a proclamation that General Leclerc proclaimed to the whole colony, based on his word of honor, and the protection of the government that he promised me, I made my submission, handed over my troops and the weapons. And yet in all times a word of honor has been binding, and the protection of a government has always been sacred. Where is then the promise of General Leclerc? It was to deceive me, then, and if he wanted to deceive me why did he not use ruses and finesse only, and not his word and the protection of the French government? Giving me one's word, and not keeping to it, it is wanting for honor. Promising the protection of the government, and acting in a different way, it is violating the laws, and failing the government itself. And the word of honor has always been followed by all sensible men and frank military men; and while I was waging war with all the enemies of the republic, I never deceived anyone by giving my word, not even any of the enemies that were waging war against me. He employed this method to deceive me. They employed all kinds of ruses and finesses; so I did the same on my side.[233]

Here is a well-known fact: the marquis of Espinville[234] was commander of Mirebalais for the king of Spain, and he had under his orders five thousand men of the infantry of the line, and 18 hundred well-mounted dragoons, and he marched several times against Verrettes and the Artibonite, during the time of the coalition against the republic. And when I gained control of all the region up to Verrettes, I attacked the Mirebalais and I had the pleasure of capturing this position and all the surrounding areas, and he became my prisoner, and everyone wanted to hurt him because he was a knight of Saint-Louis.[235] I placed him under the protection of the republic, and gave him my word that nothing would happen to him, and I

---

233. This sentence about Louverture's use of political ruse is accurate but contradicts his previous sentence. Louverture liked to fight "using ruse;" see Laveaux to Jean Dalbarade (22 Sept. 1794), F/3/199, FM, ANOM.

234. According to Isaac Louverture, his father captured the Marquis of Espinville with 800 troops after a victory in Mirebalais, insisted that he be spared, and then allowed him to leave for Havana; see Isaac Louverture, "Notes historiques sur Toussaint Louverture," 63.

235. The order of Saint-Louis, created by Louis XIV in 1693, was associated with the Ancien Régime and monarchy.

3 11

sa suré quil ce ra seullement prisonnie de geurre jus qua nouvelle ordre,
je lai faite conduire au Gonaive a vec sonnepouse, et les personne de sa
maison qui vous lai lui suivre, et pendent quil etoit sur labitations d
Grand mon prisonnie, loui et son nepouse a été respecté, jai rendus conte
au General lavaux la prise de mir ballait et toute les prisonnie, mais je
ne pas pancé de lui dire que monssieur des pinville etoit sou la protections
de la republique, en fin plussieurs rapor et des nonsations[220] a été faite conte
lui au pré du General la vaux. ce general et les menbre du consaille ce rendus
au Gonaive pour le jugé, a lors jai reclamé quil étoit sur[221] la protections
de Gouvernement francois, et que je la voit promi quant il fus prisonnie
a la prise de mir ballai et ces pour cet raisons que j ai lavoit pas lui envoié
au porde pais comme les otre, a lors le General la vaux qui command en
chef lisle jai lui et represanté que la protections du que jai la voit
promi au non de mon gouvernement et Toit sacré. et ci je croiié man
qué a ma parolle je lai ce roit plus to le conmandement, a lors le General
la vaux et toute les manbre du consaille et les otre personne qui et tè presant
Toute on santis la justice de ma reclaination.[222] Le marqui des pinville a été mis
en liberté et renvoié che lui, et il a demande a pre de sortis hor de la colonie
pour continué son service sou sa parolle de ne pas prendre les arme conte la republique
cet demande lui a et te accordé, et je me rapelle davoire recu les conpliment
Des Tous ce messieux qui étoit presant da voire soutinire l honneur et la digni
Té de mon Gouvernement; cepandant je nais pa resu educations,
ni instruit, mais mon Grobonsans ma faite connoitre quin homme doit
Tenire sa parolle sur tous un répresantans du gouvernement, a vec tous les
nation que je faisoit la guerre[223] se étoit toujour de même. il l'ias vint
a trante autre a faire[224] que jene veux pas cité et les tis moint[225] son présant;[226]
je les repete encor je demande que le General leclerc et moi paroisions en
sanble de vant un tribunal et que le Gouvernement ordonné que ton ma
porte toute mes piece de correz pondance par ce moÿent lon verras mons
innosance et tout ce que jai faite pour la republique; quoique je sant que

---

220. Like Kreyòl speakers, Louverture occasionally simplified vowels and combinations that are hard to pronounce (in this case, dropping the "i" in "dénonciations"). He did the same with "x," "r" (see "conte" in the same line), and some word endings.

221. Read: "sous."

222. Read: "réclamation."

223. Read: "avec toutes les nations avec lesquelles je faisais la guerre."

224. Read: "Il y a vingt à trente autres affaires."

225. The sound /e/ becomes /i/ in the word "tis moint" (French: témoins"). Louverture also rendered many /œ/ and /y/ sounds as /i/.

226. This is the end of the extended passage, added by Louverture in manuscript C, that does not appear in manuscripts A, B, and D and whose creolized and evocative French is typical of his personal style.

3 11

assured him that he would only be a prisoner of war until further notice. I had him sent to Gonaïves with his spouse, along with the persons from his house who wanted to follow him, and while he was on the Grand-Pré plantation as my prisoner he and his spouse were treated with respect. I gave to General Laveaux an account of the capture of Mirebalais and all the prisoners, but I did not think of telling him that Mr. d'Espinville was under the protection of the republic. Finally, several reports and denunciations were made against him to General Laveaux. This general and the members of the council proceeded to Gonaïves to put him on trial.[236] I then complained that he was under the protection of the French government, and that I had promised it when he was made prisoner at the capture of Mirebalais, and that it was for this reason that I had not sent him to Port-de-Paix like the others. Then, to General Laveaux who was commander in chief of the island, I explained that the protection I had promised him in the name of my government was sacred, and that I would sooner abandon my command than break my word. Then General Laveaux and all the members of the council and the other persons who were present, all felt the justice of my claim. The marquis of Espinville was released and sent back home, and he later asked to leave the colony to continue his service against a promise not to take up arms against the republic.[237] This demand was granted to him, and I remember being complimented by all these gentlemen who were present for having defended the honor and the dignity of my government.[238] Yet I never received an education nor instructed, but my big common sense made me understand that a man must keep his word, especially a representative of the government. With all the nations I was combating it was the same. There are twenty to thirty other cases I don't want to cite even though witnesses were present. I repeat it again I demand that General Leclerc and I appear together before a tribunal and that the government order that they bring all the pieces of my correspondence. In this manner, one will see that I am innocent and all I have done for the republic, even though I sense that

---

236. As a noble allied to Bourbon Spain, Espinville would have been considered a counterrevolutionary traitor under French revolutionary law. Louverture, however, chose to ally himself with émigrés during the 1790s, which often led to tensions with more radical Frenchmen; see, for example, Louverture to Gabriel d'Hédouville (5 Sept. 1798), Ms. Hait. 71-19 (2), BPL.

237. Under the parole system, captured officers could be released if they gave their word not to fight their captors.

238. This long anecdote, meant to teach Bonaparte about the virtues of forgiveness, also underlined Louverture's desire to be accepted as a gentleman and an honorable officer.

plus sieur piece ceronte intercepté;[227] premiere consul pere de tous les militaire juge integre defanseur des innosance prononcé dont sur mon sor,[228] mes plai et tre profond, porté les remede salutaire pour lan péché de ne jamais ouverte vous et medecin,[229] je conte entieremement sur votre justice et votre balance, salut et respec[230]

227. The following sentences in manuscript C are identical (aside from minor spelling variations) to those personally added by Louverture at the end of manuscript B. Manuscript D also contains a final appeal in Louverture's hand, but its content is slightly different. Louverture normally used manuscript D as the template for manuscript C, so one may surmise that he wrote the final appeal to manuscript D just before he handed the document to Caffarelli, leaving him no time to make a personal copy, and that he used the end of manuscript B (which he had kept with him) as the template for the last sentences of manuscript C.

228. Manuscript D: "prononcé dons sur un homme quie plus mal heure que coup pable, gairice mes plai illé tre profond, vous seul peurret portes les remede saluter" instead of "prononcé dont sur mon sor, mes plai et tre profond, porté les remede salutaire." Manuscript B is identical to manuscript C.

229. Manuscript D adds "ma position, et més service merite toute votre a tantion." Manuscript B is identical to manuscript C.

230. Manuscript B ends with Louverture's initials. Manuscript D ends with a full signature, complete with three masonic dots, presumably because this was the official copy meant for Bonaparte. Manuscript C is not signed, presumably because this was Louverture's personal copy.

several pieces will be intercepted. First consul, father of all military men, honest judge, defender of the innocent, decide on my fate. My wounds are very deep, employ the salutary remedies to prevent them from ever opening. You are a doctor, I rely entirely on your justice and your fairness.
Salutations and respect,[239]

[The C manuscript is not signed.]

239. An often-repeated tale holds that Louverture would end his letters to Bonaparte with the phrase "the first of the Blacks to the first of the Whites." But his typical send-off, as shown in this memoir, was actually "salut et respect;" see, for example, Louverture to Bonaparte (25 June 1800), Dossier 1, AF/IV/1213, AN.

INDEX

Page numbers of photographs are in italics.

Amiot, 17, 32

Baille, 11, 31–32
Baptiste, Pierre, 3, 4, 155
Bayon de Libertat, François, 26
Beard, John R., 17, 45–46
Bel Argent, 105
Belair, Charles, 3, 115, 117
Belley, Jean-Baptiste, 9
Besse, Martial, 14, 31
Bolívar, Simón, 21
Bonaparte, Napoléon, 6–8, 10, 11, 21, 30, 32, 35–36, 75–77, 83, 95, 101–103, 107, 113, 155
Boudet, Jean: 61n17, 81, 91n94, 103, 107
Brunet, Jean-Baptiste, 123–133
Bunel de Blancamp, Joseph, 26

Caffarelli, Marie-François Auguste du Falga, 11–14, 16, 25, 30
Cap-Français (Cap-Haïtien), 3, 8, 55–65, 79–81, 113, 123, 127, 134
Catholicism. *See* religion
Cauna, Jacques, 18, 22
Chancy, Bernard, 3, 107
Chancy, Louise, 38n28, 133n172
Christophe, Henry, 25, 27, 57–61, 65–67, 71–73, 85, 107–109
Clervaux, Augustin, 99
Coisnon, Jean-Baptiste, *28*, 29, 77
Columbus, Christopher, 14
constitution (1801), 6–7, *7*, 20, 145

Coupé, Marc, 57, 67, 95–97, 111
Crête-à-Pierrot, 8, 22, 89–95, 103, 107

Derance, Lamour, 21, 101
Desfourneaux, Etienne, 17, 85n73, 91n91, 151,
Desormeaux, Daniel, 13, 18, 28
Dessalines, Jean-Jacques, 4, 9, 29, 32, 55, 59, 87–97, 103–105, 113–115, 159
Dominican Republic. *See* Santo Domingo
Dumas, Thomas-Alexandre, 9
Dupin, Jean-Philippe, 73

England. *See* Great Britain
Equiano, Olaudah, 4
Espinville, Marquis of, 165–167

Fontaine, Jean-Pierre, 67–69, 109, 157n221
Fressinet, Philibert, 115

Gazagnaire, Jean, 32
God. *See* religion
Golart, Lubin, 17–18, 21, 97–99
Granville, 79
Great Britain, 6, 20, 32, 55, 147, 149–151, 161–163
Grégoire, Henri, 17

Haiti. *See* Saint-Domingue
Hardÿ, Jean, 69n36, 85n73, 105, 107–109

Jeannin, 14, 15, 18
Jenson, Deborah, 18, 28
Joux (fort de), 1, *1*, 10, 35, 155

Kerversau, François-Marie Perichou de, 73–75, 91n91, 93n99
Kina, Jean and Zamor, 32
Kreyòl, 15, 23–30, 34

Laveaux, Etienne, 19, 147–153, 167
Leclerc, Victoire Emmanuel, 8-9, 31, 57, 61, 65–71, 77–83, 89–97, 101–103, 107–109, 113–115, 119–125, 131–147, 155–167.
Louverture, Gabriel, 4
Louverture, Isaac, 4, 6, 25, *28*, 29, 73, 77, 123, 125, 135, 159
Louverture, Marie-Marthe, 4
Louverture, Paul, 3, 73–75
Louverture, Placide, 4, 6, 9, 29, 77, 123, 131, 135, 139n182, 159
Louverture, Suzanne, 4, 9, 29, 77, 119, 123, 129, 131, 135, 159
Louverture, Toussaint
　and Leclerc expedition (January-June 1802), 8–9, 19, 55–119, 159–161
　as a writer, 4, 5, 11, 13, 15, 25, 31
　capture (June 1802), 9, 19, 119–135, 157
　imprisonment and death (1802–1803), 1–2, 10–13, 30–33, 135, 139, 153–155, 159
　pre-revolutionary life, 3–5, 149, 153
　revolutionary career (1791-1801), 5–7, 19–20, 53–55, 141–153, 163–167

Maurepas, Jacques, 71–73, 93, 99
memoir of Toussaint Louverture
　editions, 17, 45–46
　historical analysis, 18–23, 34
　linguistic analysis, 23–30, 34
　literary analysis, 13–18, 34
Moïse, 5

Napoléon. *See* Bonaparte, Napoléon

Nathan, 111
Nemours, Auguste, 32

Perrin, 115
Pesquidous, 119n149, 121–123, 129n164, 133n173
Plaisir, Mars, 10–11, 33, 128n135, 133n169
Port-Républicain (Port-au-Prince), 5, 61, 73, 85, 91, 97, 139

racism, 22, 75, 105n120, 137, 141, 143
Ravine-à-Couleuvre, 8, 85–87
religion, 23, 24, 141, 145n199
Rigaud, André, 29, 31, 73n45, 99n110, 101n112, 147
Rochambeau, Donatien de, 8, 67n29, 71, 85–87, 95, 119n149
Rolph-Trouillot, Michel, 21

Saint-Domingue (Haiti)
　economy, 6, 20, 53
　map, 48–49
Saint-Marc, 55, 61, 73, 79, 81, 87, 115, 151
Saint-Rémy, Joseph, 17, 28, 45
Santo Domingo (Dominican Republic), 6, 55–57, 73–75, 143, 145
slavery, 3, 5, 20, 97, 149
Spain, 5, 20, 27, 93, 149, 151–153

Thiébault, Paul, 10
Toussaint Louverture. *See* Louverture, Toussaint

United States, 6, 20

Valdman, Albert, 27, 34
Vernet, André, 3, 75, 89
Vilton, 107–109
Vincent, Charles Humbert de, 145n198, 163–165
Vodou (a.k.a. Voodoo, Vodun). *See* religion

Wordsworth, William, 22

www.ingramcontent.com/pod-product-compliance
Ingram Content Group UK Ltd.
Pitfield, Milton Keynes, MK11 3LW, UK
UKHW042006230426
12048UKWH00009B/588